The Union of
England and Scotland

The Union of England and Scotland
1603-1608

BRUCE GALLOWAY

JOHN DONALD PUBLISHERS LTD
EDINBURGH

ISBN 0 85976 143 6

Exclusive distribution in the United States of
America and Canada by Humanities Press Inc.,
Atlantic Highlands, NJ 07716, USA

Phototypeset by Burns & Harris Limited, Dundee
Printed in Great Britain by Bell & Bain Ltd., Glasgow

Foreword

After carrying out research as a postgraduate student at Churchill College, Cambridge, Bruce Galloway was awarded his PhD in 1981. It was always in his mind to submit his thesis for publication, and by the spring of 1984 he felt ready to do so. In the interval, much work by others — on James VI and I himself, and on early Stuart Parliaments, for example — had confirmed his revisions of established views. Indeed, it is Bruce's rehabilitation of James himself, and his reassessment of the motives and mindless conservatism of opponents of the Union in the English Parliament which were the most striking conclusions of his thesis.

But at the very moment when he was preparing to embark on publication, he died in tragic circumstances. The quality of the manuscript as he left it, however, fully warrants publication, although of course the degree of subsequent revision has been necessarily modest and literal. Bruce might have wanted to make further changes, but re-reading his work as he left it, I am more than ever struck by its importance. He might have made amendments, but he would not have written a better book.

John Morrill
Selwyn College, Cambridge

Periodical Abbreviations

The abbreviations below cover periodical publications only, and are used both in the notes and bibliography. Abbreviated titles for individual articles and books appear in the second and third sections of the bibliography. Abbreviations used for manuscript collections and references appear in section A of the bibliography. A number of manuscript tracts are referred to in the notes by their abbreviated titles. These appear alongside their full titles in Appendix I to Chapter 3.

A.H.R.	*American Historical Review*
B.I.H.R.	*Bulletin of the Institute of Historical Research*
C.H.J.	*Cambridge Historical Journal*
E.H.R.	*English Historical Review*
Econ.H.R.	*Economic History Review*
H.L.Q.	*Huntingdon Library Quarterly*
J.B.S.	*Journal of British Studies*
P.S.A.S.	*Proceedings of the Society of Antiquaries of Scotland*
P. & P.	*Past and Present*
R.E.S.	*Review of English Studies*
S.H.R.	*Scottish Historical Review*
S.J.P.E.	*Scottish Journal of Political Economy*
T.R.H.S.	*Transactions of the Royal Historical Society*

Other periodicals cited in the notes or bibliography are given their full titles.

H.M.C.   Historical Manuscripts Commission (Report)

A Note on the Use of Dates

The dates follow throughout the modern year — that is, the year beginning January 1st.

Contents

Foreword by Dr John Morrill, Selwyn College, Cambridge   v

Abbreviations   vi

A Note on Dates   vi

1. Introduction: the Position in March 1603   1

2. The First Year of Union: March 1603-July 1604   15
   Appendix: Bacon's Collation of Objections to the Change in Name   28

3. Tracts and Treatises on the Union, 1603-1605   30
   Appendix: A Catalogue of Tracts   56

4. Proclamations and Commission: July-December 1604   58

5. The Project Outside Parliament: January 1605-December 1606   79
   Appendix: The Union Jack   *See Plate Section*

6. The Project Inside Parliament: November 1606-July 1607   93

7. The Project After Parliament: Union After July 1607   137

8. Conclusion   161

Bibliography   179

Index   193

1

Introduction: the Position in March 1603

1. Scope of the Book

In March 1603, the accession of James VI of Scotland to the English throne brought together two adjacent nations under the authority of a single prince. This was the 'union of the crowns' — a decisive stage in the integration of England and Scotland, as one political unit. Dynastic union conditioned Anglo-Scots relations during the seventeenth century, and led to formal political and constitutional unification in 1707. The destinies of England and Scotland proceeded in tandem after 1603 — notwithstanding periods of tension between the nations, occasionally amounting to actual military conflict.

This bald statement of historical fact is in some ways misleading. It is true, but only in hindsight. The problem may be seen in the very term, 'union of the crowns'. This was not a contemporary description of James's accession to the English throne. It is instead a piece of conventional historical parlance, which begs the question. As we shall see, there was considerable dispute in England in 1607-8 about whether the crowns *had* been united by James's accession. Many argued that 1603 had seen only a union in authority, not a union in sovereignty. The formal, political, permanent links between the countries implied by the term did not exist at the start of James's joint dominion. It was by no means clear to contemporaries that the dynastic union would be permanent, or lead to a union of the two countries in their political, economic, legal and religious institutions.

My concern is not with the 'union of the crowns' — either as an event, or a historical term. I *am* concerned generally with the subsequent integration of the two nations in these different areas of public life. More specifically, I concentrate on the project of James VI and I after 1603 to extend the dynastic union into other areas, creating a true 'union of England and Scotland'. Subsequent chapters will examine the development of this project between 1603 and 1608, in more detail than existing accounts, and analysing the main factors influencing its political progress.[1] The union of 1603 is therefore important only as a starting point, a basis, a *sine qua non*.

A project for the unification of two countries in different areas of their national life — government and the constitution, law and justice, the church, trade etc. — throws up a great deal of material of interest to specialist historians. It could indeed be regarded as a unique opportunity for a historian to examine the different institutions and systems of England and Scotland, the differing ways in which the two peoples perceived those institutions and systems, from the words of men supporting or opposing 'union' in each area. This has not generally been my aim; nor have I attempted to demonstrate how the separate

1

institutions and systems in either country evolved or interacted as a result of the union of the crowns. I consider the constitutional, legal, ecclesiastical and economic aspects of 'union' only insofar as they provide a context for the political development of James's project, or measurably affected its progress. Such consideration is, however, considerable. Inevitably, arguments for and against the union project were conditioned by how people in England and Scotland viewed their government, law, religion, society — and most important of all, each other. Our look at the union therefore presupposes statements about these real and supposed differences. The effect of the project in each area will also be charted, alongside the general account.

Before turning to James's project for further unification of his two dominions, it is important to know the position of the two countries in 1603. This is, after all, the context within which the project had to operate. This introduction is therefore concerned with examining very briefly the principal similarities and differences between England and Scotland at the turn of the century. From this 'still photograph' of Britain in 1603, I will then isolate certain themes giving the picture life and movement.

2. Constitutional and Governmental Factors

Constitutionally and politically, the two nations in 1603 seemed rather similar. Both were monarchies, subject to God, with a recognised duty to govern for the common good, within existing laws. Both provided for advice of the monarch through a Council, for legislation and taxation by Estates — representative institutions increasingly defunct elsewhere in Christendom. Offices of government, though frequently differing in name, had parallel functions and operations in either nation.

Beneath this surface similarity lay great differences — in constitutional thought, administration and the effectiveness of royal authority. The English dimension is well known, needing relatively little examination. Constitutionally, Tudor England was a monarchy limited by 'commonwealth' responsibilities to the law and to the people. The popular will was expressed indirectly, through a parliament that had a monopoly of legislation and taxation. King-in-Parliament could do things which were beyond the king's own executive or prerogative powers. The principal controversy concerned the role and rule of law. Many writers followed Fortescue in emphasising the antiquity, authority and perfection of common law.[2] A few considered such law to have survived unchanged from immemorial origins, and to be ideally suited to English needs. The implications of immutability could elevate law above Parliament or King; but generally, they were glossed rather as a moral imperative not to change law without overriding necessity. Institutionally, political life centred on a small, compact Privy Council, on certain stable offices of government (for example the Secretary of State), and on relatively infrequent parliamentary sessions. Parliament was bicameral, with rights of self-discipline and free speech. Its sittings were comparatively long, with open debate and the freedom for any member to initiate proposals for legislation. Its sphere of action was wide, uncertain, and limited only by the shadowy boundaries of royal prerogative. Parliament represented all the people, either personally or by election. Royal government carried relatively great authority, even in turbulent parts of the kingdom like the West or North. Regional Councils acted as the arms of the Privy Council, a range of local officials under the Lord Lieutenant carrying administration into the shires, and funnelling information back to Whitehall.

Scotland presents a more chaotic picture. There was much less of a consensus regarding the constitution, even on the position of the monarchy. One radical tradition subordinated the king, both to laws and people. This tradition, heavily influenced by medieval theorists such as Marsilius of Padua, exists in Major and Boece as well as in Buchanan, Knox and Samuel Rutherford's 'Lex Rex' of 1644. In this, Buchanan is the central figure — not so much for any originality as for his importance as revolutionary theorist during the Scottish Reformation.[3] Buchanan used some dubious descriptions of early Scotland, mostly from Boece, to show monarchy subordinate to the law, and elective within one royal family. The electorate were the nobility, representing as clan leaders the entire Scottish people. This theory had links with sixteenth-century Huguenot thinkers, such as Hotman, Mornay and Beza. This, by English standards, radical tradition did not command complete acceptance in Scotland, even during the heyday of Buchanan, Melville and the Reformation. Thereafter,

> The theological challenge was met by a king who was himself a theologian . . . James was an apologist . . . for a monarchy responsible to God and not to people. The laws of Scotland, he explained, did not exist before the monarchy; on the contrary, the king had been and still was the author of the laws, which he made with the consent of his high court of Parliament.[4]

The Scots constitution swung rapidly, from divines' rule to divine right.

Scottish institutions similarly displayed less definition, and more medievalism. The Council remained enormous in membership, if not in quorum or working size. It was in fact the medieval Grand Council, retaining undifferentiated judicial, legislative, executive and consiliar functions. The Scots parliament differed greatly from the English. It was unicameral, and represented not the Scottish people, but the royal tenants-in-chief. Only royal burghs sent members. Shire representatives were introduced in 1587, but even petty lairds had the right (which some occasionally exercised) of attendance. Its submissiveness to the royal will is unsurprising. Parliament sat a few days only, passing most measures without debate, after one reading of the bill and without a committee stage. The Chancellor acted as a kind of prime minister and Speaker combined, controlling the session in the royal interest. Legislative initiation rested not with the members, but with a preparatory commission, the Lords of the Articles. This contained equal representation for each Estate, selected by a system ensuring obedience to the king.[5] Most bills before parliament came indirectly from the Council, funnelled through the commission. The existence of other assemblies for legislation and taxation was another, major difference. The Scots Council could pass binding, innovative legislation, rather than merely orders restating or applying existing law. Kings might also call a Convention, summoned at short notice and bound in discussion by the terms of summons. A much less formal institution than parliament, often little more than an expanded Council, this proved particularly useful for supply. The Convention of Royal Burghs, a further assembly, met four times each year with wide powers over commercial regulation and finance. The options open to a king contemplating legislation or taxation were therefore several, with a corresponding diminution in the independence of any assembly.

This might perhaps have been expected to strengthen royal authority; but the greatest single difference between the nations politically lay in the relative ineffectiveness of Scottish government. Piggott's remarks in 1607 about the political instability of Scotland were the more damaging for their accuracy. 'They have not suffered above two kings to die in their beds, these two hundred years. Our king hath hardly escaped them.'[6] A succession of Stuart minorities and English wars had left the monarchy weak — surrounded, occasionally dominated, by powerful aristocratic factions. James's own minority had seen a bewildering sequence of plots, feuds and coups, aggravated by religious differences. In his later writings, the king was appropriately bitter about the influence of aristocracy. The three themes of noble 'honour' were

> to thrall by oppression the meaner sort that dwelleth neere them to their service and following although they hold nothing of them . . . to maintaine their servants and dependers in any wrong although they be not answerable to the laws . . . for any displeasure that they apprehend to be done against them by their neighbour, to take up a plaine feide against him and without respect to God, King or Commonweale to bange it out bravelie, he and all his kinne against him and all his.[7]

The absence of sheriffs or other local officials separate from the nobility, and the special authority given to the latter by clan leadership, rendered most of the country impenetrable to royal authority. Even in the Lowlands, feuding was more common than in English heartlands. By 1603, James had achieved considerable success in overcoming these obstacles, establishing respect and obedience to the king at a new high. This was done partly through judicious manipulation of factions, partly through a party of dependant, skilful officials owing their position to favour rather than birth — and partly through luck. Even in 1603, James's authority in his old kingdom remained more fragile than in his new.

3. Law and Justice

Discussions of the two legal and judicial systems formed a major element in tracts written about James's union project. Since these are examined in detail in Chapter 3, consideration here is brief. Again, the main contrast is between a settled, defined law in England, and a chaos of different customs in Scotland. Englishmen viewed their law as an intrinsic part of civil society — the soul of the body politic. Common law was particularly reverenced, as the distilled wisdom of immemorial centuries. Its enormous authority relied on an equal weight of precedent, which long-established royal courts were bound to follow. For many, the ability of statutes to alter this law was dubious. Equity law had been affected by the same emphasis on precedent, becoming increasingly assimilated and similar to common law, in provisions and judgement. Star Chamber apart, justice was slow and complicated, following settled procedures. Other legal systems prompted a literally insular lack of interest, as inferior, and unsuited to the free soil of England. Scots law was considered to be either a debased and adulterated version of English common law, or as unalloyed Roman law.

This attitude was partly justified. As Skene was to show, medieval Scots customary law was based on English models. Scotland, however, preserved more of the pristine feudal code in its land laws. More importantly, the Wars of Independence and alliance with France had produced major importation of Roman elements into Scots law. This reception intensified in the sixteenth century. But before Scots law was Roman, or feudal, or customary English, it was confused: an undefined and largely undifferentiated mass of separate, sometimes contradictory, provisions. There was little codification or record, and very little reliance on precedent. A doctrine of informal legal desuetude for statutes had become accepted; even an Act of Parliament might become obsolete without regular restatement. This heterogeneity was paralleled in the Scots judiciary. The most regular courts were in Edinburgh, where the Council and Court of Session sat. There were no local J.P.s, local justice relying mainly on burghal courts, presbyterian censure, and the innumerable inherited jurisdictions of great and petty nobles. Accordingly, the Scots attitude to law differed. Law was certainly of great importance, bound closely to the health and identity of the commonwealth; nevertheless, it was made by man, for pragmatic reasons, and eminently mutable. There were, of course, English lawyers who felt the same. The difference was in degree, not kind.

4. Religion and the Church

The Elizabethan church, despite considerable internal pressure for further reform, and the alienation of many sectarians (and more Catholics) outside, remained a *via media*, a broad church housing many different theological traditions. It was also episcopal, acknowledged royal supremacy, and retained a large number of 'popish' rites and practices. By contrast, the Scots Reformation advanced rapidly from its Knoxian roots to full-blooded Melvillean presbyterianism, with the abolition of 'superstitious' sacraments, the imposition of a hierarchy of ecclesiastical assemblies for discussion and discipline, apparent abolition of episcopacy and denial of temporal supremacy.[8] At the 1578 General Assembly, this programme became official policy. The two ensuing decades were however to see, if not a retreat, at least a halt to the presbyterian advance. There had always been tension between the true Knoxian reformers and the nobles who had led the Reformation; lay lords were particularly unwilling to grant the Kirk control over its property, whatever the likely benefits in an educated clergy and alleviated poor. To this was added the episcopalianism of James. The 1584 Black Acts, after the Ruthven Raid and Arran's royalist counter-coup, provided a permanent place for bishops within the presbyterian system. Arran's fall in 1585 during the 'Border Lords' coup demonstrated the influence on Scottish ecclesiastical politics of ultra-Protestant advisers like Walsingham and Davison, used by Elizabeth for her Scots policy. The presbyterianisation of Scotland culminated in 1592 in acts abolishing episcopacy and establishing annual General Assemblies. The presbyterian ministers then overreached themselves. Considerable tactlessness if not outright disrespect was shown to the crown, Melville calling James 'God's silly vassal' and preaching ecclesiastical supremacy to the king's face. One St Andrews minister even denied the jurisdiction of the Council, after being summoned for his description of kings as 'devil's children'. The turning point came with the 1596 Edinburgh Riot and the royal threat to evacuate the capital. The dying years of the century saw effective royal action to limit General Assemblies, by postponement, summoning to northern towns, or control through the commission of ecclesiastical advice, and to restore the episcopal estate in parliament. The nomination of ministers to sit in parliament as titular bishops without spiritual authority was particularly important here.

The differences in church government and discipline therefore remained significant — and were stressed by Parsons in his attack on the prospect of union.[9] Many contemporaries, however, considered these differences insignificant, compared with the broad doctrinal uniformity of the churches. Unity of religion is repeatedly cited as a major force impelling further union.[10] This close doctrinal proximity is confirmed by modern scholarship.[11] There remained another difference, in the two nations' perceptions of their churches. English apologists had presented their Reformation as a return to the original purity of the ancient English church. The Scots acknowledged their Reformation as a revolution, seeing theirs as 'a self-made church, realised through a collective act of national will'.[12] In both countries, however, the church, like the law, remained a powerful focus of national identity and pride.

5. Society and Economy

Economically, the differences between the countries were enormous. Scotland remained a poor and in some ways primitive society. Its economic base was much smaller than the English, even after allowances for differences in land mass, population and climate. Scotland was overwhelmingly rural, self-sufficient at the homestead level but subject to recurrent famine. Large areas were barren, rough pasturage or waste. Lack of proper crop rotation, poor artificial drainage and the insecurity of land tenantry-at-will all contributed to low fertility. Fishing, potentially a major resource, was under-exploited, partly because of the monopoly of (East Coast) royal burghs. James's attempts to increase Scotland's manufacturing sector were generally unsuccessful. Vested interests, notably the craft gilds, played a stifling role. Native industry *was* encouraged, by letters patent and monopolies, in many areas (for example soap, glass, linen, ironwork). James tried above all to encourage clothiers by acts favouring foreign clothmakers, as instructors to the Scots. These acts complemented the many (and widely disregarded) measures to prohibit or tax the importation of foreign cloth, and the export of native wool.[13]

Scots commerce was small in volume, involving mainly the export of raw materials (especially skins and hides) and the import of grain, luxuries and manufactures. Very little cloth was exported, save as rough clothing for the poorer classes in the Netherlands. The contrast with England's vigorous commercial activity was marked. Scots ships were as small as most of their trading ventures. Trade was dominated by a tiny merchant elite who controlled the Gild Merchant, the Royal Burghs and the Convention alike. Their overseas trips were rare, confined to a few known markets. The most important lay in the Baltic, the Low Countries, France and Spain. England was only fourth in the list of Scots trading nations.[14] Of 4500 aliens in London in 1571, only forty were Scots. The commercial inequality between the nations was therefore unrelieved by regular commercial links.

This relative poverty was reflected in social differences. Scottish burghs were small, and medieval in character. Rural society comprehended a large class of self-sufficient tenantry with little prospect of betterment and small food margins, and a small class of feudal nobility exercising jurisdiction and clan leadership over their dependants. Only in the Lowlands was there a 'middling sort' of independent farmers. Whatever view one takes of Kerridge's 'agrarian revolution', England in 1600 clearly possessed a considerable class of 'yeomen' farmers. The economic and personal subjection of tenant to landlord was less absolute than in Scotland. England possessed more arable land, and better pasture. Her agricultural wealth was paralleled by greater wealth and sophistication in manufacturing and commercial enterprise.

6. 'Cultures'

Many historians describe Scotland in the late sixteenth century as an increasing 'cultural' approximation to England: a rapprochement in language, literature, education, the arts, apparel, recreational pursuits and 'manners'. Donaldson considers this among the major 'foundations of Anglo-Scots unity'.[15] Particularly important was the extension of English language to Scotland, supplanting Gaelic and Scots alike. The anglicisation of Scots is seen in her literature, accelerated by mass importation of English Bibles. 'Already before 1603 the Scots vernacular was in fair way to being displaced as a literary language . . . in prose works generally there was a change directly from Latin to English, without an intermediate phase of Scots.'[16] This literary predominance was thus reflected in the slow development of Scottish printing. Academically and musically, Donaldson confirms Trevor-Roper's thesis of English cultural predominance.[17] Riley, however, strongly rejects the thesis of a general, steady cultural assimilation.[18] Undoubtedly, many of the changes outlined by Donaldson did occur, in the Lowlands. It was not, however, accompanied by any demonstrable growth in fraternal sentiment towards England. Rather, it seems to have been adopted in the interests of self-identification, as 'civilised' behaviour separating the Lowlander from the uncouth Highlander and Borderer.

7. Previous History

This cursory summary of the two nations in 1603 forms part of the context within which the union project developed. Other aspects, such as general relations between the English crown and parliament, will be examined later. No introduction, however, can be complete without considering the previous histories of the two countries, and the resulting attitudes of English and Scots towards each other.

Certain events and periods have apparent significance. The first, obviously, is the longstanding hostility between the nations during the medieval Wars of Independence. Despite the emphasis placed by Scots historians on the early Edwards, conflict between the nations considerably pre-dated the Bruce/Balliol controversy.[19] The practical results of the wars were the mutual isolation of England and Scotland, and the Scots alliance with France. Only in the late fifteenth century are there signs of change. The most significant events here were the 1474 marriage negotiations of Edward IV and James III, and the similar offers made two decades later by Henry VII. The success of the latter, with marriage between James IV and Henry's daughter Margaret, involved the first formal peace between the nations for 180 years, and created links between Stuart and Tudor dynasties that led directly to the union of the crowns.[20]

Henry VII's peace was temporary, ruptured almost immediately by clashes on the Borders and high seas. The provisions in the agreement contradicted Scots treaty obligations to France. Renewed hostilities after 1513 reflected partly this contradiction, partly the high-handed attitude of Henry VIII to Scotland.[21] England's failure to exploit her crushing victory at Flodden produced a decade of estrangement.[22]

Despite the Anglophile policy adopted during James V's minority, under Margaret Tudor and the Earl of Angus, conflict remained the keynote of relations during the remainder of Henry's reign. This was exacerbated by religious differences after the English Reformation, with James adhering to Rome and his two French marriages. James indeed actively courted hostility, harbouring Catholic refugees, allowing the continuation of Border raids, and rejecting Sadler's diplomatic overtures in 1540.[23]

The outbreak of war in 1542, and the campaigns of 1542-8, have been exhaustively traced.[24] However, the period had considerable importance in forming the attitudes of the two nations to each other, and to union. It therefore merits some attention. In many ways, the period was transitional. On the one hand, the campaigns contained many typical medieval features. There was the same emphasis on conquest as the means of union, the same readiness of Henry and Somerset to justify their invasions by claims to suzerainty. Thus the victory of Solway Moss and death of James V inspired English assertions of superiority as well as the marriage project between Prince Edward and Mary, Queen of Scots. However, the suzerainty theme was kept in reserve as long as the marriage remained possible. It was in 1548-9, when a French marriage beckoned for Mary, that the claims were stridently revived: in Somerset's Epistle of 1548, and in Bodrugan's Epitome.[25] The Protector scoured archives for proofs.[26] Scots reacted bitterly, the 'Rough Wooing' producing an inevitable upsurge of patriotic Anglophobia.

If these were the traditional themes of the campaign, there were also newer features: emphasising peace, brotherhood, equality and true religion. The marriage was a keystone. English ambitions in Scotland were to be achieved by peaceful means, *via* the 1543 Treaty of Greenwich. Even as they fought, burned and raped, the English protested their fellowship.[27] This use of propaganda indicated a desire to persuade rather than conquer. Henry and Somerset alike used Scots rather than English in their initiatives. Somerset particularly presented the campaign as an alliance between the English and all well-meaning Scots. The garrison policy and protection of Assured Scots were visible aspects of this alliance.[28] Somerset's proposals were appropriately fraternal, stressing Scotland's equality and independence. Scotland would keep her native laws and customs. England would abolish all her laws hostile to Scotland, and extend freedom of marriage and trade to Scotland. Unity in (Protestant) religion was also promised, along with the submergence of 'England' and 'Scotland' under 'the indifferent old name of Britaynes'.[29] This too was egalitarian, eliminating precedency in the royal style.

Somerset's proposals were unsophisticated.[30] The Protector showed little interest in Harryson's proposals for economic reform in Scotland, except as propaganda.[31] Nevertheless, the proposals are directly and indirectly relevant to James's union project. James, probably consciously, adopted Somerset's programme as part of the wider union he desired. Indirectly, the offers made by England in 1548 lessened the considerable legacy of hostility and mistrust left by the Rough Wooing. Hostility there undoubtedly was — but also a widespread feeling that the failed marriage was a lost opportunity for peace with honour.[32]

This feeling inevitably intensified after the Scottish Reformation. Even in the 1550s, there had been stirrings in Scotland against dominance by France. This was fanned by expatriate Scots protestants seeking to import the Reformation. The tangled events of 1560-7 cannot be examined here, except to stress the close involvement of England in the promotion of the protestant cause. The actual arrival of protestantism changed drastically the relationship between the nations. Scotland owed her religious and civil settlement to English assistance. The two nations were partners in restoring purity to the church, and resisting the machinations of popery. Mary's exile in England and the minority of James VI turned Scotland's attentions inward, to civil and ecclesiastical politics, away from foreign adventures. The result was unbroken peace between the nations, from Reformation to union of the crowns. James's status as likely heir to Elizabeth alternately shook and cemented this peace, notably during the turbulent 1580s. The English involvement in the Border Lords coup, the Babington Plot and execution of Mary were balanced against Elizabeth's halfway recognition of James in the Peace of Berwick.[33] The king was ambivalent during the Armada, keeping the Borders quiet but giving Catholics full rein in the Highlands.

In the 1590s, the Borders became a major instrument of policy in James's campaign for recognition.[34] We will examine Border life in more detail later. In the sixteenth century, the Borders remained an indifferently policed area of feuds, both between English and Scots, and between the surnames of the same nation.[35] International arrangements laid down by successive Anglo-Scots commissions after 1553 remained largely dead letters. Local families are found restoring castles and towers to service in the 1590s. Some of this disorder reflected the relative inability of English wardens to replace the territorial and political influence of the old noble families. It also reflected some conscious neglect by James of his duty to control the Scottish Marches — in the hope of political advantage.[36] This culminated in 1596, after Elizabeth failed to pay her annual pension. The implications of payment were more important than the sum involved. The activities of Robert Ker of Cessford and Walter Scott of Buccleuch, Warden of Middle March and Keeper of Liddesdale respectively, proved particularly odious — Scott's exploits including the famous Kinmont Willie raid on Carlisle in April 1596. The Treaty of Carlisle a year later brought some benefit; but only after Cecil's secret compact with James on succession did the Scots Council act vigorously to pacify the Marches, and establish credit in England.

8. Themes and Conclusions

From history and existing circumstances emerged certain themes and attitudes that were to prove particularly important during the years of the union project.

The first factor to be stressed is the residual hostility and prejudice of the two nations towards each other.[37] Parsons, in his propaganda against James's title, makes much of 'the aversion and natural alienation of that people from the Inglish, and their ancient inclination to ioyne with the French and Irish'.[38] We shall also see it stressed by numerous tracts on the union, notably by Craig and Thornborough.

The nature of the prejudice is also clear. 'The Scots looked on the English as selfish and arrogant, an impression which English attitudes did much to reinforce.'[39] The corresponding English stereotype of Scotland was of a poor, overpopulated country, not worth the conquest, inhabited by a primitive and disorderly people. All this was connected with deep-rooted English assumptions about their own superiority, as a nation and people. Insofar as Englishmen considered the forthcoming union, they regarded it as a subordination of Scotland to England. Parsons and his opponents are at one here.[40] This assumption of superiority went beyond the stereotype of English riches and Scots poverty. Material fortunes merely confirmed the feudal and indeed moral supremacy of the southern kingdom.

The average Elizabethan saw the old assertions to suzerainty over Scotland as simple fact. The claim was never forgotten by the later Tudors. Cecil in 1560 justified English intervention in Scots affairs precisely on these grounds.[41] Elaborate genealogies were drawn up proving Elizabeth's right to homage from the Scots king.[42] Holinshed approved the claim; so did a host of lesser historians, writers and playwrights.[43] Sir Thomas Craig found it necessary, like Major and Buchanan before him, to deny repeatedly this slur on Scots independence. Many Elizabethan lawyers seriously considered the Scots natural subjects of the English queen.[44] English and Scots alike had produced elaborate myths of natural origin, respectively affirming and refuting the claim to suzerainty. Brutus, Lucius and Arthur were invoked by the Tudors; Fergus and Gathelus by the Stuarts.[45] In England, there was particular emphasis on the antique purity and glory of their national origin. Initially rival, but increasingly consolidated mythologies linked England and the Tudors with classical and biblical antiquity. This accompanied a growth in prophetic, apocalyptic history. Studies of Revelation were correlated by Bale, Jewel and above all Foxe with English history, to justify the English Reformation and present 'an imperial vision . . . which has permanently transformed English culture'.[46] Haller's analysis of Foxe has demonstrated the growth of belief in England as an Elect Nation, preserving a primitive-Christian faith imported directly from the Apostles. Elizabeth was the culmination of this glittering history, a figure of spiritual as well as national importance.[47]

To speak only of hostility, prejudice and precedency would however be misleading. Besides the economic, religious and cultural links between the nations at the turn of the century, there was also a widespread feeling or hope that the age of hostility might have passed. Major's punning 'History of Greater Britain' (1521), with its commendation of a union between the two countries based on marriage and equality, is an early expression of this. Major praised the English polity, decrying the miserable effects of separation upon Scotland. Forty years later, Cecil repeated the theme. 'The best worldly felicity, y^t Scotland can have, is either to continue in a perpetual peace with the Kingdom of England, or to be made one Monarchy with England, as they both make but one Isle, divided from ye rest of ye world.'[48] Craig too made much of the devastating impact that disunion had had, not merely on Scotland. This generous attitude to union, most marked north of the border, grew after the Scottish Reformation. Knox regarded the character and fate of the two nations as so similar as practically to be one. This was allied to a feeling that union was the work of God. Gilby spoke of Antichrist preventing union under Edward VI lest the island become a sanctuary for true religion, and looked for a single, godly prince to lead both nations.[49] Williamson has shown the rise in Scotland of an apocalyptic vision similar to that of Foxe, but tied to Britain rather than either of the two nations.[50] This vision was strongly influenced by the survival of a British mythology comprehending Brutus, Lucius, Arthur and the Samothean links of the English patriotic tradition. These longstanding considerations of Britain as an 'Empire' were strengthened by Henrician propaganda, Tudor historiography and Elizabethan dramatic spectacle.[51] In Scotland, the British Vision was resisted by scholars like Napier, who resented its implications for Scots independence. In England, as we have seen, it went hand in hand with claims to English domination over the Scots. Undoubtedly, the tradition was helped by the prospect of Anglo-Scots union, with the possible accession of first Mary and then James Stuart as Elizabeth's successor. The considerable public debate about succession, expressed allegorically in plays, more forthrightly and dangerously in tracts, did little however to examine the likely effects or further developments such a union in authority might bring.[52] Their arguments moved opinion towards acceptance of 'union', but did not define what institutional changes unity might bring.

NOTES

1. The main general accounts of the project are: Omond, *Scottish Union Question*; Wedgwood, 'Anglo-Scottish Relations'; Ferguson, *Scotland's Relations with England*; Spedding, *Bacon* III; Willson, *James VI and I*, 'James and Anglo-Scottish Unity'; Notestein, *House of Commons*: etc.

2. Robert Mulcaster's translation of Fortescue's *De Laudibus legum Angliæ* was very popular in Tudor and early Stuart England, being reprinted several times in London. See also Skeel, 'Fortescue', and Pocock, *Ancient Constitution*.

3. For estimates of the importance of Buchanan, see: P. H. Brown, *Buchanan*; Trevor-Roper, *Buchanan*; W. S. McKechnie, ed., *George Buchanan*, Glasgow Tercentenary Studies (Glasgow, 1907); J. E. Phillips, 'George Buchanan and the Sidney Circle', H.L.Q. 1948-9.

4. Donaldson, *Scotland*, 196.

5. *Ibid.*, 284. The eight nobles on the Articles were selected first, by the (royalist) bishops. These eight then selected eight of the bishops, and the whole sixteen chose eight representatives from the third Estate. For further details of Scots parliaments, see Rait, *Parliaments of Scotland* and Terry, *Scottish Parliaments*.

6. Cobbett, *Parl. Hist.* I, Col. 1097.

7. *Basilicon Doron*, 83: quoted in Smout, *Scottish People*, 103.

8. 'Knox would have found presbyterianism unfamiliar and in some ways absurd.' *Ibid.*, 62.

9. 'Considering what the state of religion is in Scotland at this day, and how different and rather opposite to that forme which in England is maintayned, and when the

archbishops, bishops, deanes archdeacons . . . shal consider that no such dignity or promotion is left now standing in Scotland, no nor any cathedral or collegiate church . . . and when our nobilitye shal remember how the nobilitye of Scotland is subject to this day to a few ordinary and common ministers, without any head,' etc. Parsons, *Conference*, 123. See also Harington, *Tract on the Succession*, 96.

10. See e.g. *Harington, ibid.*, 30-1. A marginal note on *Parsons* 123 preserved in the facsimile edition is significant here: 'Note how he confuseth religion and church politics.'

11. Trevor-Roper, 'Union of Britain', 448. See also Tyacke's piece in Russell, *Origins of ECW*, 120-43.

12. Williamson, *Scottish National Consciousness*, 139.

13. See e.g. *Acts, Sc.Parl.IV*, 119, Lythe comments: 'It cannot be said that Scotland had acquired either a distinctive or decisive commercial policy . . . the policy towards both foreign and internal trade remained essentially medieval' — *Economy of Scotland*, 94. The best overall survey is Grant, *Scotland before 1603*.

14. Lythe, *Economy of Scotland*; Keith, *Commercial Relations*; Brown, *Early Travellers in Scotland*, 87.

15. Donaldson, 'Foundations of Anglo-Scottish Unity', in Bindoff (ed.), *Elizabethan Government and Society*, 282-314.

16. *Ibid.*, 293.

17. Trevor-Roper, 'Union of Britain', 446.

18. Riley, *Union of England and Scotland*, 2.

19. E.g. the invasion of England by William the Lion in 1174. For the events of 1291-2, see Palgrave, *Documents and Records*, i-cxxxii, and E. L. G. Stones, *Anglo-Scottish Relations, 1174-1328* (Edinburgh, 1958).

20. Bacon presents this in a prophetic manner, with English councillors protesting about the prospect of a Scots accession. 'Whereunto the King himself replied; that if that should be, Scotland would be but an accession to England . . . for that the greater would draw the less': *Henry VII*, 189.

21. Mackie, *Earlier Tudors*, 270ff.

22. Sea Eaves, *Henry VIII's Scottish Diplomacy, 1513-24*.

23. Slavin, *Sir Ralph Sadler*, esp. 77ff.

24. The best brief modern accounts are in Slavin, *Sir Ralph Sadler*; Merriman, 'Assured Scots'; Mackie, *Earlier Tudors*; Bush, *Protector Somerset*; Donaldson, *Scotland*; Ferguson, *Scotland's Relations*.

25. See Murray, *Complaynt of Scotlande*, 238-47 and 248-56. Assertions of superiority also occur in the 1544 English Act of Subsidy, in John Elder's 'Proposal for Uniting Scotland with England' (Scott, *Bannatyne Miscellany*, 3-18), and in Harryson's 'Exhortacion to the Scottes' of 1547 (Murray, *Complaynt of Scotlande*, 207-37). The claim was stressed, significantly, after the English defeat at Haddon Rig.

26. B.L.Add.MSS 6128.

27. Murray, *Complaynt of Scotlande*, 227ff. (Harryson), 239ff. (Somerset), 256 (Bodrugan).

28. Bush, *Protector Somerset*, 19; Merriman, 'Assured Scots', *passim*.

29. Murray, *Complaynt of Scotlande*, 241ff. In a report of 1543 Sadler had said that the Scots 'had levre suffer extremitye thanne cum to thobediaunce of Ingland. They woll have thaire realme free, and lyve within themselves after their own lawes and customes' (Slavin, 112). The Treaty of Haddington with the French included just such a reservation.

30. Bush, *Protector Somerset*, 10.

31. For these proposals, see 'The Godly and Golden Booke for the Concorde of England and Scotland' and his twenty-six questions (*Calendar of State Papers Relating to Scotland I*, 140-5 and 180-1).

32. Williamson, *Scottish National Consciousness*, 11ff; Craig, *Right of Succession*, 429.

33. Willson, *James VI and I*, 72.

34. See Stafford, *James and the Throne of England* for the wider campaign.

35. Smout, *Scottish People*, 104. See Chapters 2 and 5 for bibliographies of works on the Borders.

36. Watts & Watts, *From Border to Middle Shire*, 18; Rae, *Scottish Frontier*, 216-20.

37. Riley, *Union of England and Scotland*, xiv: 'Between the two peoples, at most levels of society, there was a cordial dislike and occasionally open hostility. To each the other kingdom was the ancient enemy.'

38. Parsons, *Conference*, 118. Consider the following Tudor ditty:

>   A Scot our King! That day
>   Our cripple state will need a crutch.
>   What next? In time a Scot will prate
>   As primate of our church!

W. Addison, *Essex Heyday* (London, 1949), 16.

39. Riley, *Union of England and Scotland*, xiv.

40. Parsons, *Conference*, 118-19: Harington, *Tract on the Succession*, 32, 61.

41. N.L.S.Adv.MSS 31.2.19, 139.

42. B. L. King's MSS 396, esp. fols. 28-9.

43. Wilson, *State of England*, 8; *Harington*, 61. See also Axton, *Two Bodies*, 17-20, 33-5, 94-5. Axton overemphasises the influence of Plowden, as 'discoverer' of suzerainty.

44. Craig, *De Unione*, 347.

45. See Kendrick, *British Antiquity*; Ferguson, *John Twynne*; Murray, *Complaynt of Scotlande*, etc. Axton, *Two Bodies*, 33-5 and 38-97 *passim* contains much good material on the political use of Trojan and Arthurian mythology in Elizabethan England, to confirm her 'superiority' over the Scots.

46. Williamson, *Scottish National Consciousness*, viii.

47. England became 'not a visible communion of elected saints awaiting the millenium but a people with a strong sense of there identity as a nation set apart from all others, aware of what they took to be a common past, and intent on what they took to be their apparent place and destiny in the world'. Haller, *Elect Nation*, 249.

48. N.L.S.Adv.MSS 31.2.19, 135.

49. Williamson, *Scottish National Consciousness*, 15.

50. *Ibid.*, viii-ix.

51. Koebner, 'Imperial Crown', esp. 50; Firth, 'British Empire'. Plays involving antique British 'imperium' and its descent to the Tudors are considered in *Axton*, 33-5, 77 and 97ff. For the growth of a British historiography under the Tudors, see Donaldson, 'Foundations of Anglo-Scottish Unity', in Bindoff (ed.), *Elizabethan Government and Society*, 313ff.

52. The closest concerned Parson's allegations that Scots would dominate high-ranking offices. For Harington's answer, see *Tract on the Succession*, 32.

2

The First Year of Union: March 1603-July 1604

1. Before the English Parliament

The history of the union project during James's first year as king of England has been widely considered.[1] Several themes are usually emphasised: the eagerness of James to abandon Scotland, his vainglory as a motive force for the project, his precipitate speed in pressing union against the plain wishes of England and cautious advice of councillors such as Cecil, and his excessive favour to Scots. The last theme is sometimes extended, with assertions that Scots supported the union because it tended to their particular advantage.

Each theme can be supported with some evidence. James did complete his arrangements in Edinburgh very quickly, and hurry south. The assumption of many historians is that the king was overwhelmed by his good fortune, and that this explains both his sudden departure and the rash of honours bestowed in either kingdom. This is questionable. James's speed was the natural reaction of a new king distant from his capital and anxious to secure his crown. Political insecurity can also explain the knighthoods and honours bestowed *en route*; all new monarchs were expected to be liberal in gifts, while James as a foreigner needed to establish quickly a party of Englishmen bound to him by favour. The allegation of vainglory bears closer attention. James received many panegyrics, praising his accession as the work of divine providence, and lauding his personal qualities. These were again a conventional element in any accession. Personal laudation received no particular encouragement from James, despite his alleged conceit and the emphasis on the dignity of kings in his previous writings.[2] James *did* foster the idea that the union of the crowns had been the work of God, using the king as His tool. This we shall examine in more detail later.[3] It is however simplistic to argue that James believed the panegyrists, held inflated ideas of personal mission and launched the union project as a consequence. James's encouragement for themes of divine providence can be more mundanely explained. Such ideas helped both to secure his hold over England, and advance the union project itself.

The allegation of precipitate speed is the most common, serious and mistaken theme. There is in fact very little evidence of a headlong rush towards union in 1603-4. Bacon's famous remark, that he 'hasteneth to a mixture of both kingdoms and nations, faster perhaps than policy will conveniently bear', is inconclusive.[4] Besides coming very early in the reign, the remark from its context seems to refer to a mixture of nationalities at court, not to political union. What is most notable about 1603 is precisely the absence of substantive action in this area. James restricted his activities to areas where he could use prerogative powers, without prejudicing wider discussions in parliament. These were respectively his attempts to instil peace, order and brotherhood into his two peoples, to reconcile their commercial and economic systems, to settle the government of Scotland and establish a mixture of English and Scots at court.

James was active and insistent in the first of these. In his proclamation to Scotland announcing his accession to the English crown, James ordered Scots to acknowledge Englishmen 'as their deirest bretherein and freindis, and the inhabitantis of baith his realmes to obliterat and remove out of their myndis all and qhatsumevir quarrellis . . . with ane universall unanimitie of hairtis'.[5] This theme was repeated in his later 'Proclamation for the Uniting of England and Scotland', in May 1603. The stress early in the reign on the need for a union in hearts and minds is remarkable. One area where such pious sentiments were made action was the Borders. The suppression of dissident Border clans, notably the Grahams, and the rundown of the large but now superfluous garrison at Berwick reflected partly a desire to keep order and reduce expenditure. Such actions also however reflected James's insistence that English and Scots there should be one people, enshrined symbolically under the name of the 'Middle Shires'. His policy was 'utterlie to extinguishe as well the name as substance of the bordouris, I mean the difference between them and other pairtis of the kingdome. For doing thairof it is necessarie that all querrellis amoungst thaim be reconcyled and all straingenes between the nations quite removed'.[6] As early as April 1603, James in a proclamation from Newcastle declared his intention to abolish March Laws, and govern the Middle Shires by the ordinary laws and courts of either kingdom. The same concern with concord and symbolism can be seen in lesser incidents. One such was the change in the Great Seal, conjoining not only English and Scottish arms but also those of Cadwallader and Edward the Confessor — the last undisputed kings of Celtic Britain and Anglo-Saxon England. James thereby evoked the revival of Britain and reconciliation of its peoples under a monarch of mixed blood.[7] A minor, revealing incident is the favour extended to Sir Hugh Bethell after the engagement of his daughter to the son of the Scot, Sir William Auchterlony: 'seeing we have no greater desire than that the union of these kingdoms in our person be corroborate in the hearts of our subjects of either realme . . . to establish the same to posteritie'.[8]

Commercially, the first year saw substantive progress towards union. A proclamation in April established the relative values of Scots and English currency, to encourage mutual trade. Englishmen trading in Scotland were exempted from payment of some customs, creating a virtual free trade in domestic commodities.[9] How far such relaxations were mutual is uncertain; the English Council in November 1603 proclaimed against the unlawful conveyance of goods into and from Scotland, seeking to restrict trade to the customs posts at Berwick and Carlisle.

The final area of activity lay in the settlement of government and the court. It is difficult here to separate measures taken to promote union from those made necessary by the exigencies of governing two kingdoms, one *in absentia*. The significant question is whether the measures were intended as an interim or permanent arrangement. Lee has shown that many initial measures in Scotland (for example for the education of the prince and management of the queen's estates) appear temporary. Nevertheless, the Scots bureaucracy was retained intact, officials who had accompanied James to London either returning quickly or resigning their posts.[10] The new features reflected absentee government: the establishment of an efficient post between the capitals, and the division of the Scottish Council into Edinburgh and London groups. The former was important. The king received each year over sixty public (and many more private) letters, the post acting also as the principal communications channel between London and Edinburgh Scots. In this early period, the function of these groups can be identified precisely. The Edinburgh Council was mainly executive, handling everyday matters like the Borders, but submitting major questions, with advice, to the king. The London group — Lennox, Mar, Kinloss, Sir George Home and Sir James Elphinstone — formed a coterie of trusted advisers to James on his Scottish affairs. Other London Scots acted as unofficial channels to the king, Sir Thomas Erskine maintaining a particularly lively correspondence.

In all this, there was very little to suggest imminent institutional union. English complaints about union really concerned the mixture of the two nations at court. There was resentment at the number of Scots at court, and belief that they monopolised the royal favour. The Venetian ambassador reported that 'the supreme offices are bestowed on Scots . . . everyday posts are taken from the English' in a 'high-handed' manner causing 'great chagrin'.[11]

Before examining this, some thought is necessary. There were some very good reasons why Scots might receive preferential treatment. Besides being men whom James knew he could work with and trust, old servants, they were also the people who had done most to establish the efficient government of Scotland in the 1590s. In that time, they had received relatively few rewards in cash or honours, and it was only reasonable they should expect to share James's fortune. They were also the people on whom James would be relying to maintain Scottish government, during his absence. The creation of obligations now might obviate the danger of subsequent alienation.[12]

This special pleading is partly valid, but obscures the most important truth — that there was no 'flood of Scots' into English government. The number of Scots coming south was small, especially after James's proclamation forbidding unlicensed passage.[13] Fewer still secured official positions in London. James overwhelmingly rewarded his Scots servants with pensions and cash rather than positions — to their chagrin, as the French ambassador makes clear.[14] The king then required his servants to return home, resuming their posts in the Scottish government. The residue of 'official' Scots in London comprised three groups. A few were advanced into minor government posts, and denizenated.[15] The second group was James's inner ring of counsel on Scots affairs. These five were likewise denizenated, and admitted to the English Council.[16] Their influence on English affairs was, however, small; they were occasionally appointed to Council committees, but did not form part of the quadrumvirate (Cecil,

Worcester, Suffolk and Northampton) with most influence on royal policy. They were outnumbered not only by established Councillors, but by Englishmen raised to the Council during James's first years. Of the five, only Home received a governmental post, and that briefly.[17] Their admission may be seen either as a convenience measure, to give them a recognised standing at court, or as a symbol of the united, British Council James hoped eventually to create.[18] The third and largest group comprised Scots given places in the Household, notably the Bedchamber and Privy Chamber. Their overall number was small, but sufficient to establish a definite presence, particularly in the queen's service.[19] Two factors apply here. It was entirely natural that the king and queen should continue in their immediate entourage personal servants who had shown loyalty and goodwill. Equally, they could in practice have only one such entourage. Since James was king over both countries, it would have insulted Scotland grossly had his entourage been entirely English. This principle of equality surfaces in de Beaumont's report of James's intention, to have seven of each nation in his Bedchamber.[20]

The presence of Household Scots undoubtedly caused resentment, as de Beaumont showed. Willson considers this discontent justified, the Scots acting as major sources of patronage. This is at best unproven.[21] Certainly, some Englishmen were displaced, and others disappointed. More significant is the spread of discontent to classes in England whose own chances of favour were non-existent. Scots at court were an issue around which crystallised the residual hostility and suspicion of the two nations.[22] The evidence for friction in 1603 is considerable. French and Venetian ambassadors were for once in agreement here. Arthur Wilson later recalled that 'the streets swam night and day with bloody quarrels' between Scots and English.[23] James was forced in July 1603 to issue a proclamation against Scots insolencies, and in April 1604 to order the arrest of 'Swaggerers' who were ambushing Scots in London.[24] In Scotland, there were already signs of unhappiness with absentee government, and fears that future union would bring an unequal settlement.[25]

By March 1604, James had moved gradually to promote the idea and reality of union, stressing the need for amity between his peoples. Simultaneously, the new contact between English and Scots had aroused old contentions, ensuring that 'union' would be a controversial subject in 1604.

2. The English Parliament in 1604

Discussion of the union project during the English session of March-June 1604 has long been affected by the controversy over relations between the early Stuarts and the House of Commons. The session has usually been interpreted in a 'whig' manner, emphasising the importance of parliament, of the Lower House within parliament, and of those in the Commons who spoke against 'royal interests'. Politics was thus seen as a battleground between a 'Court Party' of dependants and a relatively well-organised, fixed-membership 'Opposition' seeking to rectify grievances, secure parliamentary privileges, and expand the scope and effectiveness of the House through committee systems and threats to withhold supply. To Notestein in particular, the significant issues of the session were wardship, purveyancing, the Merchant Adventurers and the disputed Goodwin/Fortescue election. These questions of grievance and privilege allegedly created conflict with a king unused to and unsuited for the patient management of long, powerful English parliaments. The result was the Commons' 'Apology', 'a bold declaration of right, a lecture to a foreign king upon the constitution of his new kingdom'.[26]

The whig tradition has of course been questioned for some time. Recent scholarship has stressed the defects of parliament: its infrequent meetings, the erosion of its legislative monopoly by proclamations, and of its fiscal position by the growth of extra-parliamentary sources of revenue. Parliament's concern with historical 'rights', based on precedent, becomes last-ditch conservatism under pressure from the inexorable logic of Divine Right monarchy. Through-out Europe, parliamentary institutions were giving way to the absolute sovereignty of the king. When an English parliament sat, it was intended as a national show of solidarity, to consider an emergency like war or a major constitutional question. Arguments were rare even in the Lower House, the two chambers normally cooperating in obedience to the king. Where 'opposition' did surface, it usually reflected divisions within the court and Council.

This general reassessment has meant radical reinterpretation of the 1604 session, particularly on grievances and privilege.[27] The Buckinghamshire election has been relegated to a dispute between Commons and Council, James himself showing strict impartiality. His 'high-handed, dictatorial command' to the Commons to confer with the judges, and subsequent decision to admit neither candidate without fresh elections, becomes a compromise enabling the Commons to surrender without losing face. The programme of grievances advanced by Wroth on March 23 is considered a *royal* initiative, to secure composition of feudal purveyancing and wardship dues.[28] Purveyancing and the 'monopoly' of the Merchant Adventurers survived because of internal divisions in the Commons, while the failure to agree on wardship reflected only the deteriorating relations of king and Commons during May 1604.

Any independent discussion of the union must take account of and influence these rival interpretations. Two features stand out. Firstly, the union was undoubtedly intended as the major issue of debate, and in fact occupied more parliamentary time than any other subject. Secondly, modern insistence on the cooperation of king and Commons cannot obscure the exasperation of both sides by June 1604. The 'Apology' may never have been submitted to James. The king may have been more careful in his final speech to distinguish between the well-affected majority and knavish minority in the Commons than is generally believed. Nevertheless, that speech remained a blistering admonition. Contemporary records leave no doubt about the royal disfavour.[29] The same records indicate that the main source of contention was the union.

It is at first sight difficult to understand why the project raised so much controversy. Gardiner, Notestein and other historians believed that it was James's original intention to secure a substantive union in 1604, and that parliamentary resistance compelled him to accept as second best a preparatory commission. This is totally inaccurate. The central proposal had always been just such a commission, 'with power onlie to report to the nixt parliamentis'.[30] The other union proposal was similarly limited: a change in the royal style from 'King of England, Scotland, France and Ireland' to 'King of Great Britain', etc. Its purpose was symbolic, emotive, to mark the unity and equality of his twin peoples. It was a change James could make without parliament, by proclamation; his desire for parliamentary ratification reflected his emphasis on hearts and minds. He wanted a demonstration of goodwill towards the principle of union, by the highest public representatives. James's speech on March 19 opening the session blatantly appealed for such a show of solidarity. It also established many themes used later, by himself and by pamphleteers: the comparison of this union with that of York and Lancaster under Henry VII, its achievement by divine providence, manifested in their long peace and existing unity in language, religion and continent. It emphasised James's direct, personal relationship with 'Britain'. 'What God hath conjoined then, let no man separate. I am the husband, and all the whole isle is my lawful wife; I am the head and it is my body; I am the shepherd and it is my flock.'[31]

Inexplicably, the speech was followed by a month of silence on the union. On April 13, however, replying to a Commons vote of thanks for his handling of the Goodwin-Fortescue case, James set out his union programme for this session and later years. 'His wish, above all things, was at his death to leave: one worship to God: one kingdom, entirely governed: one uniformity in laws.'[32] His present purpose was however for a preparatory commission, and a change in style. These proposals were elaborated in joint conferences of Lords and Commons on April 14. Debate in the ensuing fortnight concentrated entirely on the style: a confused, sometimes acrimonious discussion, producing much argument in the Commons. Those supporting the change, including Bacon, emphasised the proclamatory power of the king, the antiquity of 'Britain', the divine providence theme and the title's symbolic importance in securing a union of hearts and minds.[33] Various arguments were advanced against the change in the first three days of debate, notably by Sandys and Fuller. Many objections concerned not the style but the principle of union. Fuller threatened mass immigration of Scots. There was much discussion about English precedency. Sir Maurice Barkley urged that Scotland, as the 'less honourable' kingdom, should seek the change first. Fuller used the Henrician precedent of union with (subordinate) Wales, to argue for a commission examining Scots law before any union. Sandys too spoke of England's precedency in the existing style, believing that Scots should yield and accept the famous name of England. The spectre of English suzerainty was duly resurrected as justification, on April 20. On the same day, the Commons decided to oppose any change in name before union in government.

Precedency apart, the most important objection was the alleged legal effects of a change in style. This too was stressed by Sandys, an enigmatic figure whose precipitate rise in the Commons came in these debates.[34] He argued firstly that a parliament commissioned to discuss English affairs could not consider 'Great Britain', and secondly that a change in style would invalidate the laws, oaths, legal instruments and institutions (including parliament) currently established under the name of England.[35] This line of resistance involved no offence to James or Scotland, and was repeated by M.P.s whose previous opposition had been more emotive.

The reaction of James and his supporters came on April 20-21, with a royal audience in St James's Gallery. James underlined the limited nature of his immediate programme, even excluding from the scope of the Commission the 'fundamental laws' by which England and Scotland were governed. Legal union would thereby be restricted to abolition of laws of hostility, and 'a participation of such lawes as were good in each and defective in the other'. After answering several objections to the new style (that the change was dishonourable, that many titles were better than one, that Scotland would not assent), he said he would forego the change if any confusion in the laws might result. To clarify his position beyond doubt, he delivered a statement of intent in the form of a bill.[36]

This intervention did not prevent increasingly confused and heated debates during the following week; nor did a further message on April 24 guaranteeing freedom of speech and referring the legal question to the judges notably cool the situation. To follow this discussion in detail would be repetitive, the previous arguments being elaborated on successive days. At first, the Commons refused conference with the Lords, submitting only on April 23. Later, the possibility of declaring James 'Emperor of Great Britain' was mooted, reviving a proposal by Sir William Morrice on March 31. Since 'Empires' embraced several kingdoms, the legal difficulty would have been avoided.[37] Percival renewed the threat of a flood of Scots, into English lands and offices. A committee was eventually appointed under Bacon to compile a list of objections to the change, for the next conference. M.P.s competed to add arguments to the list. The most important speech was again by Sandys, on April 26, restating his objections in a form adopted by later pamphleteers. Distinguishing between unions by marriage, election and conquest, he argued that only the last brought union in laws, offices or styles. 'Great Britain' would not only abrogate existing laws, but prevent legislation by either national parliament. Neither could legislate for 'Britain', or for part of an indivisible new kingdom. The change therefore entailed a complete union, James alone having any constitutional authority. No proviso could avoid this. The oath between king and subject, treaties running in the name of England and the diplomatic precedency of the king abroad would all be affected.[38]

The list was completed on April 27, and reduced to a scheme for conference. To analyse it would only repeat the themes above, but it is worth noting briefly its basic assumptions. Two are already clear: the legal pretext, and the loss of England's rightful precedency over Scotland. The other main assumptions were that the change had no good purpose, lacked precedent, and would be unpopular. Despite later importance in tracts on the union, the objections did not at the time have any decisive impact. Although used in conference on April 28, they were rendered unnecessary by the opinion of the judges — agreeing with the Lower House. The new style, if taken by Act, would entail 'an utter distinction of all the laws now in force . . . all processes, all writs, all executions of justice, yea the very recognition of the king in this parliament'.[39] James consequently abandoned his proposal.

The Commons had shown little willingness to make any public demonstration of goodwill on the union. While the legal pretext was from James's viewpoint an entirely valid argument, most other objections raised were profoundly offensive — implying distrust of him or depreciation of Scotland. The latter was particularly unfortunate, as likely to alienate the Scots even as they were asked to show support for union. It is in this context that one must see James's sharp message of May 1, accusing the Commons of 'jalousie and distruste, ather of me the propounder, or of the maitter by me propounditt'.[40] Their reaction was a motion to make reply to the king. This was headed off into committee by Bacon, Hastings and Sir Richard Leveson, but from here grew the 'Form of Apology and Satisfaction'. The central role of union in the deterioration of relations is again clear, the debate on the name providing the immediate occasion of protest as well as the background of mutual dissatisfaction.

By contrast, the Act of Commission passed with great ease. Outlines were agreed in conference with the Lords on May 2. The Commission would be established by statute, framed (most unusually) by a joint subcommittee of the two Houses. The number and nomination of Commissioners would be decided by each House, but the number was to be 'competent', and include a mixture of common and civil lawyers, government officials, merchants etc. It would sit between parliamentary sessions, starting on October 1 in the Painted Chamber at Westminster, empowered only to prepare proposals for parliament. By May 10, the number of Commissioners had been agreed, and a draft bill introduced into the Lords. This reached the Commons two days later, a list of Commissioners being agreed in the ensuing days. The Lower House did find 'certain doubts and differences' in the Bill, establishing its own committee on May 22 to examine these — the first union committee on which Sandys sat. There followed a conference with the Lords on a 'provision or restriction', and an agreement that Commissioners should not be bound on return to parliament to support its proposals. The amended bill was finally engrossed by the Lords on May 28, and passed by the Commons five days later.

Throughout, only two areas of disagreement arose between king and Commons. The first was phraseological. The original draft had included fulsome commendation of union, with long references to divine providence, unity in continent etc. It dismissed the 'shadows and fears' of those concerned about the dangers to existing privileges with a brief pledge not to alter fundamental laws, and anticipated a union of 'such points of incongruity and disconvenience as the several laws and customs . . . may bring forth'.[41] It was couched in petitionary form. The eventual Act by contrast included a lengthy preamble on the pledge (probably the 'restriction' inserted by the Commons), reducing the commitment to further legal union to cover only elimination of hostile laws. The petitionary form and references to divine providence were excised, leaving it altogether a more grudging and equivocal measure. The second disagreement concerned a tract by John Thornborough, Bishop of Bristol, answering the Commons' objections to the change in style. Thornborough's 'Discourse' was already in print by May 26, when the Commons made a complaint that it breached parliamentary privilege. The book was formally examined by both Houses, its author being required to apologise on June 5 for any breach of privilege he might have committed. Sir John Holles believed that this comparatively lenient treatment reflected royal intervention.[42]

The development of union in the session raised many questions of general interest. To an extent, it confirms the 'whig' thesis of organised opposition in the Lower House. Nevertheless, the feeling remains that the union was very much a special case, which cannot safely be used for generalisations about the court/Commons relationship. Many M.P.s opposing the style appear in 'whig' histories as 'government men', and there is evidence for covert support for the opposition within the Lords and Council.[43] The English reaction against the project clearly ran deeper than feelings on other issues before parliament. The extraordinary mistrust of 1604 thus reflected an extraordinary issue.

3. Scotland

The union project has traditionally been considered as an episode in English parliamentary history, Scottish attitudes being quickly passed over. Some historians have portrayed the Scots as highly unionist, hoping to obtain rich lands, benefices and posts in England. This is to accept the Commons' propaganda at its face value.[44] Manuscript evidence for 1603-4 is minimal. Nevertheless, enough survives to demonstrate not only Scotland's ambivalence to union, but also her influence on political developments. By Autumn 1603, French and Venetian reports show the same things: increasing hatred and discontent between the nations, the Scots deciding to have agents at the English parliament to report on proceedings there, and leading political figures in Scotland agitating against any change in their ancient laws and privileges.[45] In March 1604, even as the English session began, we find Mar assuring James of Scotland's goodwill to union, providing a saving on such changes were made.[46] Simultaneously, the same report speaks of Englishmen opposing Scots access to English offices and privileges unless Scotland accepted English law. Several Commons speeches after April 18 groped tentatively at this, the main theme of opposition to union in 1607. This throws into sharp relief James's assurance on April 21 excluding fundamental laws from the Commission. Rather than being an answer to English fears about the change in name, as it is traditionally regarded, it reflected crown policy agreed before parliament, and partly under Scots influence.

Scots wariness before the English parliament turned during the session into bitter resentment. The progressive prorogations of the Scots parliament necessitated by Commons resistance delayed the start of substantive consideration from April 10 to July 3, exasperating many. Scots were alienated by the arguments used in the Commons about precedency, and the poverty of Scotland.[47] The growth in acrimony is traced in the letters of those statesmen working hardest to counteract it — Cecil, Mar and Balmerino. On May 3, Cecil urged Balmerino 'in no sort to suffer bruicts unanswered, so to possess the mynds of that parliament there (which may be collected out of some particular and idle speaches comon in multitudes)'.[48] His concern was justified. Subsequent letters from Mar and Balmerino refer to 'malicious speechis sentt heir and spred in this cuntrie', and to English debates 'exasperat[ing] some sores that the best physicians of both states will be troubled to cure . . . most of us all could be rather content in our wonted condition nor to match with so unequal a party'.[49] Ambassadors show the Scots parliament resolving to eschew any union involving alteration of their laws, or an end to the French alliance, proposing York or Berwick as a site for the Commission and opposing certain names on the king's list of Commissioners as being too closely associated with English interests.[50]

It was to this resentment that James addressed himself, in an admirable soothing letter to the Scots parliament on June 12. Reporting the passage in England of the Act of Commission, he swore on his honour that 'als wele in all the speichis as actionis of this our parliament heir, nathing . . . [wes] done or utterit whiche mycht tend ather to the reproche in honour or the prejudging of the liberteis and freedomes of our ancient and honourable realme'.[51] He would always consider the honour and weal of Scotland as equal to the English. Eye witnesses were sent with the letter to confirm this rose-tinted presentation of the English debates.

The Scots Act of Commission passed on July 11; but there remain hints of resistance and disenchantment. A list of Commissioners submitted by James was replaced with one drawn up by parliament.[52] The Scots Act included a saving on fundamental laws not only in the preamble (where it was not legally binding) but also in the main text. This change was the more notable as James had required parliament to match the English Act 'worde be worde'. Even more remarkable was the success of Morton in securing a supplementary Act, excluding changes in the Kirk from the scope of discussion available to the Commissioners.[53] The first year of Jacobean rule from London and talk of union had filled presbyterians with apprehension, of measures to 'Anglicanise' the Kirk. The outcome of the Hampton Court Conference, monitored closely in Scotland and lamented by James Melville in the Edinburgh presbytery, was regarded as the start of just such an alteration.[54] This was despite James's promise before leaving Scotland not to tamper with Scots discipline or doctrine.[55] Forbes believed that James's policy before 1603 of encouraging 'bishops' in Scotland reflected desires for union, and that these strengthened after his accession.[56] Such fears surfaced before the parliament in demands by the Synod of Fife and Commissioners of General Assembly for a new Assembly, to discuss union. This demand was the more strident because of (substantiated) fears that James intended to prorogue the scheduled 1604 Assembly.[57] The Scots Council and king rejected this demand. Parliament would do no more than appoint Commissioners to discuss union. The Kirk was represented in parliament, by its 'bishops'; and James's promises to the church still held. The ministers were unconvinced. 'The Realmes could not be united, without the Union and Conformitie of the Kirks Government, and Worship; and how could the Kirks be united, unlesse the one give place to the other?'[58] Morton's Act may be considered the result of such fears, and a reaction to events in England. James's attitude is unclear. He was already pledged against alterations in either Scots religion or fundamental law, and did not upbraid the parliament for either caveat. Nevertheless, the king must have been disturbed by Scotland's lack of enthusiasm, and there are indications of disfavour shown to various of the nobles in parliament.[45] In Scotland as in England, James had secured his Commission, a first step towards unity. In both nations, he had made cautious advances, with the maximum use of propaganda and emphasis on unity in hearts and minds. Prejudices were shown on either side, England fearing Scots monopoly of the royal favour, and asserting ancient superiority, Scotland fiercely repudiating claims to precedency and regarding the maintenance of laws and the Kirk as a touchstone of nationhood.

NOTES

1. See esp. Willson, *James VI and I*, 'James and Anglo-Scottish Unity'.
2. E.g. *Basilikon Doron, The Trew Law of Free Monarchies*, etc: James I, *Works*.
3. See below, Chapter 3 (esp. note 1).
4. Spedding, *Bacon* III, 77.
5. *Reg.PCSc.* VI, p. 552. See also *ibid*, 558 and *Larkin & Hughes*, 18-19.
6. *HMC.Salis.MSS* XV, p. 405: Watts & Watts, *From Border to Middle Shire*, 133-4.
7. *HMC.Salis.MSS* XV, 69. See Kendrick, *British Antiquity*, 35. An excellent example of the seal is affixed to B.L.Eger.Charter 370.
8. S.P.14/9/1.
9. N.L.S. Adv.MSS 34.2.2. II fols. 321 and 328. See also Lythe, 'Union of the Crowns', 222.
10. Lee, 'Government of Scotland', 42.
11. *Cal.S.P.(Ven) 1603-7*, 33, 43-5.
12. Donaldson, *Scotland*, 218: Craig, *De Unione*, 430ff. For a perceptive English comment before 1603 on the king's need to reward Scots servants, see Harington, *Succession*, 32. James's lavish farewell bestowal of honours in Edinburgh is notable: *Reg.PCSc.* VI, liv.
13. *Ibid.*, lxiv and 602.
14. B. L. King's MSS 124, fols. 27-8. The Venetian ambassador also notes the return of the Scots, rationalising that they were 'bought off' by Cecil: *Cal.S.P.(Ven) 1603-7*, 70. For gifts to Scots early in the reign, see B.L.Add.MSS 12497, fols. 153-60.
15. E.g. Alexander Douglas, admitted Keeper of the Council Chamber with Humfrey Rogers, 13 May 1604: *Act, PCE*, 498. James's later declaration against such promotions is in S.P.14/10/40.
16. *Acts, PCE*, 496-7.

17. He was made Chancellor of the Exchequer, in succession to Fortescue.

18. For Scots fears of this, see *Cal.S.P.(Ven) 1603-7*, 106-8.

19. P. R. Seddon, Patronage and Officers in the Reign of James I (unpublished Ph.D thesis, University of Manchester, 1967).

20. B.L.Add.MSS 30640, fol.97.

21. The reference Willson cites is Winwood, *Memorials* II, 57; this however concerns discontent at court at the excessive deference of Sir Thomas Lake. Accusations of Scots dominance at court are in S.P.14/7/59 and the 'Advertisements of a Loyal Subject to his gracious Sovereign, drawn from the Observation of the People's Speeches': Scott, *Somers Tracts* II, 144-8. See also Burgess's apology in S.P.14/8/85.

22. See esp. Wilson, *History of GB*, 25-6 and the 'Advertisements of a Loyal Subject'.

23. Wilson, *History of GB*, 28. *Cal.S.P.(Ven) 1603-7*, 94; B. L. King's MSS 124, fols. 27-8 and 73; B.L.Add.MSS 30640, fols. 24-5. James was naturally swift to suppress specific instances of insult on either side: S.P.14/8/85.

24. S.P.14/7/29.

25. See e.g. *Spottiswoode*, 476.

26. Willson, *James VI and I*, 249. The other main traditional interpretations are: Willson, *Privy Councillors* and 'Earl of Salisbury'; Notestein, *House of Commons*; Mitchell, *House of Commons*; Wallace, *Sir Edwyn Sandys*; Rabb, 'Sir Edwin Sandys'; Gardiner, *History of England*.

27. See esp. Munden, 'Growth of Mutual Distrust'. I am grateful to Mr Munden for permission to consult his unpublished M.Phil thesis, The Politics of Accession — James I and the Parliament of 1604.

28. Tyacke, 'Session of 1604', 141.

29. S.P.14/8/93: *HMC.Portland MSS* I, 13.

30. *Reg.PCSc.* VI, 596-7. Notestein etc. presumably rely on *Cal.S.P.(Ven) 1603-7*, 151-2. James adopted this programme almost certainly on Cecil's advice: *HMC.Salis. MSS* XV, 346 and B.L.Add.MSS 30640, fol. 63.

31. Tanner, *Constitutional Documents*, 26. For an — extremely — novel interpretation of this speech, see Enright, 'James and his Island'. I find Dr Enright's thesis of a surviving archaic kingship ritual more interesting than useful.

32. *CJ* I, 171.

33. *Ibid.*, 176: Spedding, *Bacon* III, 191. The debate was launched on a motion by the Speaker: *HMC.BUCC.MSS* III, 87.

34. Sandys had been an M.P. in 1593, a minor 'government man'. Later, as Cecil's client, he had been employed in Scotland, before 1603. For his background and rise see Rabb, 'Sir Edwin Sandys', Wallace, *Sir Edwin Sandys*.

35. *CJ* I, 177-8 and S.P.14/7/75. 'The Name urgeth and inwrappeth the Matter: — We shall prejudge the Matter.'

36. Spedding, *Bacon* III, 194: S.P.14/7/75. Copies of the bill are in B.L.Harl.MSS 292, fol. 131 and Lincoln's Inn Maynard MSS 83:4. Debates during this period are recorded in detail by Carleton at S.P.14/7/74 & 76A.

37. For the evolution in meaning of 'Empire', see Koebner, 'Imperial Crown' and Firth, 'British Empires'. Great Britain was widely termed an empire after 1603, e.g. by John Dee, Speed and, of course, Camden.

38. *CJ* I, 186: S.P.14/7/63 & 64.

39. S.P.14/7/85.

40. Winwood, *Memorials* II, 20-1: Cobbett, *Parl.Hist.* I, Cols. 1021-2.

41. Spedding, *Bacon* III, 204-6.

42. *HMC.Portland MSS* I, 13: LJ II, 306.

43. *HMC.Portland MSS* I, 12-13: *Cal.S.P.(Ven) 1603-7*, 151; B.L.Add.MSS 20640 fols. 98-103 (esp. fol. 98v).

44. For English beliefs, see *CJ* I, 361: 'Scotland was so greedy of this union . . . as they cared not for the strictness of any conditions'.

45. *Cal.S.P.(Ven) 1603-7*, 94, 106-8; B.L.King's MSS 124, fols. 27-8, 53, 73, 148. See also N.L.S.Adv.MSS 33.1.1. I, Nos. 16 & 22.

46. B.L.Add.MSS 30640, fols. 63 & 71.

47. Ibid., fol. 126; *Cal.S.P.(Ven) 1603-7*, 153-5. De Beaumont's words have precise significance: Scots fear English claims that 'l'Escosse peut et doit être adioustée et comprise soubz la domination d'icelle ainsi que l'Irlande'.

48. S.R.O.MSS G.D.156/6/3 (Elphinstone Papers).

49. S.P.14/8/9 & 10. See also *HMC.Salis.MSS* XVI, 86, 98-9.

50. *Cal.S.P.(Ven) 1603-7*, 153-4, 63; B.L.Add.MSS 30640, fols. 98ff, 126, 157, 166.

51. *Reg.PCSc.* VII, 457-9.

52. *Ibid.*, 461.

53. *Calderwood*, 481-2; Scot, *'Apologeticall Narratioun'*, 125-6; Forbes, *Certaine Records*, 375-6; Melville, *Diary*, 560; Row, *History*, 223.

54. For reactions to the conference, see *Calderwood*, 473-7. This makes clear the concern of the Scots clergy for 'relief of the good Brethren of the Ministrie in England' (473). *Spottiswoode*'s interpretation (478-9) is predictably different.

55. *Row*, History, 222: Scot, *Apologeticall Narratioun*, 124.

56. Forbes, *Certaine Records*, 373-5. 'So farr was his Hienes sett to promove the Union of the two Kingdomes, that becaus he was maid to judge it dificille to reduce England to a conformitie in religion to Scotland, he inclyned to suffer Scotland to be brought to ane uniformitie, at least in government, with England' (375).

57. For the prerogation and the subsequent meeting in Aberdeen of ministers from St Andrews, see Row, *History*, 224ff; *Calderwood*, 482-4; Scot, *Apologeticall Narratioun*, 128-9; Melville, *Diary*, 560-4; Thomson, *Acts of the Kirk*, 1009-12.

58. *Calderwood*, 479; *Scot*, 127: *Forbes*, 375: *Melville*, 554-6.

APPENDIX

Bacon's Collation of Objections to the Change in Name

This was the list of objections to the change reported by Sir Francis Bacon to the English House of Commons on 27 April 1604, under the full heading: 'Objections against the change of the name or style of England and Scotland into the name or style of Great Brittany; to be moved and debated in the Conference between the Lords and the Commons; and to that end by the Committees of the House of Commons collected, reviewed, and reduced to order, for their better instruction'. The version below is the most complete of many manuscript lists, and that used by Spedding, in *Letters and Life of Lord Bacon*, Vol. 111, pp. 197-9.

The objections are of four several natures or kinds:
   Matter of generality or common reason.
   Matter of estate inward, or matter of law.
   Matter of estate foreign, or matter of intercourse.
   Matter of honour or reputation.

The matter of generality or common reason hath two parts:
   That there is no cause of the change.
   That there is no precedent of the like change.
   The first objection therefore is: —
   That in constituting or ordaining of any innovation or change, there ought to be either urgent necessity or evident utility; but that we find no grief of our present estate, and foresee no advancement to a better condition by this change; and therefore desire it may be showed unto us.
   The second objection is: —
   That we find no precedent, at home or abroad, of uniting or contracting of the names of two several kingdoms or states into one name, where the union hath grown by marriage or blood; and that those examples which may be alleged, as far as we can find, are but in the case of conquest.

Matter of estate inward, or matter of law, hath three main heads: —
   The first, that the alteration of the name of the King doth inevitably and infallibly draw on an erection of a new kingdom or estate, and a dissolution and extinguishment of the old; and that no explanation, limitation, or reservation can clear or avoid that inconvenience; but it will be full of repugnancy and ambiguity, and subject to much variety and danger of construction.
   The second is an enumeration or recital of the special and several confusions, incongruities, and mischiefs which will necessarily and incidently follow in the time present; as,
   In the summoning of Parliaments, and the recitals of Acts of Parliament:
   In the seals of the kingdom:
   In the great officers of the kingdom:
   In the laws, customs, liberties and privileges of the kingdom:
   In the residence and holding of such Courts as follow the King's person; which by this generality of name may be held in Scotland:
   In the several and reciproque oaths: the one, of his Majesty at his Coronation, which is never iterated; the other, in the oaths of Allegiance, Homage, and Obedience, made and renewed from time to time by the subjects.
   All which acts, instruments, and forms of policy and government, with a multitude of

other forms of Records, Writs, Pleadings and Instruments, of a meaner nature, run now in the name of England, and upon the change would be drawn into incertainty and question.

The third is a possibility of alienation of the Crown of England to the line of Scotland, in case his Majesty's line should determine (which God of his goodness defend); for if it be a new-erected Kingdom, it must go, in the nature of a purchase, to the next heir of his Majesty's father's side.

The matter of state foreign, or matter of intercourse, consisteth of three points: —

The first is, that Leagues, Treaties, foreign Freedoms of Trade and Traffic, foreign Contracts, may be drawn in question, and made subject to quarrel and cavillation.

The second is, that the King's precedence before other Christian Kings, which is guided by antiquity of kingdoms, and not by greatness, may be endangered, and his place turned last, because it is the newest.

The third is, that the glory and good acceptation of the English name and nation will be, in foreign parts, obscured.

The matter of honour and reputation standeth upon four points: —

The first is, no worldly thing is more dear to men than their name; as we see in private families, that men disinherit their daughters to continue their names: much more in States, and where the name hath been famous and honourable.

The second is, that the contracted name of Brittaine will bring in oblivion the names of England and Scotland.

The third is, that whereas now England, in the style, is placed before Scotland, in the name of Brittaine that degree of priority or precedence will be lost.

The fourth is, that the change of name will be harsh in the popular opinion, and unpleasing to the country.

3
Tracts and Treatises on the Union, 1603-1605

1. Introduction

The accession of James had been greeted in England with a mass of pageantry, and in both nations with numerous encomia.[1] These cannot strictly be considered tracts on the union project. Their primary concern was celebratory, lauding the character of the new king, his good fortune, and the splendid future opened up to both kingdoms as a result of his accession. They were commentaries on the union of the crowns, rather than examinations of the further union that James might wish to achieve. Nevertheless, they were important both as propaganda for 'union' in general, and as the first statements of themes which were to become common in debates and writings on the further union. The encomia and pageantry are notable for their extravagant praise of unity as a general principle in human affairs, their references to existing unities between England in Scotland (in continent, religion etc.), to divine providence as the author of this union, to James as His tool, and to the revival of the antique unity and glory of Britain.[2] These are all themes which this chapter will have cause to examine in more detail.

Encomia were an essential part of the installation of a new king, and had little direct political relevance to the development of royal policy. Our examination will concentrate on a much larger and more influential body of literature, written specifically about the union project during the first two years of Jacobean rule. This body of tracts and treatises is considered here, after examination of the 1604 parliamentary session, for good chronological reasons. It was during the period between May and October 1604 that the bulk of the literature was written.

The tracts are listed and briefly described in the Appendix to this chapter. Their range was considerable. Surviving treatises vary in length from a single manuscript folio to several hundred pages — the longest being Sir Thomas Craig's *De Unione*, one of the few to have attracted the attention of historians. Craig apart, the longest works are those of Hayward, Thornborough and Russell, between twenty and twenty-five thousand words, the majority of the other tracts falling between five and fifteen thousand. Eleven of the treatises were printed contemporaneously, while several others appear in sufficient manuscript copies to suggest a considerable private circulation. The bulk of the material, the high percentage of printed matter and the circulation of manuscript tracts may be taken as confirmation of contemporary references to the union as a major subject of public discussion. Nine of the tracts were by Scots (including two by the Anglo-Scot John Gordon), seventeen by Englishmen, and one by a Dutchman (Albericus Gentilis) resident in England. Four of the

30

printed treatises were Scots, while Cornwallis's *Miraculous and Happie Union* received simultaneous publication in both capitals. This, however, distorts the real balance between the two nations in printed material. Gordon's two sermons were preached and printed in London, and predominantly reached an English market.

The variation in authorship is similarly marked: clergymen of both churches (Thornborough, Gordon, Pont), practitioners of Scots law (Craig), common law (Bacon, Doddridge) and civil law (Hayward, Albericus Gentilis), established scholars (Spelman, Savile), lesser men of letters (Cornwallis, Russell, Maxwell), and those like Pont, Gordon, Hayward, Bacon and Craig who habitually produced scholarly works as an adjunct to their main careers. Their political activities and importance differed accordingly. Doddridge and Bacon were well-established English politicians, who had made their views on union known during the parliamentary session of 1604. Craig was appointed as one of the Scots Commissioners for the Union, as one of the king's nominees. The tracts of Gordon and Savile were written by command of James or those closest to him, and so acquired particular political significance. By contrast, authors like Saltern, Russell, Hume and (at this time) Maxwell had no political influence or close connections in high places. Between these extremes lay a group of writers with public standing and political connections but no special access to the seat of policy on the union question. These included Thornborough, Hayward, Cornwallis, Spelman and Pont. The motive in writing their treatises is often uncertain. Some were undoubtedly penned with an eye to royal favour — but which? It would be simplistic to dismiss treatises supporting the union as automatically or necessarily self-seeking. To prove a desire for favour, corroborative evidence is required: the submission of the treatise unasked to the king, fulsome flattery, or previous attempts to secure patronage. Hayes and Maxwell clearly fall into these proofs. Bacon (in 1603) and Hayward both wrote tracts commending the union during times of personal disfavour. However, some of the treatises arguing most strongly for limitations on the union also contain fulsome flattery, or were submitted to James: Russell's 'Treatise of the Happie and Blissed Unioun' and the anonymous reply to Thornborough are examples. Many were written by those to whom substantial favour had already been shown, and were thus the work of royal servants counselling their king or providing propaganda for the project. Bacon's second tract, and those of Savile and Doddridge, were meant as counsel. Thornborough, Gordon and Pont provided works with primarily propaganda effect. Cornwallis and the author of *Rapta Tatio* appear rather as inveterate scribblers and essayists. Above all, there is no hard evidence that any author falsified his beliefs while writing about the union. Some, like Russell, Hume and Spelman, were clearly moved by blinding concern about the future of their respective nations. Most were written to advance genuine, tenable proposals on the question.

The final area of variety is also the most important. This was the difference in their attitudes to and proposals for the union. A few tracts were explicitly opposed to any union beyond that in sovereignty established by James's accession. Many more fulsomely praised the project, without examining in any depth what a 'union' should comprise. Some, like Bacon, seized this nettle, outlining programmes for unification in law, institutions, commerce and the outward marks of government. Others instead justified limitations on further union, particularly in the legal and institutional field. This variety, however, hides a more fundamental agreement in approach. The tracts are overwhelmingly arguing about the same things — the principle of unity, the change in the royal style, the advisability of further union in the same specific areas of public life. Their cases are argued in a very similar manner, with the same sources being used to support their arguments: biblical and ancient philosophical texts, historical precedents and mythological beliefs, 'common reason'. The same arguments, supported by the same examples, recur — reflecting an underlying set of assumptions both about the union itself and the manner in which it should be debated. This common intellectual context allows us to describe the tracts accurately and briefly, by examining them in groups of arguments used: for and against the general principle of British unity, for and against the title of Great Britain, proposals for and limitations on further union.

2. The Principle of Unity in Britain

The arguments contained in the first group are those supporting the general principle of British unity, but not defining the nature of or constituent elements in such a 'union'. Considerable scholarship was exhibited in this area, themes being drawn from many sources including philosophical and theological thought, biblical and historical precedent, mythology, the Qabala, the world of nature and 'common reason'. The propaganda importance of these arguments should not be underestimated, despite their lack of apparent contribution to the development of the union project.

   These general arguments fall neatly into two categories: the secular and the religious approaches. The central theme of the first was that unity brought prosperity, disunity misery. Several tracts, such as that of Russell, use Livy's comparison of the bodies politic and human: as union between the parts of the body was essential for survival, so unity between classes and geographical regions of the body politic was necessary for survival, safety and prosperity. A more sophisticated analogy was that drawn by Bacon's *Brief Discourse*, between political union and unity in nature. Union brings strength to nations, as the Sun's conjunction with bright stars in Leo brings heat to the month of August. Most writers relied for supporting evidence on historical precedent. Innumerable precedents were cited for united kingdoms proceeding to fame and fortune, while disunited territories fell prey to invasion, sedition and malaise. British history in particular was invoked, Craig dedicating a long section in *De Unione* to prove that 'the separation of the crowns of the island is the cause of all the calamities which have befallen Britain'.[3] Division among Celtic tribes helped the

Romans, while the Danes similarly profited from the disunity of the Anglo-Saxon Heptarchy. Medieval hostility between England and Scotland prevented the success of English arms abroad, as did the later division between the Houses of York and Lancaster. United, Britain was doubly strong, 'the renown and safety of the inhabitants and free denisons . . . encreased, the enemie's feare augmented and his pride abated'.[4]

This equation of unity with strength and success is a potent underlying feature in most of the tracts. The religious approach is rather less frequent, but had deeper implications for the union project. Christian theology and classical philosophy were used to show unity as a divine principle, the work of the gods. The unity of God Himself, of His universe, of man with God before the Fall and later through the Crucifixion of His son were all emphasised. Correspondingly, division became the mark of Satan. The separation of man from God by original sin, of Adam's family after the expulsion from Eden and of the Heavenly Host itself through Lucifer's rebellion received extensive treatment. This common-place equation of Divinity and Unity (for example by Russell, Gordon, Thornborough and *Pro Unione* required relatively little supporting material, so ingrained was it in public consciousness. Gordon, however, did invoke the Qabala, analysing the Hebrew word for 'union' into three parts with the mystical meanings of knowledge, life and door. Union therefore became 'the door whereby we enter by knowledge into life and eternall felicitie'.[5]

To these and other writers, the relationship between unity and prosperity reflected not the operation of earthly laws, but divine decree. The precedents they used to demonstrate the relationship were notably more ancient and biblical than their 'secular' counterparts. Particularly favoured was the precedent of Israel under David, Solomon and their successors — the established image of James as a 'British Solomon' adding a flavour of direct analogy here.[6] The lesson was simple: purity of religion is rewarded with unity, and consequent prosperity. Idolatry and resistance to divine commandment are punished by disunity and misery. The logical consequence of this was to regard the union of the crowns as the work of God, a reward for the reformation of religion in England and Scotland. The treatment by Pont and Russell of England's offers of union in 1547-8, and its rejection through the machinations of Catholic bishops, was therefore designed to do more than demonstrate religious unity as a *sine qua non* of political union. It reflected the hand of God, both then and in the union of 1603.

The divine providence theme is widespread, appearing in James's speech at the opening of the English parliament, and in the majority of the tracts. In most, however, it formed only a passing or rhetorical flourish. Certain writers, however, saw it as an integral and indeed central part of their approach to union. If union was the work of God, they argued, then James must be His tool and servant. This was to invest James with some of the divine mystique and authority already assumed for the principle of British unity. To resist James's proposals for further union implicitly flew in the face of God's will. Russell in particular attacks the English M.P.s on these grounds. The thesis of a divine mission vested in the king is also implicit in the insistence of Cornwallis, *Rapta Tatio* and *Pro Unione* that decisions on the project should be left entirely to James's personal judgement.

This theme was extended still further in the tracts of Gordon and Russell. They postulate a personal royal mission, not only to unite Britain in true religion but also to purify all Christendom of its idolatry. Indeed, the mission was vested not only in James, but in Britain itself. Many tracts followed the encomia and pageants of 1603 in emphasising the ancient unity of Britain, presenting the project as 'The Triumph of Re-United Britannia'.[7] The principal elements here were mythological — the foundation of Britain by the Trojan hero Brutus, its early reception of pure Christian teaching under the Romano-British monarch Lucius, and the defence of Britain by Arthur. These were highly significant precedents. Brutus provided links with classical and, through John Bale's allied Samothean mythology, biblical antiquity, while Arthur combined patriotism with the Holy Grail. To resurrect Britannia revived ancient glory. Gordon and Russell concentrated on Lucius, significant as the first Christian king and a man acknowledged by the Pope of the time to have complete ecclesiastical jurisdiction in Britain. Lucius symbolised the religious independence and purity of Britain. Gordon explicitly represents British churchmen like Bede and Wycliff as zealots struggling for true British religion against the tyrannical practices of Rome, while James himself became, in Russell's terms, 'a vive Lucius'. Britain was touched with divinity, the very name, in Qabalistic lore, meaning 'Covenant of God There'. Effectively, Gordon is doing for Britain what Foxe's *Book of Martyrs* did for Elizabethan England — creating a belief in the inhabitants that they constituted an Elect Nation, singled out for greatness and eventual salvation.[8]

The theme of a divine mission was politically important. Nevertheless, few other treatises relied so heavily on their general arguments for 'unity'. Most tracts using general arguments did so as an introduction to their chapters on the royal style and the further union. Moreover, such use did not necessarily presuppose support for union in these other areas, because general arguments could not define what kind of 'union' was to be desired. To oppose unity as a principle was unthinkable, treasonable, because it implied denunciation of the union of the crowns and therefore of James's own sovereignty. The nearest approach to this can be seen in the long, discursive but incidental passages in Craig, Spelman and Russell lamenting the effects of the existing union on their respective nations. It was perfectly possible for such writers to extol 'unity' and then recommend limitations on further union. Spelman and Russell did precisely this. Spelman thus began his treatise with a demonstration of unity as strength, only to conclude on a negative note: 'Let us see what manner of union it is that must supporte this our greatness and felicity. Is it union of lawes, union of freedomes, union of inheritance? No, but union of our loves, of our strength, of our obedience'.[9]

3. 'Great Britain'

The discussion in the tracts of the change in the royal style was dominated by the list of objections produced by the English Commons on April 27, 1604, and reproduced as an Appendix to our previous chapter. The importance of this list is unsurprising. The objections were widely copied and circulated in manuscript[10] and given added publicity by their reproduction in Thornborough's *Discourse*. Four other tracts (*Pro Unione*, the Trinity College MS, and the treatises of Hayward and Craig) answered the list in full, others like the 'Discourse on the Proposed Union' selecting a few objections from the list for reply, and generally commending the change. As a result, there was much more discussion of the name of Great Britain than of any other single proposal for union.

The first of the four headings contained in the list of objections was 'Matter of Common Reason', alleging that the change had (a) no 'general necessity or evident utility' to justify such an innovation, and (b) no precedent. The tracts are almost unanimous in reply to the first objection. Names are seen as potent things, holding the imaginations of the people. To maintain separate names for England and Scotland would continue their longstanding connotations of hostility, and thereby risk new hatred. A new style would 'imprint and inculcate into the hearts and heads of the people, that they are one people and one nation'.[11] The Greeks and Swiss were frequently cited here, as multiple polities associated under a single name. The objection on precedent in fact telescoped no fewer than three distinct arguments used in the Lower House: that 'Britain' was itself a harsh, foreign and unknown term, that there was no precedent for changing the royal style by Act of Parliament, and that there was 'no president at home nor abroad, of uniting contracting of the names of two several kingdomes or states into one name where the union hath growne be marriage or bloode' rather than conquest. This third argument was that on Bacon's list, and was answered by the five main tracts with examples of just such unions. Many also took the opportunity to recite precedents for 'Britain' itself, including Brutus, Roman Britannia, and the use of *Rex Britanniae* by Anglo-Saxon kings like Athelstan. Here, the tracts were on solid ground. Professor Hay has demonstrated that, by 1600, the name was widely used to comprehend England and Scotland. Its considerable diplomatic heritage included use by Edward I, by the Council of Constance in 1414-18, by Edward IV in his marriage negotiations with Scotland, and most importantly by Henry VIII and Protector Somerset in their propaganda campaigns, 1542-8. James's own mother had assumed the title 'Queen of Great Britain' in 1584, at the suggestion of the Bishop of Ross. Alongside this ran a powerful literary tradition, drawing particular strength from the Arthurian legends, and including sixteenth-century works as diverse as John Major's *Historia Majoris Britanniae* and Cervantes' *Don Quixote*.[12]

The tracts' answers to 'Matter of Common Reason' were generally convincing. It was in the second section, 'Matter of State Inward', that their position appears weakest. The central principle of the objections here was 'that the alteration of the name of the king doth inevitably and infallibly draw on an erection of a new kingdome or estate'. This would extinguish in law the separate nations of England and Scotland, and threaten a range of government instruments and institutions (parliamentary summons, acts, seals, offices of the crown, laws, customs, privileges, oaths and courts) currently existing under the authority of the 'King of England'. The laws governing the succession might even be affected, with England conceivably passing to a new Scots dynasty.

Many contemporaries expressed frank scepticism that a change in style should have had such an effect in law. Savile defined these objections as 'trickes and sharpness of wit to overthrow that by wreting of law and wrangling which they had no liking should go forward'.[13] But two factors made counter-argument more difficult. The first was the judges' opinion upholding the objection. The second was its own, probably deliberate, lack of absolute clarity. The danger of extinction arose only through taking the new style by Act. This was unprecedented, and would have the force of new law, superseding all done under the English style. James might safely take the new name by proclamation, since this had no power to make new law.[14] This distinction did not appear in the objection, perhaps because the majority of M.P.s opposed any change, however achieved. As a result, writers could easily misunderstand the real point at issue. Certainly, their answers to the legal technicality often seem inadequate. Craig and Thornborough referred to 'Great Britain' as a restitution, not alteration, Craig also arguing that it 'encompassed' the existing names. Unfortunately, no legal doctrine of restitution or encompassment existed. Only Hayward tackled the legal pretext directly, denying that the change would erect a new estate. He dismissed the judicial opinion as devoid of legal force *ex camera*, and compared the question to the dispute raised under Mary Tudor whether laws passed under the name of a king remained in force under a queen. Even Hayward, however, advised the inclusion of a *caveat* in the Act, stating that the change should not be construed to affect the validity of existing instruments or institutions. The 'Discourse on the Proposed Union' advised a similar provision, while Thornborough desired a clause retrospectively altering all previous references in laws and instruments to the separate national names. These expedients implicitly denied the Commons' separate assertion, 'that no explanation, limitation or reservation can clear or avoid that inconvenience'.

The tracts demonstrate particular confusion over the lesser objections in this section, notably concerning the king judging English cases in Scotland and England passing to a Scots dynasty. The Trinity College MS was quick to point out the English chauvinism implied by these objections, but totally missed the point in its assertion that, under the law of nations, the failure of the Stuart line would return Scotland to a Scots dynasty and England to an English. This would not be true if 'Great Britain' were a single, new estate. The best answers here were by Russell and *Pro Unione*, pointing simply to James's wealth of progeny — by divine providence.

The two remaining groups of objections came under 'Matter of State Foreign' and 'Matter of Honour and Reputation'. The first objection in the former transported the legal pretext into international relations, arguing that the change threatened all leagues and treaties, giving nations wishing to escape their diplomatic ties an opportunity to do so.[15] Craig and the Trinity House MS again miss the legal point with their talk of 'encompassment', while Thornborough and *Pro Unione* lamely argue for new diplomatic initiatives to establish alliances under the altered style. It is again Hayward who pinpoints the legal question, arguing that treaties relied for their force only on the law of nations, which was '*bona fidei*'. Princes using a pretext of this kind to escape a treaty would lose their reputation in other countries. The second objection here, relegating the new nation of Britain to the lowest diplomatic rank, elicited a varied response. All respondents surprisingly accepted that the antiquity of a kingdom rather than its greatness determined precedency; but while Hayward and the Trinity College MS simply denied that a new name would be held to imply a new kingdom, Thornborough and Craig alleged further that the restoration of so ancient a name as Britannia should actually elevate her rank. As the reply to Thornborough stated, this was unlikely to impress envious foreign courts.

Answers to the remaining objections were more cogent. The final objection under state foreign, that the glory and good acceptance of the English name would be diminished, provoked few tears. Thornborough alleged that the name of Great Britain would thereby shine the more strongly, while the Scots author of the Trinity College MS remarked simply and sourly that 'I wish it [i.e. the name of England] were such as they do esteme of it'! This objection was connected logically with the four objections under 'honour and reputation': that there was nothing dearer than a name, that the new style would consign 'England' and 'Scotland' to oblivion, that England would lose her precedency over the northern kingdom, and that the change would be unpopular. The tracts' answers to these are generally consistent. Several point to the numerous changes in name by foreign nations, and condemn the Commons' example of fathers disinheriting their daughters to maintain the family name. This was in answer to the first objection. Hayward, the Trinity College MS and the 'Discourse on the Proposed Union' prophesied that popular and literary use would save the old national names from oblivion. The argument about precedency produced from Craig a revealingly reflex denial that Scotland had ever acknowledged English claims to superiority — although the objection clearly referred to the precedency the name of England had in the royal style. Other writers condemned this inequality in the style, Hayward asking pertinently whether England should 'contend for general precedence with thcm, with who we intend, or at least pretend desire to be one'.[16] All the five main respondents saw time and usage as the answer to the alleged 'harshness' and unpopularity of the new name.

As this summary implies, the tracts provided much more argument for than against the change in style. Only the reply to Thornborough openly supported the Commons against their critics. Four other tracts, all English, showed rather less than enthusiasm for the alteration. Doddridge merely commented that a change in name was the 'most absolute union of kingdoms' that could be imagined, and should follow the achievement of unity in other fields. Savile, Spelman and the 'Discourse Against The Union' concentrated on demonstrating the truth of one objection, that changes in style were unprecedented except in unions achieved by conquest. Savile devoted eight of his thirty-three chapters to this, and wished 'with all my heart his Majesty would be pleased the names of England and Scotland might still continue'.[17] This said, he then denied that the change would be impossible, or inconvenient. Spelman showed much greater reluctance, referring to the Britons as 'an obscure and barbarous people' whose memory was best overlooked. Although examining 'Albion' and 'Great Britain', his heart lay elsewhere. Reviewing precedents for united names, he 'proved' union to occur only where one existing name swallowed up another. Turning to British history, he then demonstrated to his own satisfaction that the kings of England had always held dominion over Scotland, yet never felt it necessary to take its name separately into their title. As an inferior dominion, 'Scotland' was automatically comprehended within 'England' — and so could be dropped from James's existing royal style! His subsequent retreat from this revealing assertion of precedency is unconvincing, and brief.[18]

Overall, the honours of the debate belonged distinctly to the supporters of the new style. Only the legal technicality of the new estate had failed to elicit a convincing reply. Here, James already had means to avoid the difficulty. Hayward, *Pro Unione*, and above all Bacon's 'Certain Articles' urged the king simply to take the name by proclamation, Bacon enclosing a draft with the treatise. James, of course, did precisely that.

4. Discussion of the Further Union

While the arguments over the style and for the principle of unity occupy a predominant place in some tracts, there are very few which do not include — if only in passing — proposals for further union in specified areas of public life, or limitations on such further union. In most tracts, it is this discussion of further union which predominates. Generally, the areas considered for union are the same: law, the higher institution of government, its outward marks such as seals and currency, offices, religion and commerce.

(a) The Law

Of these areas, union in law predictably attracted most attention, both then and in subsequent historical examination.[19] Pocock has depicted the attitude of early Stuart Englishmen to their law as a form of reverential conservatism. According to him, many writers considered common law in particular to have survived without change or addition from immemorial antiquity to the present. It was thus vastly older than Roman Law, different if not opposite in inspiration, more conducive to liberty and ideally suited to the needs and character of England.[20]

While all but a few accepted the mutability of common law by statute, there remained an immense suspicion of such 'innovation'. Particular reverence was paid to 'fundamental law', a powerful, ill-defined term used variously to describe the laws governing the royal succession, the crowning heights of the law or the entire corpus of common law. James, in the context of union, considered the fundamental laws of England to be those 'whereby not only his regal authority but the people's security of lands, livings and privileges . . . are preserved'.[21] Some considered these immutable; all agreed that they could only be altered with great danger. The 'Divine Providence' and 'Discourse on Three Types of Union' conventionally describe such alteration as 'pure bondage'.

To quite an extent, the tracts confirm Pocock's thesis. Many of the treatises considering legal union start by an assertion of the immemoriality and quasi-immutability of English law, and of its perfect suitability to the nation and national life. Such beliefs inevitably affected their consideration of legal union. On the one hand, the unique nature of common law was considered to render union an impossibility. Englishmen of the period tended to see Scots law either as a debased common law, or more commonly as a mixture of feudal and Roman codes, antithetical in attitude to common law. Legal reconciliation would therefore be difficult, while no alteration in English law could be contemplated. On the othe hand, the immemorialist attitude to law presupposed a belief in an unusually intimate relationship between the law, and public and private life. Law was the soul of the body politic, the adhesive by which the uncertain structure of the commonwealth was kept together. There could thus be no significant union without reconciliation of English and Scots law. Taken to its logical conclusion, the only acceptable possibilities were no union (save that in sovereignty achieved by the accession of James) or one involving Scots submission to common law. Thus we find Savile commenting on the lawyers in parliament urging the necessity of legal union, while Spelman and the common lawyer Doddridge described it as an essential but most difficult part of any union programme. Each tract sees the change in terms of a Scots submission to English law.

This prospect clearly caused apprehension in Scotland, and met predictable resistance in Scots treatises as in their political discussions of 1603-4. Scots attitudes to law during this period are often considered to differ fundamentally from the immemorialist English tradition, the lack of codification, clear authority and antiquity in Scots law creating a more utilitarian, less reverential view of the law and its function in society. This difference did not prevent the inclusion of many quasi-Pocockian statements in the Scots treatises. There was extreme suspicion of alterations. Russell fondly cited Plato's dictum about the maintenance of wicked laws to uphold the authority of law itself, and the example of the Locrians, among whom any man proposing a new law wore a noose about his neck.[22] The real cause of resistance, however, was plainly patriotic. Scots, as we have seen, regarded the maintenance of their laws and privileges as a touchstone of nationhood. Hume, the Trinity College MS and Russell are united here, the last becoming plainly emotional: 'Sall all this be lost in ane day, and that be our auin voluntar consent? Sall ane frie kingdome, possessing sua ancient liberteis, become ane slave?'[23]

The only Scots seriously entertaining the prospect of legal unity are Pont and Craig. The former considered the subject only in passing, and tempered his approval with reference to continental unions where no reconciliation had occurred. Craig's position is more complicated. In his previous *Ius Feudale*,[24] Craig had challenged the immemoriality of common law, tracing its origin to a medieval feudal code already received (and in a purer form) by Scotland. He had then advocated legal union by a return to these feudal roots. How seriously this proposal was advanced is uncertain. In his later introduction, Craig merely attacked those who emphasised the differences between the two systems of law: 'There exists a fundamental identity between the principles underlying the legal system of the two countries; and in comparing them together, I found the closest affinity of method in legal argument, expression and analysis,'.[25] It was therefore a work of propaganda as much as a formal proposal. In *De Unione*, Craig retreated further, including a long section on the similarities of the two codes, but resolving eventually against unification. Craig possibly felt constrained here to justify the Instrument of Union produced in December 1604, and so to eschew legal union at this stage. More probably, the alienation of Scots opinion during 1603-4 had affected Craig, inducing a nationalistic reflex similar to that of Russell.

This combination of English immemorialism and Scots patriotism would appear to have left relatively little room for legal union. One possibility was to hijack English immemorialism. *Ius Feudale* was paralleled here by a little-known English work, George Saltern's *Of the Antient Lawes of Great Britain*. Published in May 1605 to supplement a now lost tract on union, this similarly attempted to bridge the gulf between the two systems of law, by asserting a common, antique origin. In this case, the origin was the laws of God, allegedly adopted entire by the 'British' King Lucius — another approach to Gordon's Elect British Nation. Saltern's work does not, however, appear to have had much influence on popular beliefs, or royal policy!

More important than Saltern were the large number of English writers who do not fit into the Pocockian mould. These abandoned immemorialism, assessing law in utilitarian terms, and working upon the assumption of its absolute mutability. Prominent here were the lawyers Hayward, Bacon and Albericus Gentilis. Other writers, like Cornwallis, Thornborough and the author of *Rapta Tatio* revealed the same assumptions in their general commendation of legal union, by compromise. The attitude of Hayward and Albericus Gentilis reflected a wider campaign by civil lawyers, including Cowell, to demonstrate the similarities between common and Roman law. This would mitigate the English stereotype of the civil law as foreign, authoritarian and papist.[26] The opportunity offered by the union project was fully grasped. Hayward in particular attacked the common law's pretensions to immemoriality, praised the virtues of absolute legal reconciliation, and concluded with a programme of gradual unification in the fundamental laws leaving local customs and privileges unchanged. Bacon's position is even more interesting, given his eminence within the legal profession and known enthusiasm for reform and codification of the common law. In the *Brief Discourse*, he too praised unity in laws as a source of permanence in united kingdoms, citing historical precedents in support, and concluded that it would be 'a matter of curiosity and inconvenience to seek either to extirpate all particular customs, or to draw all subjects to one place or resort of judicature or session. It sufficeth that there be an uniformity in the principal and fundamental laws both ecclesiastical and civil'.[27] A year later, in 'Certain Articles', he has moderated and defined this project. The repeal of statutes demonstrating hostility between the nations is advised, and of the local Border customs. The 'Middle Shires' would then house an experiment in legal unity, special courts administering a mixture of English and Scots law. Reconciliation elsewhere would entail only the definition of certain major offences — capital cases, non-capital penal cases concerning the public state, and cases where a deed in one country prejudiced the estate of the other. These included misprision of treason, incest, praemunire, removal of bullion, libel and conspiracy to commit treason across the border. Union in the institutions of justice would be limited to a new, prerogative court about the king, freedoms and liberties being defined in a fresh (British?) Grand Charter. This was a considerable, visionary programme, proposed with the Anglo-Scots Commission in mind. His failure to recommend union in fundamental laws is notable, but probably reflected only their exclusion by Act from the scope of the Union Commission.

(b) Government and Offices

It is noteworthy how much more discussion there is in the tracts of union in law and fundamental law than in the institutions of justice and government. Only a few writers consider union in government, and these concentrate exclusively on arrangements for the parliaments and privy councils. Hume, 'Pro Unione' and Bacon's 'Certain Articles' all favour parliamentary union, the second even advising James to call Scots to his next English session by prerogative summons. 'Pro Unione' also advises the elevation of Scots onto the English Council, and of Englishmen onto the Scots. Bacon is more cautious, leaving the Councils to royal discretion but advising a united parliament in which the Scots should have one-third of the seats. To achieve this proportion, the small number of English peers should be drastically increased. Hume, with his strong Scots sympathies, favoured a British parliament in York, and a mixed Council composed equally of Scots and English. All seem to have considered the proposed parliament in an English light, although Bacon did favour importing the Lords of the Articles as a preparatory commission. Doddridge and 'The Divine Providence' each advanced federal unions. Both favoured three parliaments, the third being a joint British assembly to handle causes of equal concern to either nation. 'The Divine Providence' echoed 'Pro Unione' in support for mixed Councils, while also pressing for joint meetings of the two Councils on matters of common concern.

Union in lesser institutions of government was considered only by Bacon, and rejected. Discussion centred instead on two subsidiary areas. There was wide agreement about the need for unity in the 'outward marks of government' — seals, coins, crowns, weights and measures, the flag. Bacon and Craig in particular described such union as necessary to instil a sense of unity and fraternity in the two peoples. The second area was the eligibility of one nation to the offices of government in the other. This was overwhelmingly discussed in terms of Scots gaining English positions. It is not surprising to find this major English fear of 1603-4 reflected in the tracts, Spelman above all emotionally threatening a deluge of Scots into offices of power throughout England:

> Make the SS free of England, what will be the sequell? First many of their nobles and principall gentlemen will strive to creepe themselves as neare the Court as they cann. And reason they shold for who doth not desire the influence of the prince. But our houses our landes our livings shall be bought up in all places the City and country shalbe replenyshed with SS: the Court shall abounde with them. And they having favour of the prince to begg and capacitie by the lawes to take, shall not only obteyne leases and inheritances in all partes of England but the offices of ftate and government also. And whereas the Lawes of England do not permitt any Alien nor denizen himself to beare any office tuching the peace of the lande, no, not the meane office of a Constable, nowe by this Union the SS shall become capiable of the high Constableshipp of all England.[28]

The depth of these feelings is remarkable. Hayward spoke of such English jealousies, scornfully condemning those of 'dazzled judgement' whose whole case against the union was 'that all the sweete of the land will hereby be drawne from the auncient inhabitants of the same'.[29] He considered this prejudice to be so deeply ingrained as to make participation in offices impossible 'untill by benefit of time, the bond of union bee made fast indissoluble'. He also followed 'The Divine Providence' in referring to the danger of promoting Scots to positions requiring knowledge of English law. Other writers were less equivocal in support of participation. All the Scots authors favoured it, unsurprisingly, as did Cornwallis, Thornborough, *Rapt Tatio* and 'Pro Unione', the first pair citing historical precedents for its necessity, the second also emphasising the complete authority of James over such appointments. All mentioned English fears, stressing in reply the small numbers of Scots in England and the absolute impartiality of the king.[30] In this discussion of offices, there is absolute unanimity on the question of the Scots' status in common law. Doddridge, Bacon, Spelman and the Trinity College MS agree that Scots born after James's accession were English subjects by law, able to inherit and bequeath property in England, be free of customs, taxes, subsidies and other duties laid on aliens, and be equally preferrable to crown offices. Given the controversy over this question in 1606-8, such agreement is highly significant.

(c) Religion and Trade

Religion and trade were the two remaining areas of public life to receive most attention in the context of further union. The treatment of religious unity is noteworthy in several ways. Firstly, writers unanimously regard it as essential for general union, the greatest of all possible bonds between the peoples. This being so, it is surprising how few schemes for church unity were advanced. 'The Divine Providence' advised a federal ecclesiastical government, with general assemblies for each nation and an overall British Convocation. Unity in ecclesiastical law was also proposed. Doddridge went further, advocating union in church discipline through gradual anglicisation of the Kirk, and implicitly condemning presbyterianism as 'popular'. The 'Discourse on the Proposed Union' likewise asserted the historical primacy of the Archbishop of Canterbury over Scotland, Scots bishops allegedly being consecrated at York in Anglo-Saxon times. One might have expected a storm of Scots protestation in reply, about the superiority of the Kirk and its independence. Hume, and to a lesser extent Russell, did indeed include long passages supporting the integrity and privileges of the Scots church. Hume, indeed, went so far as suggesting an ecclesiastical union based on the exportation of presbyterianism to England. These writers were clearly influenced by the continuing worries in Scotland about the danger to the Kirk that might arise by union. Hume's two treatises are the nearest approach to a fusion of presbyterianism with the apocalyptic, British vision of Gordon: the same picture of a British nation united under a reformed church that was to inspire the Covenanters four decades later. Generally, however, the treatment of religious union is self-congratulatory. Writers insisted that the two nations were already effectually united in religion. While Bacon soberly recorded their uniformity in doctrine and diversity in government and discipline, the latter differences were ignored or dismissed as irrelevant by Savile, Pont, Craig, Gordon, Thornborough and 'Pro Unione'. Existing unity in religion — confirming recent research by Tyacke on the Calvinist base of the English church under Bancroft — was one of the most common themes used by writers to justify unity in other areas.

The principle of commercial unity was widely praised but scarcely examined.[31] Only Bacon and Craig outlined concrete proposals for unification. 'De Unione' merely advocated exemption from Alien's Custom, not even including the other proposals of the Anglo-Scots Commission on which he had sat. Bacon's 'Certain Articles', before the Commission, went rather further, proposing mutual eligibility to the great commercial companies, and a single system of imposts and customs throughout Great Britain. Opposition to the principle came entirely from England, and described commercial union in extravagant terms as a threat to English trading interests. The leading tracts here are Spelman's 'Of the Union' and the 'Discourse on Three Types of Union'. Both allege that free trade would empty the royal treasury, and that goods would in future enter Britain through Scots ports where duties were cheaper. Spelman produced a variety of unconvincing but much-repeated arguments to show that the Scots would come in short time to dominate British trade. Their small ships could sail when the large, armoured merchantmen of England had no wind, while the hard life and diet of Scots sailors would enable their masters to undercut the English. Scotland would gain access to rich English commodities, offering little in return but poor fish and worse cloth. Free trade would bring dearth to England, the Scots transporting all her corn into their own country. All these arguments would reappear in 1606, with another major theme contributed by Savile — the inequity of Scots trading privileges in France, allowing the Scots to undersell England at home and abroad.

(d) The Historical Case for a Limited Union

From the three previous sections, it might seem that the supporters of further union had a preponderance, if not monopoly, of the discussion. There remained, however, a large and internally very cohesive group of arguments against further union, established primarily and overtly on historical precedents. These precedents recur consistently, seven in particular providing the majority of references. These were the unions of Castile and Leon, of Castile/Leon and Aragon, of Spain and Portugal, of France first with Normandy and later Britanny, of the Netherlands with Austria, and of Poland with Lithuania under the Jagellons. The various unions in Scandinavia were also regularly cited. It is notable that these precedents are all medieval or sixteenth-century, and continental. Of various English and Scots unions which could have been cited (for example England and Spain under Phillip and Mary, Scotland and France under Francis and Mary Stuart), only that of England and Wales, significantly, received any attention. The seven core precedents are matched by seven tracts in which they formed the central element. These were Savile's 'Historical Collections', Doddridge's 'Brief Consideration', the four discourses 'On the Proposed Union', 'On Three Types of Union', 'Against the Union' and on 'Union by Cocurrency', and the Trinity College MS. The discourses 'On the Proposed Union' and 'On Three Types of Union' were relatively unsophisticated in their use of historical precedents, assuming all to be of equal value and the same type. Their conclusions, after examining this undifferentiated mass, were correspondingly more general than those of the other five — namely, that unions do not usually involve assimilation in laws, or the institutions of justice and government. Their stance on privileges was equivocal. The 'Discourse on Three Types of Union' allowed a union in 'privileges of person', including the right to hold, inherit and bequeath all property, and have office or parliamentary place in the other country, as a natural subject. Doddridge, however, whose own differentiation of precedents is incomplete, argued strongly against participation in offices, citing as precedent the Spanish/Portuguese union where Portugal retained her own offices and filled them entirely with Portuguese.[32]

The other tracts refined these basic themes by dividing all the precedents into different types. Some were clearly inapplicable to the present case, the union of two non-sovereign states (seignories) and the union of a seignory to a sovereign but not suzerain state being the principal examples. The three types most commonly discussed were: first, consolidation — the union of a seignory with a sovereign state holding its suzerainty; second and third, the union of two absolute and sovereign states under one monarch (a) by conquest and (b) by peaceful means, such as inheritance, election or marriage. The clearest exposition of these categories is in the opening chapters of Savile's 'Historical Collections'. Examination of the precedents in each category showed them to have different consequences. In a conquest, the conqueror might impose any conditions he desired on the subjugated state, extinguishing all competing titles and achieving a union in name, laws, institutions etc. simply by substituting those of the conquering nation. The settlement of the conquering nation, however, remained inviolate and unalterable. This followed the civil law doctrine of Conquest Right, originated by classical jurists like Gaius and received into continental constitutional thought during the Middle Ages.[33] Nevertheless, the argument here was notably conducted not in legal but in historical terms. The same is true of consolidation, where precedents were used to show that the name, laws, privileges and institutions of the fief were automatically replaced on union by those of the suzerain state. This is again an argument about feudal law conducted within a historical context, by men ignorant of or antagonistic to feudal and civil traditions. Finally, the peaceful union of sovereign states was considered on precedents to involve no reconciliation of laws, institutions, customs or indeed anything other than the person of the king and the allegiance of his subjects. This is the message above all of the 'Discourse Against the Union', after examining no fewer than nineteen unions by marriage, election and inheritance.

This was in effect a fully-fledged historical philosophy of union, applicable in several different ways. The most obvious was of course to declare England and Scotland sovereign states uniting peacefully, thereby debarring further or institutional union. The discourses 'Against the Union' and 'On Three Types of Union' took this line, as (eventually) did Savile. There is *no* concrete proposal in any tract to treat Scotland as a fictive conquest. The theme was however raised several times in the parliamentary debates of 1604, notably in Northampton's speech answering allegations 'that in this union equalitie was not desired but a conquest'.[34] The Scottish counterpart may be seen in two reports by the Venetian ambassador,[35] and in the Trinity College MS. Both pointed to a feeling north of the border that England, as James's second kingdom, might be declared 'accessorie'. In both cases, however, its use was incidental, defending Scotland against English assumptions of superiority.

These English claims were more serious, and demonstrated themselves very clearly in the third use of the historical union philosophy. Several English writers were willing to assert that the union was in fact a consolidation, Scotland being an historical fief of England. If so, Scotland could be brought to immediate unity by the imposition of the English name, laws, institutions and privileges. 'Union by Cocurrency' expressly urges this course of action on the king: 'A perfect consolidation . . . being grounded upon this title will be easy, and one withall so firme that no exception or accident can ever dissolve it'. Spelman's attempt to exclude 'Scotland' from the royal style springs from the same roots. By contrast, the 'Discourse on the Proposed Union' justified the new style precisely on grounds of English precedency, since it had been taken by Anglo-Saxon kings to register their suzerainty over the Scots. Finally, Savile himself was clearly attracted by the possibility, examining with approval the English claims and dismissing Scots objections as 'meerly frivolous and false'. Nevertheless, as we have seen, Savile eventually turned away from this line to that of the peaceful union of sovereign states, taking his stance accordingly against the union in style, laws, parliaments or liberties. This was the most popular use of the historical philosophy in the tracts, and was to be of considerable importance in the parliamentary debates of 1606-7.

5. Conclusions and Summary

(a) General Conclusions

The tracts comprise several hundred thousand words of text on the union, and contain a wealth of material of great interest to political, religious, economic and legal historians. In this examination, I have concentrated on the material's political significance. The treatises give us almost too much information about attitudes and factors influencing the political development of the project. Firstly, they may be taken to confirm the main themes in our analysis of the 1604 parliamentary session. The sheer bulk of the material confirms the issue's importance in the political scene of 1604. The willingness of Bacon, Russell and Savile to submit very different tracts on the union to the king indicates that James was not publicly committed to any single programme, to be forced through at top speed. Savile indeed was knighted shortly after submitting his tract commending a limited union. The arguments used by so many tracts to justify the 'urgent necessity' of the change in the name, as fostering a sense of unity in both peoples, provide a credible alternative to the simplistic allegations of royal vainglory. The answers of writers to the Commons' objections highlight their diversity, showing the many different strands within the 'opposition' of the Lower House. Finally, the bitterness roused by the English session, both between king and Commons and between the nations, is echoed in the widespread condemnation of the Lower House by English and more particularly Scots treatises.

It is more difficult to prove that the tracts influenced later political developments. The proclamation on the change of style, the issuing of the 'Unite' coinage in October 1604 and the other measures to obtain unity in the 'outward marks of government' in 1604-5 strongly recall the advice of Bacon and other authors. By contrast, the Anglo-Scots Commission ignored most of the proposals for further union, being bound in scope by the bans on discussion of the fundamental laws and religion contained in the Scots Act of Commission. Since subsequent debate followed the Commission's recommendations, the proposals in the tracts might at first sight seem to have become irrelevant. Nevertheless, the enormous overlap between the arguments in the tracts and in the parliamentary debates of 1606-7 implies a considerable indirect influence. Questions like the Scots trading privileges in France and the lack of legal reconciliation in peaceful unions of sovereign states, first fully enunciated in the tracts, became major elements in the opposition to enactment of the Commission's programme.

Above all, the tracts are useful in revealing the intellectual context in which the political debate took place, the ways in which people in either country saw 'the union', and the assumptions and beliefs underlying those attitudes. Most of this concluding section will isolate and concentrate on differences between three groups of tracts — the English, the Scots, and those whose arguments seem most clearly to reflect royal attitudes. These groups, however, shared many assumptions and beliefs. Firstly, they were united in their assumptions about the correct sources of arguments to be used in discussing an issue of this kind. Generally, this discussion is marked by its lack of a comparative or analytical approach. Comparisons between England and Scotland are limited to occasional assertions of an existing unity in manners, apparel, language, religion and continent. There is little comparative analysis of their constitutions, institutions of justice and government, social and economic systems, or even (Craig and Bacon aside) their laws. The debate instead ran at a more superficial level, on the general advisability of union in certain areas of public life. The main sources used were the Bible, ancient philosophy, 'common reason' and above all historical precedent. Much has been written about the links between history and politics in the early modern period.[36] Books of history were written as general political advice (Major, Macchiavelli, Guiccardini) or polemic for a particular policy. John Hayward's own 'Life of Edward VI' was suspected of the latter, while he and Bacon both later wrote histories to promote Anglo-Scots unity.[37] The link between the Earl of Essex and Tacitan historians like Savile is also well-known.[38] Inevitably, history was regularly used by those in power to glorify the nation or dynasty, either by showing its heroic past or giving it a politically significant mythological origin. English politicians in particular avidly sought historical precedents to justify their positions on questions of policy or constitutional interpretation. The origin of parliament, Magna Carta and 1066 all received particular attention under the early Stuarts, who also fostered research in support of extra-parliamentary methods of finance: fiscal feudalism, impositions, ship money, baronetcies etc. The union was thus only one issue where historical precedents were invoked. It is however an especially good example both in the tracts and in general political discussion, perhaps because the project was new and had no tradition of argument built up in Elizabethan times. It was also a project whose ultimate scope was unclear, making an appeal to history, as an independent authority, the more attractive.[39]

The three groups of tracts similarly shared many common assumptions about the nature of 'unity', as a general principle. Unity was good, approved of by philosophy, touched with divinity. As a general rule, and predictably, it was equated with 'uniformity'. Only rarely was it suggested that cultural diversity might actually enrich a political union. This emphasis on the need for uniformity in public behaviour led to a concentration by all the tracts on the systems governing that behaviour, namely religious doctrine and law. By contrast, there was relatively less interest in discussing union of the institutions by which these systems were operated. If Scots and English behaved alike, they might safely be governed differently — an important assumption saying much about the ultimate purpose of James's project. The main differences between the tracts lay in other areas of belief — notably about the immediate scope of the union, and about the 'correct' relationship between the nations.

(b) Royal Tracts

It is often difficult to separate a 'royal' tract — one whose arguments seem most closely to reflect the attitudes of James himself — from the mass of English and Scots treatises. The danger of circular argument is obvious. Several criteria have been used in selecting the group; tracts written by royal command, or the command of a close associate; printed tracts, since these required government approval for publication; tracts not only seen but approved by the king; and above all, tracts whose central themes reflect those used in James's own speeches and messages on the union. 'Pro Unione', Bacon's two tracts, Thornborough's discourses, Gordon's sermons and printed works like Pont, Hayward, Cornwallis and *Rapta Tatio* all qualify. Savile and Doddridge also belong to the group, but are notable for their different, 'English' perspective, while Russell occupies a similar halfway position between the royal and Scots groups.

These tracts are united by several features. They all contain high praise for the principle of unity, many giving over a great deal of space to discussion of its virtues. There is absolute agreement on the divine origin of unity, and on the part played by divine providence in bringing about this particular union — echoing James's speech of March 19, 1604. As we have seen, this was used by several to condemn opposition to the king's wishes as flying in the face of God. There is a danger here in over-emphasising the importance of the providential and particularly the missionary element in 'royal' thinking. The key figure here is of course John Gordon, with his vision of James as a divinely inspired unifier not only of 'Britain' but of all Christendom. Russell and Maxwell also press the theme. It is impossible to assess how much credit James gave to these messianic ideas. As Williamson has shown,[40] his early scholarship was heavily imbued with apocalyptic elements, reaching its fruition in his meditation on Revelation, Chapter 20. That work had implicitly personified him as a British David, and laid the ground for Gordon's more sophisticated edifice of a British Elect

Nation. Similarly, James was obviously eager to encourage such speculations.

His favour to Gordon and to other 'apocalyptic' Scots clergymen like Patrick Galloway, the swift printing of the sermons and his occasional references to the memory of Arthur and Brutus are all significant here.[41] Finally, the inclusion of the short second tract on union with France and Spain in Savile's work (written by commandment) and the later campaign against Cardinal Bellarmine all confirm James's adherence to 'lofty ideas . . . [of] universal agreement and concord', and suggest a measure of royal credence in the apocalypse. However, the missionary theme formed only one element in the tracts, and not one which regularly found its way into James's own writings and speeches. There, the king goes no further than referring to divine providence as the root of union, and to the close relationship between himself and the reunited island of Britannia. James also made gestures towards other figures of historical and mythological significance, who would not fit into the missionary theme. The quartering in the Great Seal of the arms of Cadwallader and Edward the Confessor is one example; while James's frequent references to the York/Lancaster division and Henry VII were given particular point by his own descent from the first royal Tudor. The naming of Prince Henry could thus be considered analogous to Henry VII's own use of Arthurian symbolism in the christening of his eldest son. It is important to remember that all the Tudors had engaged in similar posturings. Henry VIII's flirtation with Constantine the Great has been admirably demonstrated by Koebner.[42] The later elaboration of the Constantinian heritage under Elizabeth to create the Foxean Elect Nation in England met with similar royal encouragement. Nevertheless, Elizabeth had equally taken on other roles from time to time, such as Gloriana, Cynthia, and arguably the Virgin Mary.[43] In short, there is no doubt that James was attempting to use historical, mythological and biblical symbolism to give his dynasty and kingdom of 'Britain' the appropriate mystical flavour. To do so legitimised his hold in either nation, and strengthened the bonds between them. Such legitimation had been the original purpose of James's own meditation. What is dubious is the extent to which James allowed his own actions to be swayed by this grand apocalyptic vision of a purified Christendom under British rule approaching the Eschaton. The relative caution of his first year and his proposals for the 1604 parliaments suggest a more modest and gradual approach to union.

Gordon apart, the 'royal' tracts have a very clear and much more limited picture of the aims and scope of the union project. Above all, these treatises emphasise the need for a unity in the hearts and minds of the two peoples, and so they absolutely supported union in the outward marks of government — the name of the kingdom, its flag, its seals and coinage, etc. These symbolic changes were essential to instil a sense of unity and brotherhood into the two peoples. Similarly, there was very general support in the group — Savile, Doddridge and Russell being (important) exceptions — for union in the laws. The 'royal' attitude to law was utilitarian rather than reverential, and there were few qualms expressed about altering or reconciling the laws. Again, the concern for uniformity in public behaviour surfaces, with considerable emphasis on the existing unity in 'manners'. Support for union in other areas, such as the institutions of justice and government, was sporadic; but there was universal agreement on the need for mutual participation in offices — again, to establish an awareness of fraternity.

The royal tracts are united in their picture of the project's long-term purpose. This was seen as the consolidation of the two nations in mutual amity and secure obedience to the Stuart dynasty. The emphasis on union in hearts and minds, and on uniformity in public behaviour, came from this awareness of the fragility of the existing union in sovereignty. James's own gradualist approach to the project, seeking the maximum public display of support for every change and relying heavily on the use of printed propaganda, is thus confirmed almost as a form of emotional engineering. His attitude is made most clear in a letter to Cecil on November 22, 1604: he was 'fully resolved that the smallest beginning of this happy errand at this time with the hearty applause of all parties will imprint such a general apprehension in the hearts of all the people . . . that the union is already made'.[44] The institutional changes also needed to secure his hold over the two kingdoms could follow in due course.

(c) English Tracts

English tracts on the union not associated with the 'royal' group present a very different picture. The main treatises in this category are Spelman's 'Of the Union', 'Union by Cocurrency', the reply to Thornborough and the three discourses 'Against the Union', 'On the Proposed Union' and 'On Three Types of Union'. Savile and Doddridge's tracts must also be associated with the group, on the arguments they advance. As a rule, these tracts either omit or include only very short passages of praise for the general principle of unity, and make few references to divine providence. The precedents used to support their arguments are notably later than the other two groups, which include many biblical and classical precedents in their text. The English texts are generally very lacking in religious content, even when this might be cited to support their general position on the union. In particular, there is no trace of the English apocalyptic vision being used against the Scots. The English tracts are remarkably lukewarm about union. There is some mild satisfaction at the elimination of a menace on their northern border, but very little support for any union deeper than that in sovereignty already achieved by James's accession to the English throne. The need for a unity in hearts and minds, and in public behaviour to secure the hold of the Stuart dynasty over England and Scotland was not perceived, except by Spelman. In particular, the historical philosophy of union was used to justify opposition to union in laws, outward marks of government, institutions of justice and administration, and usually the change in style also. Mutual participation in offices and trade was seen as benefiting the Scots, at England's expense. On law, as we have seen, opposition was strengthened by native beliefs in the immemoriality and quasi-immutability of the common law, a theme that surfaces many times in the treatises. Any advances towards union involving alterations in the public systems and institutions of England were rejected out of hand.

Above all, there was a very general feeling that Scotland was the lesser partner in this union, and so should make any concessions necessary for it to become substantive. This feeling went well beyond mere hostility to Scotland, although such prejudice undoubtedly existed among many Englishmen. It was rather an almost universal assumption or prejudice of precedency. Scotland was seen as inferior, not merely in resources, military prowess, historical glory and cultural achievements but in feudal and indeed moral terms as well. Inevitably, the union project had revived the age-old controversy concerning English suzerainty over Scotland. This has been touched on in our first chapter. To modern eyes, the debate seems arid, pedantic, irrelevant, a tedious English recital of alleged homages done by Scots kings to their English counterparts from Alfred to Edward III, each case being refuted at equal length by Scots scholars. Patriotic mythologies had been invoked on both sides to give the correct flavour of immemoriality — England seeing the origin of her superiority in the division of Britain between Brutus's three sons, Scotland inventing an older origin in Scotia, daughter of a Greek mercenary captain in the service of the Pharaohs.[45] The absurdities and tedium of these laborious efforts should not blind us to their continuing political importance. As we have seen, the debate over suzerainty was still very much alive in 1604. Levy, McKisack and Kendrick have demonstrated that belief in the Brutus myth, the least credible part of the English case, remained high in the early seventeenth century. Even chroniclers writing at the height of the union debates in 1607 could treat English suzerainty as accepted historical fact.[46] Craig's own refutation of Holinshed, *De Hominio*, had been written as recently as 1602. The parliamentary debates of 1604 in England had contained explicit claims to suzerainty, and the use of precedents (like the union of England and Wales) redolent of consolidation.

Prejudice, precedency and a belief in the immemoriality of English systems and institutions were therefore potent factors in framing the English response to union — namely, to oppose further union involving changes in English law and institutions, proposing instead the submission of Scotland to English systems.

(d) Scots Tracts

Williamson's examination of the Scots public consciousness during the reign of James VI contains much of direct relevance to the union. This is particularly the case in his treatment of Gordon and the apocalyptic mission. Williamson has shown that the theme of a British Elect Nation taking the leading role in the apocalypse dated back at least as far as Knox, and was by 1603 a major element in Scots attitudes to the prospect of 'union'. It is therefore unsurprising that all the writers on the union including the theme (Russell, Gordon, Maxwell) were

Scots. We have already examined its close links with Jacobean ideas. The failure to produce an apocalyptic vision based on Scotland alone is remarkable. Nevertheless, the intensity of the British vision may again easily lead to the obscuring of other attitudes to the union. Generally speaking, the Scots tracts on the union do not rely on the apocalyptic vision for their arguments. Only in the work of Gordon and Maxwell is it a dominant element. Nor, as Williamson suggests, are they dominated by a blinding concern for the independence of the Scots Kirk — as we have seen. The 'secret' lies elsewhere.

The Scots tracts not associated with the royal group are Hume's two tracts, Craig, Russell and the Trinity College MS. These share many of the features of the 'royal' group, notably in their fulsome praise for the principle of unity, their absolute certainty about the divine origin of the union, and their tendency to use ancient and biblical precedents as a result. Particular stress is placed by authors like Pont and Russell, and to a considerable extent Hume, on the unity in true religious doctrine as a cause and mark of the union. In Pont's case, this emphasis reaches almost Gordonian levels. The coming together of two nations in peace and true religion is linked with the universal extirpation of idolatry; but Pont specifically rejects the vision of antique religious purity presented by Gordon and Russell, seeing no particular mission either in Britain or James. Hume apart, there is no presbyterian insistence on the need for a British covenant; at most, the references in Pont and Russell to the sins of the English may be cited.

The Scots tracts generally accept in full the need for unity in hearts, minds and affections, and refer openly to the previous bitter hostility between the nations. They therefore support a union in the name, in outward marks of government, and mutual participation in trade and offices. These are very significant areas, since proposals for union in each presupposed an equality between the countries. Even more than the English tracts, the Scots saw the union in terms of precedency — in their case, an admission of English superiority they would never be prepared to make. No opportunity was lost to condemn the English parliamentary 'opposition', not merely for the opposition itself but also for the haughty assertions of precedency that accompanied it. No real or imagined challenge to the dignity of Scotland is left unanswered. It is remarkable that in a tract commending union, Craig should refer to the haughty remarks of his English fellow-Commissioners, and should think or find it necessary to include long sections defending Scotland from accusations of laziness, poverty, barbarity, cannibalism and ignorance, and denying that Scotland had ever under any circumstances admitted any kind of inferiority to the crown or nation of England.[47] English claims were met not with assertions that England was 'accessorie' to Scotland, but with a vigorous demand for a union based on strict parity. The Scots support for the 'indifferent' name of Great Britain is therefore especially marked. In these demands, medieval and sixteenth-century precedents from British history were invoked, to point a partisan moral: that since England had striven so mightily hard for union in the past, by force of arms, she should now willingly embrace without cavil the peaceful and equal union which had fallen so providentially into her lap. This was particularly emphasised with the offers of marriage and union made by Henry VIII and Protector Somerset in the 1540s. As we have seen, the arrival of Reformation in Scotland had altered Scots attitudes to the 'Rough Wooing', many Scots following Knox in praise of Somerset's offers. The emphasis by Somerset on equality was the key here. The name, commercial unity and the maintenance of Scotland's existing laws and privileges had all been proposed — as marks of equality. The same demands duly appear in the Scots tracts of 1603-4 — consciously adopted, or a parallel response to certain unchanging circumstances of union. The reservation on ancient laws and privileges may, as Williamson suggests, have been strengthened by presbyterian desire for an autonomous church in an autonomous state, its position defined by a codification of Scots law.[48] In general, however, the maintenance of the 'auld estaitt' was nothing more nor less than a touchstone of equality and sovereignty. Many Scots writers rejected any legal reconciliation, even one involving equal changes to either code. This fear of admitting precedency often overcame Scottish pride in having James as king of England. Craig, Pont and Russell all included passages lamenting the *de facto* diminution of Scotland by the union of the crowns:

> Our naturall prince far resident from us, the publict resort of this cuntrey far decayit, the nichtbour cuntrey daylie florisching . . . this unioun tendis only to magnify the ane, preiudge the uther, Ingland to joyse all, Scotland in effect nathing, and to be as it were ane pendicle of thair kingdome, we to lose our ancient glorie forevir.[49]

Russell's final plea truly summarised the attitude of Scotland: 'Giff thairfoir it salbe an unioun, lett it be in a plaine paritie, without alteratioun of our estaitt'.[50] The two nations were therefore very much at odds, and could only agree to go their separate ways. England would admit no further union save one that confirmed her precedency. Scotland would never consider such a confirmation, demanding equality as the central element in any acceptable settlement.

NOTES

1. See e.g. the following: J. Gordon, *Panegyrique of Congratulation for the Concord of the Realmes of Great Britaine in unitie of Religion and under one King*, London 1604; Sir T. Craig, *Serenissimi et invinctissimi Principis Jacobi Britanniarum et Galliarum Regis στεφανοφορια*, Edinburgh 1603; R. Ayton, *Ad Iacobum VI Britanniarum Regem, Angliam petentem, Panegyris* — printed in *Delitiae Poetarum Scotorum*, 1937; D. Sinclair, *De auspicatissima Inauguaratione Jacobi Primi, omnium Britanniarum Regis, Concilium Deorum*, Paris 1603; G. Thomson, *'Ανακεφαλαιωσις, sive de reductione regnorum Britanniae ad unum principem, poema*, London 1604. The best discussions of these panegyrics are in Bindoff, 'Stuart Style', 205 and Axton, *Two Bodies*, 131-2.

2. The universal use of 'Britain' in their titles is remarkable. See also the sentiments of Sam Daniel's poem on the union of the crowns (Bindoff, 'Stuart Style', 205):

> Now Thou art all Great Britain and no more;
> No Scot, no English now, nor no debate:
> No borders, but the Ocean and the Shore.

3. Craig, *De Unione*, p. xii.

4. B. L. Royal MSS 18A.XIV, fols. 13-14 (Pont).

5. Gordon, *Ενωτικοη*, 7.

6. The best example is J. Williams's funerary sermon of 1625, *Great Britain's Salomon* (London, 1625). It does however date back to 1604: see e.g. Thornborough, *Joyful and Blessed Reuniting*, 269.

7. This was the title of a masque produced by Anthony Munday in 1605, for Lord Mayor Sir John Holliday.

8. For England, see Haller, *Elect Nation*. Some English Puritans in 1603 had prophesied an apocalypse — see esp. the preface to Andrew Willett's *Ecclesia Triumphans* (Cambridge, 1603). The Scots dimension is covered in Williamson, *Scottish National Consciousness*.

9. B. L. Sloane MSS 3521, fol. 3r.

10. E.g. B.L.Harl.MSS 292:58 & 60, S.P.14/7/59 & 76B, B.L.Add.MSS 38139 fol. 38v, etc.

11. Spedding, *Bacon* III, p. 227 (Bacon, 'Certain Articles').

12. Hay, 'Gt Britain', 55-67.

13. B.L.Harl.MSS 1305, fol. 11r.

14. See esp. Manwood's report on the debate of 23 April 1604: B.L.Add.MSS 38139 fol. 27v.

15. For this possibility, see *Cal.S.P.(Ven) 1603-7*, 195.

16. Hayward, *Treatise of Union*, 54.

17. B.L.Harl.MSS 1305, fol. 10r.

18. B. L. Sloan MSS 3521, fol. 7r.

19. See esp. Levack, 'Union of English and Scots Law'.

20. See esp. Pocock, *Ancient Constitution*.

21. S.P.14/7/75. For a full discussion, see Gough, *Fundamental Law*.

22. N.L.S.Adv.MSS 31.4.7 fol. 6.

23. Ibid., fol. 5.

24. Its date is open to doubt. The 'Epistle Dedicatory' talks of a legal commission, which suggests 1607-8 (see below, Chapter 7). It is however clear that the body of the text was written long before. *DNB* and Tytler, *Sir Thomas Craig* date it as 1603, Girwan (*Sources and Literature of Scots Law*) as 1600. The last is probably correct: *De Hominio*, written in 1602, speaks of it as a previous work.

25. Craig, *Ius Feudale*, ix.

26. Levack, 'Union of English and Scots Law', 102-3.

27. Spedding, *Bacon* III, 97.

28. B. L. Sloane MSS 3521, fols. 9v, 11r (fol. 10 misplaced).

29. Hayward, *Treatise of Union*, 2-3.

30. E.g. Cornwallis, *Miraculous and Happie Union*, 10-11.

31. It was praised by Pont, Russell, the Trinity College MS, 'The Divine Providence', Doddridge, Bacon and Craig — amongst others.

32. Modern scholars agree: Braudel, *Mediterranean World* II, 1176-85.

33. Sutherland, 'Conquest and Law'.

34. S.P.14/7/41 & 42. Note the use of the Protector Somerset precedent.

35. *Cal.S.P.(Ven) 1603-7*, 106-8 and 153.

36. See esp. the following: Fussner, *Historical Revolution*; Fox, *English Historical Scholarship*; Skinner, 'History and Ideology'; Levy, *Tudor Historical Thought*; Campbell, 'Use of Historical Patterns'; Sharpe, *Sir Robert Cotton* (esp. 116, 152-4, 165, 227 and 251

for Cotton and the Union).

37. Goldberg, 'Sir John Hayward', 233-44; Bacon, *Henry VII*; Sir J. Hayward, *The Life and Raigne of King Edward the Sixt* (London, 1630).

38. Levy, *Tudor Historical Thought*, 237-56 *passim*; Benjamin, 'Sir John Hayward', 275-6.

39. For the use of historical precedents in political debate on the union, see for example Winwood, *Memorials* II, 35 and *HMC.Salis.MSS* XVI, 345.

40. Williamson, *Scottish National Consciousness*, 39, 80-2.

41. E.g. in his Audience of 21 April 1604; Spedding, *Bacon* III, p. 194.

42. Koebner, 'Imperial Crowns', 29-53.

43. Haller, *Elect Nation*, 245.

44. *HMC.Salis.MSS* XVI, 363.

45. See J. Harryson's 'Exhortacion to the Scottes, to conforme themselfes to the honourable, expedient and godly union betweene the two realmes of Englande and Scotland': in Murray, *Complaynt of Scotlande*, 220ff.

46. Harington, *Tract on the Succession*, 61; Ayscu, *Historie*, 94-5.

47. Craig, *De Unione*, 232, 331, 353-5 *et passim*.

48. Williamson, *Scottish National Consciousness*, 10-16.

49. B. L. Royal MSS 18A.LXXVI, fol. 8.

50. Ibid.

APPENDIX

A Catalogue of Tracts

This is a brief list of the principal tracts and treatises examined in Chapter 3. Abbreviated titles used in notes and the text are bracketed after bibliographic information. All lengths given are approximate.

SECTION ONE: SCOTS TRACTS

1. Sir Thomas Craig, *De Unione Regnorum Britanniae Tractatus*. Written 1604-5, updated in 1607, published 1909; ed. C. S. Terry, Scottish History Society, Edinburgh. 95,000 words (*De Unione*). MS in Latin, N.L.S.Adv.MSS 24.1.1.

2. John Gordon, Ενωτικοη, *or A Sermon of the Union of Great Brittaine*. October 1604. Printed, London. 16,000 words (Ενωτικοη).

3. John Gordon, *The Union of Great Brittaine, or England and Scotland's Happinesse in being reduced to unitie of Religion*. April-December 1604. Printed, London. 12,000 words (*Union of Great Brittaine*).

4. Robert Pont, *De unione Britanniae dialogus*. May-October 1604. Printed, Edinburgh. 11,000 words (*De Unione*). Latin: a contemporary MS translation is in B. L. Royal MSS 18A.XIV.

5. John Russell, 'Ane treatise of the Happie and Blissed Unioun betuixt the tua ancienne realmes of Scotland and Ingland', etc. May-October 1604. 24,000 words. Manuscript only: N.L.S.Adv.MSS 31.4.7 and B. L. Royal MSS 18A.LXXVI (latter is later, and extensively altered) ('Treatise of the Happie and Blissed Unioun').

6. An anonymous and untitled treatise in Trinity College, Cambridge. May-October, 1604. 13,000 words remaining, introduction lost. Manuscript: Cam.Trinity College MSS R5.15, No. 10 ('Trinity College MS').

7. D. Hume, *De unione insulae Britanniae, tractatus primus*. 1605. 12,000 words. Printed, Latin. (*De unione I*).

8. D. Hume, 'De unione insulae Britanniae, tractatus secundus'. 1605. 17,000 words. Manuscript, Latin: E. U. L. Laing MSS Vol. III, 249 (Ibid. II).

9. J. Maxwell, 'Britain's Union in Love'. 1604. Manuscript: a scheme for a tract, 1000 words. B. L. Royal MSS 18A.LI ('Britain's Union in Love').

SECTION TWO: ENGLISH TRACTS

1. Sir F. Bacon, *A Brief Discourse touching the Happy Union of the Kingdoms of England and Scotland*. 1603. Printed, London: reprinted in Spedding, *Bacon* III, pps. 89-99. Many MS versions survive: e.g. B.L.Harl.MSS 532:7. 4000 words (*Brief Discourse*).

2. Sir F. Bacon, 'Certain Articles or Considerations touching the Union of the Kingdoms of England and Scotland'. June-September, 1604. Manuscripts: B.L.Add. MSS 41613, fols. 37-47, Queen's College Oxford MSS XXXII fols. 129-37, etc. Printed in Spedding, *Bacon* III, 217-47. 8000 words (plus 2000-word draft proclamation) ('Certain Articles').

3. Sir William Cornwallis, *The Miraculous and Happie Union of England and Scotland*. Printed March 1604, London and Edinburgh. 9000 words (*Miraculous and Happie Union*).

4. Sir J. Skinner *or* N. Douglas, *Rapta Tatio: The Mirrour of his Maiesties present gouernement, tending to the union of his whole iland of Brittonie*. April-October 1604. Printed, London. 8000 words. (*Rapta Tatio*).

5. John Hayward, *A Treatise of Union of the two realmes of England and Scotland*. November 1604. Printed, London. 20,000 words. (*Treatise of Union*).

6. John Thornborough, *A Discourse plainly proving the evident Utility and urgent Necessity of the desired happy Union of England and Scotland*. May 1604. Printed, London (*Discourse*). 6000 words.

7. John Thornborough, *Joyful and Blessed Reuniting the two mighty and famous kingdoms of England and Scotland*. January-April, 1605. Printed, London (*Joyful and Blessed Reuniting*). 22,000 words.

8. Albericus Gentilis, *De Unione Regnorum Britanniae*. 1605. Printed, London, in *Regales Disputationes Tres*. 11,000 words (*De unione*).

9. Sir Henry Spelman, 'Of the Union'. May-October, 1604. Manuscript: B. L. Sloane MSS 3521. 8000 words ('Of the Union').

10. Sir Henry Savile, 'A Treatise of the Union'. May-October, 1604. Numerous MSS copies: Bod.Misc.MSS 3499, B.L.Harl.MSS 1305, S.P.14/7/40,72 & 73. 20,000 words ('Historical Collections').

11. Sir John Doddridge, 'A Brief Consideration touching the Union of the two kingdoms in the hands of one king'. March-October, 1604. Several MSS: B. L. Sloane MSS 3479, fols. 59-67, B.L.Lansd.MSS 486, pps. 77-84, etc. 6000 words ('Brief Consideration').

12. Anon., 'A Brief Replication to the Answers of the Obiections against the Union'. June-October, 1604. MS: B. L. Stowe MSS 158, fols. 34-9. 4000 words ('Reply to Thornborough').

13. Anon., 'Union by Cocurrency of ye Homager State with ye Superior'. 1604. MS: S.P.14/7/80b. One chapter from a long work, now lost: 500 words ('Union by Cocurrency').

14. Anon., 'Pro Unione'. April-October, 1604. MS: Cam.Caius College MSS 73/40 No. XVII. 7000 words ('Pro Unione').

15. Anon., 'A Discourse Against the Union'. 1604. MS: S.P.14/7/65 & 66. 7500 words ('Discourse Against the Union').

16. Anon., 'A Discourse on the Proposed Union between England and Scotland, founded on the opinions of historians ancient and modern'. May-October, 1604. MSS: B.L.Harl.MSS 6850 fols. 35-43 and 50, B.L.Harl.MSS 292:55, S.P.14/9/37.1. 6500 words ('Discourse on the Proposed Union').

17. Anon., 'A discourse on the Union as being triple-headed: in head, in laws, and in privileges'. 1604. MSS: B.L.Harl.MSS 292:59, S.P.14/7/61-62. 750 words ('Discourse on Three Types of Union').

18. Anon., 'The Divine Providence in ye misticall and reall union of England and Scotland' etc. April-October, 1604. Several MSS: e.g. B.L.Add.MSS 38139, fols. 42ff. 3000 words ('The Divine Providence').

4
Proclamations and Commission: July-December 1604

1. Introduction

The concentration by authors like Notestein on the parliamentary history of the Jacobean union has led to neglect of two other stages in the development of the project. One of these was the widespread discussion of union by the tracts and pamphlets examined in Chapter 3. These dated predominantly from the late spring and summer of 1604. The second neglected stage was the Anglo-Scots Union Commission. Lightly touched on by historians as background to the great parliamentary debates of 1606-7, the Commission was in some ways the most decisive of all the phases. Its proposals determined the scope of the parliamentary debates in 1606-7; and the arguments used during its discussions, often reflecting previous usage in the tracts or the session of spring 1604, recurred in 1606-7 as the principal themes of debate. It is for this reason that we have devoted an entire chapter to the history of the Commission.

The importance of the Commission was fully appreciated before its first meeting, by contemporaries on all sides. Besides its domestic discussion in the treatises, the union became in the summer and autumn of 1604 the subject of intense diplomatic activity, involving particularly the French ambassador. De Beaumont regarded the union in the same light as many of the tracts — namely, as a project strongly detrimental to French interests. In practice, it would remove the threat of Scots involvement in Anglo-French disputes, or even switch that involvement to support for England. This might make English policy towards France more aggressive, and effective. Union could also be used by England as a lever to break the formal diplomatic links between France and Scotland, the 'Auld Alliance'.[1] This immediate prospect was the more dismaying given the diplomatic isolation already threatened by James's policy of peace and concord with Spain. These Spanish overtures were then in a final stage of negotiation. De Beaumont therefore urged his king to finance 'soubs main' a specifically anti-unionist party among the more malcontent Scots nobles. His advice was couched in terms hardly flattering to the 'Auld Allies' themselves. 'Ceux de cette nation sont pauvres et avares, et subiets de se laisser corrompre, je persiste à la suplier de se resoudre de bonne heure, et sur l'occasion qui se presede d'en obliger quelques-uns des principaux par des pensions et gratifications'.[2] The French king, worried that news of such activities might reach the ears of James and impel him still further towards Spain, adopted a more cautious policy. De Beaumont was to court prominent Scots, notably through promises of places in a military company being established under the Duke of Albany. The purpose was however only to build up a general goodwill among the most influential of the Scots — in effect, creating a party dedicated to the maintenance of the Auld Alliance rather than to the defeat of the union project.[3]

De Beaumont's abortive plotting is the more interesting for its clear confirmation of resistance to the union in Scotland. The Scots are portrayed as a nation affronted by English pretensions to superiority, resolved to maintain Scots privileges in France and their own domestic laws and institutions — both for themselves and as marks of nationhood. Putting names to the disaffected 'party' is more speculative; the ambassador's direct Scots contacts are kept anonymous, and seem to have been mainly low-level intermediaries. Lennox, Hamilton, Huntly and Argyll are however identified as being committed to the French alliance, Huntly and Argyll with a definite anti-union bias. The Venetian ambassador adds Marischal and Moray to the list.[4]

French fears of danger to her Scots alliance were justified. The inequity of Scots trading privileges and naturalisation in France recur as English arguments during the Commission, the alliance being more directly attacked as a threat to internal English security by Savile and a curious document prepared in England shortly before the Commission and innocuously described by the Public Record Office as 'A Discourse of Naturalisation'.[5] This is in fact no less than a memorandum of arguments against substantive union, naturalisation in particular being regarded as favourable to the Scots. The direct continuity between this memorandum and themes used by the English Commissioners suggests a high-level origin for the Discourse, and will result in considerable reference during this chapter. In general terms, it may be taken as further indication of substantial English feeling against further union on any but her own terms.

2. Government Preparations

Against this backcloth of resentment and diplomatic manoeuvring, government preparations continued. These may be conveniently divided into two parts: firstly, attempts to improve attitudes to the project by gestures of symbolic and future unity; secondly, direct arrangements for the meeting; and discussions of an agenda.

The 'gestures of symbolic and future unity' were of course the two royal proclamations of early Autumn 1604 — on the change of style, and on the issue of the 'Unite' coinage. In both cases, timing and content were highly significant. The proclamation changing the royal style was read in London on October 20, the same day as the first meeting of the Commission.[6] That on the coinage was delayed until mid-November — but still occurred during its early deliberations, and was sufficiently close to the previous proclamations to emphasise their connections in an overall programme of unification.

The importance of these proclamations as symbols of unity requires little demonstration. Admittedly, the proclamation on the coinage did have practical functions. It repeated the earlier proclamation of April 8, 1603,[7] reconciling the relative values of English and Scots currency on the basis of £12 Scots to £1 sterling. This was itself useful, both proclamations emphasising the commercial advantages of reconciliation and the needs of Scots nobles to pay Scots coin to their creditors. A long period of decline in the relative value of Scots coinage was thereby ended, and relations between the two currencies were placed on a more stable and permanent footing.[8] The technical virtuosity of the latest measure, balancing the different proportions of gold and silver coinage in the two nations, and the greater weight of the English pound,[9] tend to obscure a much wider, propaganda significance. The coins issued covered an enormous range, from the Scots half-shilling (equivalent to an English halfpenny) to the great Unite or Sceptre.[10] They were not merely valid in either kingdom, but uniform (and uniformly high) in fineness throughout James's dominions. This consistency went well beyond the necessity to counter contemporary allegations of debasement.[11] It was glorificatory, guaranteeing a ready and permanent reception of the coins at home and abroad. The names and stamps were however the most incontrovertibly unionist aspect of the issue. Their names — Unite, Britaine Crown etc. — were redolent of unity. Most bore symbols of both nations, the Thistle Crown for example having on different sides the crowned thistle and an English crowned double rose. On each, James was portrayed in his new role as 'King of Britain, France and Ireland'.[12] Their slogans were entirely unionist in implication. The similarities and differences between James's final inscriptions and those drafted by Cecil are revealing.[13] Both emphasise divine providence, Cecil including quotations from Ephesians 2.14 (*Ipse fecit utraque unum*) and Ezekiel 37.20 (*Erunt unum in meum manuum* — wrongly tagged as 37.14). The final inscriptions, however, predictably laid greater stress on James's personal mission, the historical precedents for the union and the work remaining to be accomplished. The Double Crown repeated the Henry VII theme, with *Henricus rosas regna Iacobus*. Cecil's retrospective *A duo fac unum est* became personal and prospective, as *Faciam eos in gentem unam*. James returned to the theme of divine providence in *Tueatur unita Deus* (Half and Thistle Crowns), and above all *Quae Deus coniunxit nemo separet* (silver 60s Scots piece). The last looked not only back to James's speech at the opening of the 1604 English session of parliament, but also sideways to the marital symbolism contained in the proclamation changing the royal style.[14] The currency thus broadcast both the fact of unity and the theme of a divine mission working through history to fulfilment under James. Its immediate impact was dulled in Scotland by a delay in issue, the parallel proclamation not being read there until March 1605.[15] The intention was plain, however.

The proclamation of Great Britain was even more patently geared to register unity in the hearts and minds of the peoples. It was launched with appropriate pomp and ceremony, with the extra apocalyptic strains of John Gordon's 'Ενωτικοη' (read before James on October 28): 'At the Great Cross in Westminster the King was in most solemn manner proclaimed King of Great Britain . . . in the presence of Sir Thomas Bennett, the Lord Mayor of London, the aldermen in Scarlet, with the heralds and trumpeters, all mounted'.[16] Its phraseology was correspondingly majestic. The basis was undoubtedly the draft proclamation submitted by Bacon with his 'Certain Articles' in the Summer.[17] But it was remodelled, in certain minor ways. Bacon's references to punishment of those impugning the style, to James's equal favour and to the use of prerogative power to avoid abrogation of the laws were all muted, though not excised. By contrast, the final proclamation laid more stress on the Imperial Crown of Britain, on James's just title and descent from Henry VII (again!), and on the further changes of substance to be expected from the Commission. The themes of divine providence and personal mission were likewise heavily emphasised. In its other particulars, the proclamation answered the Commons' objections to the change in name — notably in its denial of vainglory, and its citing of domestic and continental historical precedents for such changes. The legal danger was evaded partly by the fact of proclamation, but also by the final provision (or proviso) excluding the new title of Great Britain from 'any legal proceeding, instrument or assurance'.[18]

James's authority to take the name of Great Britain into his style by proclamation was unquestioned.[19] As a measure designed to instil unity into the popular imagination, however, it was (at least in England) counter-productive. Bindoff's sources for antipathy to the title[20] are all far too late to be useful, but much contemporary evidence is available. Dudley Carleton, in a previous memorandum, had already indicated the dangers involved in taking the name at this stage. 'The misconceaving vulgar will take this to be done out of humour to cross the proceedings in Parliament rather than out of any sound reason, and such as skoffingly have given out that so the k: had the name, he would not much care for the matter may come happely this neare the marke'.[21] Carleton's analysis proved correct. The 'Advertisements of a loyal Subject' and De Beaumont both describe the English *plebes* as scandalised by the change, while a letter written in December 1605 dismissed the proclamation scornfully as 'to no purpose without compounding the people or government'.[22] Once again, James's relatively sophisticated propaganda use of symbolism got little response.

These proclamations were the most spectacular manifestations of state activity during early Autumn, but by no means the only preparations made for the Commission. On September 15, its venue was proclaimed: October 20 in the Painted Chamber, Whitehall.[23] Consultations had already started by mid-September on an agenda or programme, leading Scots Commissioners being called down for discussions with their English counterparts as early as the end of August 1604.[24] Scots thus summoned included Vice-Chancellor Fyvie, Secretary Balmerino, Lord Advocate Hamilton, the Comptroller (Lord Scone/Sir David Murray) and the Lord of Berwick. De Beaumont considered this an attempt to win over particularly the Scots Commissioners to easy acceptance of union, by promises and rewards.[25] A more sober examination of the grants made during the last six months of 1604 to Commissioners of either nation reveals however very little evidence of bribery. Eight English Commissioners received grants of some kind before the Commission, three others together with two Scots (Elphinstone and Fyvie) being rewarded after its termination in December.[26] Among those rewarded, however, were men self-confessedly intending to offer nothing to any purpose, like Zouch,[27] and even Hoby, who refused to subscribe the Instrument. The most significant grants were to Bacon (an annual pension of £60 and a place as King's Counsel), Cecil (made Viscount Cranborne) and Fyvie. In the two latter cases, service was obviously due for recognition by an elevation in rank, while Bacon's fairly minor rewards probably reflected his support for union in the parliamentary session and his work on the 'Certain Articles'.

Bribery apart, the place of these advance discussions in the history of the Commission is uncertain. Records of their debates, if ever kept, have been lost with the mass of English Privy Council archives from 1604, leaving only hints. The surviving letter of summons from James to Hamilton — 'Tam o' the Cowgate' — suggested not only discussions about currency matters, but also trade and customs. Commercial union also appears as a major element in the few surviving state papers from the weeks before the Commission. These are a note by Cecil of the king's thoughts concerning a programme of union,[28] some rough drafts (by the Secretary?) of possible clauses for acts on matters of particular difficulty,[29] a list of English laws antipathetic to the Scots[30] — and the 'Discourse of Naturalisation' mentioned above. The other concerns of these papers were naturalisation, hostile laws and provisions for the future adminis-tration of justice on the Borders. Each of these will be examined more closely in the sections on individual parts of the Commission's programme. The important point here is that even before the first meeting of the Commission, an agenda for discussion had apparently been agreed between the leading statesmen of the two nations — and it was a programme which did not include the union of laws, religions or parliaments.

3. Overview of the Commission

The Commission that assembled on October 20 was a carefully selected, homogeneous body of forty-eight Englishmen and thirty-one Scots. Each delegation contained a balance of great nobles, statesmen, gentry, civil and common lawyers, clerics and merchants — a representation in miniature of all the groups that would normally be found in an English or Scots parliament.[31] This homogeneity was deliberate, James having instructed the Scots to match the list of English Commissioners 'with personis of lyke qualitie and rank'.[32] The main difference between the two groups is the very much larger number of privy councillors among the Scots Commissioners — which says rather more about the size and composition of the two Councils than about the Commission. There were a number of noteworthy absentees from the Commission, on either side. Scots absent included several great nobles alienated from the mainstream of Jacobean government by religion (for example Huntly) or inclination (Hamilton), together with all the London Scots — Home, Erskine, John

Murray, Alexander Hay, the Earl of Mar and the Duke of Lennox. The effect was to make the delegation firmly representative of the Edinburgh establishment, and of unadulterated Scots interests. There is some evidence that the exclusion of Lennox and Mar in particular reflected the suspicions of the Scots parliament in July 1604.[33] On the English side, the most notable absentees were the M.P.s who had argued most forcefully against the union and the change in name — such as Fuller, Sandys and Percival. The Commons' willing approval of a list representing the religious, civil and legal establishment of Jacobean England is a salutary qualification of their 'opposition' in 1604!

Within either group, a few names stand out — largely those called down for advance discussions in September. Spedding and Masson justifiably identified two couples as the powerhouses of the Commission: Fyvie and Cecil being the two delegation leaders, and Bacon and Sir Thomas Hamilton cooperating closely as the prominent figures on the legal and commercial questions. The other major Scottish figure was Balmerino.

The first meeting of the Commission was quickly adjourned until October 29, due to the absence of some Scots.[34] From October 29 to the signature of the Instrument on December 6, however, the Commission met every few days. Given the controversy over their conclusions in 1606-7, and the time spent by other seventeenth-century Anglo-Scots union commissions, the speed of their deliberations is impressive. Within six weeks, proposals were debated and agreed, only Hoby — a pensioner of the French king — refusing his subscription to the Instrument. The reasons for this swift and easy passage are fairly clear. In part, it reflected an amicable social and working relationship between the two groups. Craig and Neville[35] alike stress, with evident surprise, this amiability. Neville noted the Scots' 'modest and respective carriage', Craig telling us that the English had rather expected a 'fiery display of Scottish *pervervidum ingenium*'. This conciliatory demeanour was answered by a 'spirit of accommodation', contradicting Scots expectations of an 'arrogance and contempt of our nation'. Other sources too note the remarkable identity of interest between the two groups.[36] This was however rather a symptom than a cause of the ease of debate. Nor can the ready socialisation outside the Commission be invoked confidently as an explanation. Procedurally, the Commission adopted an open-forum discussion very different from the closed national caucuses and exchange of papers favoured by some other seventeenth-century union commissions. But this was quite as likely to produce lengthy and acrimonious debates, as the discussions on naturalisation on November 15 (with its eventual reference back to caucus) was to show.

The real reasons for the speed and success of the Commission have already been touched on, and can be summarised in the word 'control'. The two groups of Commissioners were homogeneous, because that had been the royal wish. More important was the limited nature of the agenda agreed for discussion. Issues like trade and naturalisation were very far from uncontentious; but advance consideration by leading statesmen could eliminate or evade many controversial points before the Commission even met. The exclusion of religious, legal or parliamentary union similarly ensured concentration on areas where agreement was more possible. In the Commission, most substantive business was carried on in sub-committees, meeting between full sessions and producing firm proposals for debate and decision. Both the Commission itself and the sub-committees were dominated by a small number of English and Scots statesmen, who had established a good working relationship and broad plans of discussion beforehand. Cecil and Fyvie were especially important here: exchanging papers on matters involving points of policy, conferring privately on issues before discussion in full Commission, agreeing on alterations for the meetings of Commission and sub-committees alike. De Beaumont significantly singled out Fyvie as the orchestrator of the Scots delegation.[37] The anonymous Commissioner and M.P. who wrote in 1606 about the meetings is particularly cogent, singling out a handful of Commissioners on either side who monopolised discussion: 'Those amongst us who spoke at all or at any time, publickly, they were not above eight at most, and whereof the great lawyers were none (Sir Francis Bacon only excepted). To those that did speak also the matter was new, never before propounded, read or heard argued by them'.[38] No doubt many Commissioners, like Zouch, came to the meetings with 'no substance but good wishes'. Even Neville is found appealing to Winwood for information on naturalisation and customs in the union of Spain and the Low Countries, in order to keep abreast of discussions between the leading Commissioners. The author of Harleian MS 1314 — the 'Paper Booke' — is less reliable in his insistence that the Commission was not only rigged, but rigged in the Scots' favour. There is little evidence of this. The Booke's arguments are self-contradictory: the domination of discussion by leading Scots is considered evidence of prior orchestration in their national interest, while the parallel predominance of Cecil, Bacon and other great Englishmen is presented as oppression of the lesser English Commissioners. Central to its argument is the belief that the leading English statesmen subordinated national to personal interest, seeking royal favour through acceptance of the Scots' 'demands'. This when the Scots 'found themselves at any time conquered with our reasons . . . then his Ma.tie (to whose eares they never wanted accesse) . . . graciously stept in (for them I will not say) playing the princely Umpire by some gracious letter publick yet expecting absolute yielding from us in express words, wherein he accordingly prevailed'. This is highly questionable. Some nobles did entertain the Scots lavishly — breeding jealousy among other English Commissioners, and eliciting a letter of warning from the Scots themselves to the king.[39] But on the one issue where the Scots did appeal to the king — naturalisation — they were, as we shall see, overruled.

   The Commission was therefore an efficiently managed body in which most substantive discussion took place offstage, between two small groups of statesmen genuinely seeking solutions that defended their own national interests. Discussion began (after settlement of procedural questions) with the abolition of hostile and Border laws. The list of such laws produced by the sub-committee on November 2 followed that drawn up in consultations before the

Commission. Debate then turned to trade and customs, starting on November 6 with an examination whether 'hostile' laws prohibiting the import and export of certain goods should be abolished in their application to the other country. The following week saw extensive debate generally on commercial union — access to companies, freedom of trade between the nations for domestic use, difficulties raised by Scots privileges in France and lower customs. The Commission agreed on a bond to prevent abuse of domestic commercial freedom, and on a mercantile sub-commission to examine Scots privileges abroad. Naturalisation occupied the middle of the month, the seven hours of debate on November 15 being the centrepiece. The outstanding difference between them was submitted to the king himself for resolution, his decision being accepted reluctantly by the Scots on November 24. In trade, the form of the bond was resolved after reference to the Barons of the Exchequer on November 22. Arrangements for administration of laws and justice on the Borders were then completed with debate on the remand and trial of criminals in either realm. The Instrument was engrossed and prefaced — the preface occasioning disagreement with James, who demanded a strengthening in its unionist phraseology. This delayed final signature until December 6. Three copies of the Instrument were made — one for either Chancellor, and a third for the king. Strict secrecy was enjoined on the Commissioners, not to publicise the contents of the Instrument before the next parliamentary session. In practice, however, there was no shortage of Commissioners willing to divulge details of the provisions to their friends and allies.[40]

4. Hostile and Border Laws, Justice

Of the three main issues, the least contentious and first debated was that of hostile and Border laws. Although considered *en bloc* by the Commission, these were in fact a heterogeneous group of laws, passed under differing authorities for different purposes. The first category comprised national statutes passed in times of emergency, prohibiting community or mutual aid in the Border shires between English and Scots. These had at various times been forbidden to marry each other, provide each other with horses, victuals, weapons or other military necessaries, hold land by homage in the other kingdom, let or sell land to their counterparts, use each other's boroughs/burghs or markets, etc. Many acts strengthened the defence of the Border against the other nation, or forcibly repatriated Scots or English who had crossed the frontier. In theory, these statutes established a strict Iron Curtain between Carlisle and Berwick. The reality was very different. Some acts, particularly on Border defence, had been confirmed by Elizabethan parliaments; but long decades of peace had caused the prohibitions to be ignored. One should not regard these acts as a deliberate, permanent system to prevent communication between the peoples; they were *ad hoc* measures enacted in times of hostility that fell into desuetude after the immediate crisis had passed. Their importance to James was again symbolic, as memorials to the centuries of Anglo-Scots enmity. Untouched, they would be a formal stain on the principle of unity; abolition, while contributing little to the substantive progress of unification, was a gesture of brotherhood, and also of intent — a flourish in the general direction of legal uniformity.[41]

The second, and more important, category of hostile laws was the local legislation of the Border shires themselves. Tough[42] has identified four sources of non-statutory Border law, supplementing and largely supplanting the operation of common law. These were: conciliar orders, especially common in Scotland;[43] ordinances of the Lieutenants or Wardens; constitutions of Carlisle and Berwick; and customary March Treasons appended to the form and order of Warden Courts. Some of these laws were truly 'hostile', involving prohibition of aid or community. Borough constitutions forbade the appointment of Scots as officers or mayors.[44] March Treasons denied the unlicensed marrying or 'trysting' of English and Scots, wartime victualling, the payment of homage to a native of the other kingdom, and so on. Some measures were intended to enforce national commercial protectionism, by prohibition of import and export of certain goods. Most Border laws, however, served rather to combat the actual hostility, and intermittent anarchy, of the two peoples. These provisions fell into two parts: the definition of crimes, and arrangements for trial and punishment of offenders. These were increasingly codified after 1450 by individual agreements between English and Scots Wardens, and by international treaties devised by joint Commissions. The crimes covered were predictable: murdering or wounding a subject of the other realm, burning, spoiling or stealing his goods, receipt of stolen goods or fugitive malefactors, rape, acts of clan war such as the siege of fortified houses, economic exploitation including the sowing of corn, pasturing of sheep and cattle, fishing and hunting in the other kingdom, together with perjury, false accusation, excessive claims for the value of stolen goods, etc. Provisions for the exercise of justice were also included in the Treasons and treaties. The institutions and manner of Border justice have occupied many historians, most recently Rae, but remain both confusing and confused. On the Scots side, it is often difficult to distinguish Warden, Steward and Justice Courts, jurisdiction being further complicated by private heritable rights, burgh magistracies and commissions of justiciary made to men often with no official standing in government of the Borders. The most effective means of justice were the county eyre, the Edinburgh High Court of Justiciary, and the summary raid through the shires by armed forces under command from the Council. English Marches similarly ignored ordinary systems of justice, such as sessions of the peace.[45] Private jurisdictions and Warden Courts reigned supreme. Warden Courts were cumbersome, proclaimed beforehand at all markets and requiring in theory the attendance of all gentry, clan leaders and freeholders. Trial was by jury, the March Treasons occupying the place of common law crimes. Warden Courts were generally ineffective in suppressing Border feuds, the treaties themselves providing for summary execution of 'justice' by offended against offender. Provisions included raiding for the recovery of recently stolen goods, hot pursuit and execution of fugitive offenders by Wardens, and despatch of red-handed murderers without redress. The greatest difficulty lay with the raider who had successfully returned to his own country. Allowing Wardens to pursue and operate over the frontier had created some major international altercations. The other principal expedient was the Day of Truce — international gatherings where the two Wardens in command of opposite Marches assembled in a convenient place, usually hard by the Border. Each brought a number of persons accused previously in a letter from his counterpart, together with witnesses and an assize jury. The Scots assize tried Scots offenders, and *vice versa*. In practice, Truce Days were even more cumbersome and less effective than Warden Courts. Few offenders were actually captured by the Wardens, and fewer still convicted. The determination of James to abolish the entire apparatus, demonstrated in his proclamation from Newcastle in 1603 and his measures for pacification of the Border shires, was therefore the more comprehensible.

The Commission had three main tasks, therefore: repeal of national statutes in which opposite nationals were classified *per se* as hostile; abolition of all Border laws, customs and ordinances, as marks of separation distinguishing the 'Middle Shires' from other parts of the new Great Britain; and establishment of new arrangements enabling the operation of ordinary laws and courts in the area to be effective. These tasks had already been identified before the Commission assembled. Abolition of hostile statutes appears in Bacon's 'Certain Articles', and in the 'Discourse of Naturalisation'. The Proclamation of Great Britain describes a legal opinion, that certain of these hostile laws had automatically expired on James's accession. The same opinion had also advised abolition of Border laws and customs.[46] For Border justice, Bacon's bold proposal of an experimental court governing both sides of the frontier through a mixture of English and Scots law was ignored. Cecil's 'Certayne Clauses' concerned only the tidying up of Border laws and courts, with a separate Commission to allot lands of debateable nationality between England and Scotland, and divide them into judicial units.[47] The Commission was quick to tackle the issues raised. On October 29, it established a sub-committee of lawyers to examine and collate hostile laws: Herbert, Dunne, Bennett, Bacon, Hobart, Hesketh, Hubbard and Tanfield for England, Hamilton, Skene, Sharpe and Craig for the Scots. A comprehensive list of Acts was produced, and examined in caucus, then in full Commission on November 2. It was agreed that the proposed bill should contain a reference to abolition of all other hostile laws that might subsequently be discovered, and of all clauses redolent of hostility in borough constitutions. The replacement of other Border customs by common and statute law in either kingdom was formally agreed on the same day.

The Commission then turned to arrangements for enforcement of justice. Short- and long-term problems arose here. The English Commissioners on November 20 demanded the provision of mechanisms for the redress of March Treasons outstanding since the death of Elizabeth. It was decided merely to advise the parliaments of this difficulty, and the requirement for some commission to settle outstanding Border causes. The long-term problem was that of fugitive malefactors. No common or statute law mechanism existed to impose justice on a raiding criminal after his safe return over the Border. The two possible options were extradition and reciprocal jurisdiction. Offenders could on complaint be seized in their native country and either sent for trial in the country of offence, or tried by their own law and courts for crimes committed elsewhere. Fyvie and the Scots favoured extradition, by application between the Councils.[48] The English reaction can only be inferred from the clause agreed on November 24, permitting extradition only in cases of murder, false coinage and forgery of legal instruments. Even here, the case might be tried in the offender's native country if no approach from a J.P. across the Border was received. The implication — of resistance to extradition — fits well with the debates on the subject in the 1607 English session of parliament; there, the Commission's own compromise was considered a plot to deliver Englishmen into the tender hands of Scots justice!

5. Trade and Customs

As we saw in our last chapter, the tracts showed a lot of support for the principle of commercial union, but little consideration of what such a union should comprise. The main exception, Bacon's 'Certain Articles', recommended the mutual access of merchants to the major commercial Companies, and equalisation of customs and impost rates. The latter was repeated in Cecil's 'Certayne Clauses'. Noting James's determination to achieve a 'sharing of all priviledges, trade and other Admenitys', Cecil drafted two clauses for possible proposal by the Commission. These limited rather than advanced commercial union. In particular, they advocated the continued imposition of Alien's Custom on Scots until lower Scots imposts had been raised to English levels, and commercial privileges in France either abolished or extended to Englishmen.

Mutual access to the Companies was passed by the Commission on the nod. Covertly, there was opposition. The 'Paper Booke' records in a contemporary note 'my L. of N.'s' (Northampton's?) opinion that royal favour would bring a mass influx of Scots into the Companies, oppressing lesser English merchants. Such access was however an inevitable concomitant of the Commission's stance on naturalisation; while in practice, the small number of major Scots merchants and their concentration outside London rendered the change cosmetic rather than substantial.

The other main commercial provisions eventually agreed were the exemption of either country from the other's prohibitions on import/export of certain goods, and from the payment of customs when transporting goods between the nations. These propositions occasioned much debate. Exemption from prohibitions arose from the wider exercise to abolish hostile laws. The legal opinion before the Commission had considered many commercial statutes as fit for abrogation.[49] It was therefore predictable that the list of prohibitive laws set

before the Commission (November 6) should have come from the Bacon/
Hamilton sub-committee on laws. Prohibited exports included goods of war,
bullion and treasure, but above all raw materials: wool, leather, coal, skins, fish,
cattle, sheep etc. Prohibited imports meant made-up cloth. This reflected
contemporary European protectionism, to encourage domestic manufacture by
conservation of raw materials and prohibition of external competition. The
decision on exemption was taken quickly, in two days of full Commission on
November 8 and 10. Again, some had secret qualms, notably 'my L. of N.' His
view, 'which he dared not adventure yesternight', was that the free export of
wool to Scotland would encourage Scots clothiers, and lead to unemployment
among English spinners and weavers.[50] This paralleled the wider discussion on
re-export, examined below. While the virtual identity of English and Scots law
on prohibited goods ensured that raw materials transported between them
would not pass directly into overseas markets, they might eventually travel
abroad as finished goods.

Much more discussion survives on exemption from customs. Duties were at
this time relatively uncomplicated, dividing neatly in England into an ordinary
custom of 5% (1s in the £) and an extra, Alien's Custom of 1¼% (3d in the £) for
foreign traders. The Commission's proposals were to make no charge on goods
between the countries, if intended for domestic use. Alien's Custom would also
be lifted. The latter again followed logically from the propositions of the
Instrument on naturalisation. Opposition to both exemptions came entirely
from England. Some pointed to the decline in royal revenue that would result.[51]
This was James's problem, however, and one viewed by him with equanimity —
as his use of prerogative powers in 1603 to exempt English traders in Scotland
demonstrated. Others cited the danger exemption posed to English manufacturers. The result was to exempt from free passage a range of raw materials:
while no longer prohibited exports, these would be subject to ordinary custom
— a provision which went far to negate the real freedom of trade proposed.
Most objections proceeded from a belief that the Scots merchants were already
in a superior trading position, making freedom of trade economically disastrous
for England. Given the rudimentary state of Scotland's industrial and
mercantile base, this seems curious. Riley dismisses the English fears as
'ludicrous . . . English commercial competition threatened to ruin Scotland'.[52]
Some of the arguments are indeed unconvincing. The 'Discourse of Naturalisation' echoes Spelman: the smallness of Scots ships, their mean furnishings, the
low wages and bartering habits of Scots sailors, the 'impetuosity' of national
character all somehow become decisive Scots advantages. But more substantial
reasons were produced, following Cecil's condemnation of lower Scots imposts
and Scots trading privileges in France. Both implied the possibility of Scots
advantage, through re-export. English goods travelling custom-free to Scotland
might be shipped abroad onto Continental markets, paying only low Scots
custom. Foreign goods might similarly find their way through Scotland to
England at prices undercutting the English merchant. Differential customs had
already been widely discussed in England, notably by Bacon, Spelman and the

'Discourse'. The last, like the 'Paper Booke', saw the actual rates of Scots custom as irrelevant; if Scots exported goods north without impost, 'they may easily imbezill those commodities from thence, being a kingdome full of harboroughs' and empty of revenuemen. The answer was to limit free trade to goods intended for domestic use, and enforce this with a bond or certificate. This was agreed on November 12, and the matter of its form and operation was referred to the Exchequer Barons. The eventual format was identical to the bond required of merchants conveying goods between English ports.[53] The Scots exporter would have to deposit a sum of money with English customs equal to the value of the merchandise, reclaimable upon production of a certificate by a Scots customer confirming its unloading in Scotland for domestic use.

The problem of Scots privileges in France, affecting predominantly inward trade, raised more difficulty. There is evidence of an orchestrated campaign here, led by Cecil and Ellesmere, using the carrots of free trade and naturalisation in an attempt to rupture the Auld Alliance.[54] The English certainly disliked and mistrusted the French connection. Savile and the 'Discourse of Naturalisation' both considered it a danger to English security. Inequity in trading privileges was therefore only one reason why the Alliance came under attack. The inequality was nevertheless emphasised, particularly by the 'Discourse': 'The Scotts in France do trade as freely there with the same Immunities, as the Naturall French, not paying any such Impositions for theire Merchandize as the English'. A Scots domination in Anglo-French trade was therefore likely to result from union. In practice, it proved impossible to assess the Scots 'advantage'. A memorandum comparing English and Scots privileges considered the difference minimal; since Alien's Custom did not exist in France outside Normandy, the Scots advantage in Bordeaux described by the 'Discourse' was illusory — while Scots privileges in Normandy were limited to goods passing to Scotland for domestic use.[55] Consideration continued nevertheless, dominating the commercial discussions. A privileged Scots merchant could import goods direct from France to England, exempt from Alien's Custom in either country. On November 6, the Commission established the principle that 'how much the Scottish or English merchante may save in buying of their commodities at a lower rate, by means of any privilege . . . so much the Scottish shall advance their custome in England'.[56] This was a compromise between free trade and the continuation of Alien's Custom proposed by Cecil.[57] A Committee was appointed: Cecil, Northampton, Neville, Ridgeway, Stafford and Billingley for England, Linlithgow, Balmerino, Blantyre, Melville and Carnegie for Scotland. Merchants of either nation were examined on their customs rates and trading privileges. It was then agreed (November 12) that the differences between privileges in Bordeaux were minimal, but that a sub-commission comprising two merchants of either nation should be established to examine privileges elsewhere in France and report direct to the next parliament — supplementing the statement of principle in the Instrument.

The Instrument therefore represented a moderate advance towards free trade and commercial union. No customs union was included; to have done so would have been ruinous for the infant Scots manufacturing sector. Restrictions on otherwise free trade would prevent the Scots receiving any advantage by this differential, or by their naturalisation and other privileges in France. Mutuality in prohibited exports and access to the Companies were a gesture towards a future British commercial system.

6. Naturalisation and Offices

Less material has survived on naturalisation and the Commission than on its other work; which is unfortunate, since all sources attest its importance and controversiality. Neville is explicit: 'The last Article begat more debate and contestation than all the rest, as that which touched the Freehold of the principall of both Sides, and imported them most in their particular, the one Side to seek, the other to exclude'.[58] This concentration might on previous evidence seem surprising. Even Spelman agreed on the legal position of Scots in England. It was universally accepted that the Post-Nati — those born after March 24, 1603 — were by law natural subjects in either kingdom. This was confirmed in November 1604 by an opinion of the Crown Law Officers.[59] The Commission accordingly agreed (November 24) on the nod that Post-Nati should and indeed did by law have full rights of succession, inheritance, purchases and office, as natural subjects. Parliaments would therefore be asked only for a declaratory law formalising this situation. The unanimity and perfunctory nature of this debate is important, given the laborious contentions of 1606-7.

The real controversy lay over the future status of the Ante-Nati, born before 1603. Bacon's 'Certain Articles' advanced the curious opinion that these were now legally denizens in England — a limited form of naturalisation normally extended to aliens by grant under letters patent. James had denizenated a number of Scots in 1603, while the 1604 parliament had passed several private acts of naturalisation for prominent Scots. General denizenation without patent was however unprecedented, and it was more usual to consider the Ante-Nati as aliens. The legal opinion and Commission took this line.

The Ante-Nati thus required substantive, enabling legislation to become subjects in England. They were also more likely to arouse contentious opposition. The Post-Nati would not in practice be eligible for the rich livings, offices and posts — so obsessive to the English — until they had grown to maturity, by which time James would probably not be living, and his successor would be a prince raised predominantly in England. Opposition to naturalisation of the Ante-Nati can be found before the Commission, notably in Spelman and the 'Discourse of Naturalization'. The latter saw great equality in mutual naturalization, contrasting the richness of England with Scots poverty: 'All the Poor People of that Realm . . . will draw nearer the Sonn, and flocking hither in such Multitudes, that death and dearth is very probable to ensue'. English craftsmen would be undercut by parsimonious Scots and reduced to penury, while the great offices would be monopolised by Caledonians. James might already use his prerogative (i.e. denizenation) to prefer individual Scots; 'yet I think it a wiser course humbly to obey him than to be the Instruments of our own harm, and it is farr better to open a Wicket by the which they may be let in one by one, then to open the greate Gate without restraint'.

Debate in the Commission began on November 13 with a motion by Fyvie. The great debate two days later appears in the Journal as a brief but appetising reference. The subject was 'argued and debated by the Commissioners on both sydes with great gravitie, iudgment will and learning . . . and this point especially handled, whither the naturalisacon should be absolute . . . or with certaine limitacons'. Discussion occupied seven hours, from early afternoon to late evening. Fortunately, other sources exist: correspondence between Cecil and James, the description of proceedings in Craig's *De Unione* and Harleian manuscript 1314, and above all Dudley Carleton's digest of the discussion on November 15.[60] Carleton shows the debate following entirely national lines, the English rejecting naturalisation unless coupled with a ban on holding offices. Their proposal was naturally resisted by the Scots. While not objecting to an informal agreement against office-holding, the Scots considered a formal reservation to be a mark of disunion, an infringement of the royal prerogative and above all a slur on the Scots nation as unequal and grasping. They questioned whether Ante-Nati *were* aliens, calling the separation of a day (i.e. between them and Post-Nati) 'silly'. They argued that they must be as natural in England as their countryman, the king, and that naturalisation with reservation granted them less than they already had in France. The last touched a deep English nerve, condemning the French naturalisation as a device to keep Scotland hostile. The English rejected an informal agreement as giving liberties on trust, and piously fell back on visions of the perfect union to justify limitation here. Carleton: 'Our maine retreit was that granting the naturalisacon was to give them all they lookt for, and then the Union of laws and privileges wch must make the perfect Union would scarce follow'. This ingenious theme reflected and may have been lifted bodily from the 'Discourse of Naturalization'; it also anticipated a major argument of 1606-7.

The discussion was inconclusive. The Journal states that 'the tyme was so farre spent without resolucon the farther proceeding therein was deferred untill Saturday' — when the Scots Commissioners were absent *en bloc*. Carleton and other sources make it clear that the Scots had refused to accept the English reservation, and appealed to the king.[61]

James's response requires special examination. Harleian MS 1314 saw him granting the appeal, and imposing a settlement favourable to the Scots by command. Neville denies this flatly: 'In the End the King was won to our Side, and so it was concluded in this Form'.[62] In fact, James did accept the necessity of a reservation, but insisted on its containing certain features. Firstly, the limitation must be expressed as a royal declaration of intent, not binding his prerogative or implying its subordination to the will of Commission or Parliament. This reflected legal advice in a letter by Cecil,[63] as well as the Scots argument on November 15. Cecil advised that no reservation would prevent denizenation and preferment of individual Scots. James also demanded that the reservation apply equally to either nation, no form of words implying insult or derogation to Scotland, that no timespan be mentioned, and that Scots should not be left feeling that their position had deteriorated.[64] He also protested strongly against English fears and jealousies, on November 24:

> Never Scottishmen did either directly or indirectly make suite to me for any such preferment as is mentioned in the Act; And . . . I was ever rooted in that firme resolucon never to have placed Scottishmen in any such roome, till first tyme had begone to weare awaie that opynion of different Nations; and secondlie, that ialous apprehension of the Union had been worne awaie; and thirdlie, that Scottishmen had bin brought up here . . . And when all this were done, I would ever all my life prefer an Englishman to a Scottishman, for any such place. Caeteris Paribus . . . I am not ignorant, nor voide of meanes, to show my thankfulness to my subjects of Scotland, withowt any such preferments.[65]

The reservation put forward by James[66] was therefore a royal declaration not to prefer Ante-Nati of one nation to offices of government and justice in the other, till 'Time and Conversation have increased and accomplished an union of the said Kingdoms, as well in the Hearts of all the People, and in the Conformity of laws and Policy in the Kingdoms, as in the Knowledge and Sufficiency of particular Men'.[67] This satisfied the English, but not the Scots. The latter received the news on November 20 in Commission and immediately adjourned into caucus. Craig speaks of 'heated dispute among our own Commissioners, whether to agree to the inequality of status or to break up the Conference'.[68] They did however eventually agree the provision, November 22–24, with only a few minor amendments to make it mutual on either side. The result was thus the proposal advanced in the Instrument: an enabling Act to naturalise the Ante-Nati, subject to a royal promise on limitation of offices. To many Scots, these limitations represented a step backwards. Craig strove to show that Scots had never been aliens in England, and that the Instrument granted no more than their existing common law rights.[69] Many English believed that, reservation or no, the Scots had carried the day. Harleian 1314 and de Beaumont agree here, the latter calling the proposals 'more generous to the Scots than one expected. Several of them [i.e. the English Commissioners] say that they have done it to please the king now while hoping that the Parliament will never confirm what they have agreed'.[70] In fact, the agreed proposal was a compromise, achieved after hard debate.

7. Analysis and Summary

On December 6, the Commission ended its proceedings in the royal presence, amid much self-congratulation from Cranborne and the leading Commissioners.

The Instrument was triplicated, one for each Lord Chancellor and the third for James himself. The king thanked his Commission, which then dispersed.

What should we make of the Instrument? We have already examined its provisions, individually. A long list of statutes of hostility were proposed for abolition by Acts of Parliament. English and Scots common law and courts were to become the only methods of justice on the Borders, with March Treasons, Wardens' Courts, etc., being abolished. The very name of the Borders was to be expunged in favour of the 'Middle Shires'.[71] Outstanding causes were to be settled by some unresolved means, and provisions made for trial of fugitive offenders by either extradition or reciprocal jurisdiction. Hostile clauses in borough constitutions would be abrogated.

In trade, English and Scots would be eligible for membership of each other's great commerical Companies. Imports and exports prohibited by statute would freely pass between the nations. Trade between them in goods for domestic use would be free of custom, except for a range of raw materials mostly on the old list of prohibited exports. A bond system similar to that operating internally in England was advised to prevent abuse of free trade. Strangers' Custom would no longer be charged on Scots in England, or vice versa. If Scots paid less by privilege in France, they would face a corresponding customs surcharge for French goods in England. The Bordeaux wine trade had been examined, and shown to contain no difference in privileges; other parts of France would be examined by a special sub-commission of merchants reporting to the parliaments.

Finally, the legal status of Scots in England and English in Scotland would be clarified by two Acts: one *declaring* the Post-Nati to be natural subjects in both kingdoms under existing law, the other naturalising the Ante-Nati with a royal declaration of intent against preferment in the other kingdom until a perfect union in sympathies and institutions was achieved.

The proposals of the Commission appear very modest in comparison to the extensive programmes in the union tracts, and James's own rhetorical flourishes towards perfect union. Nevertheless, there is no reason to see the Commission as a setback. The three wider areas of union which lay on the periphery of the Commission were of course religion, laws and parliaments. Given the belief in existing doctrinal unity, religious union could therefore be only in church discipline and hierarchy. The Venetian and French Ambassadors[72] report an attempt by the Archbishop of Canterbury to have the question of his primacy over Scotland included on the programme. However, there is no evidence of support from James and Cecil, or of prior preparation for such a move.[73] Lacking such support, it faced the united opposition of the Scots Commissioners. To the Scots, religious union lay beyond their commission, and raised offensive implications of inequality between the two nations. The evidence for parliamentary and legal union is again fragmentary. Union in parliaments *does* occur in Cecil's note of the king's intentions before the Commission; but this is its only mention, and may refer to the king's long-term rather than immediate plans. References to legal union require more attention.

The subject was usually raised by English Commissioners — but this does not, as Omond believed, amount to an attempt at 'a uniform system of laws for the two countries; a proposal to which the representatives of Scotland would not listen'.[74] Instead, its use was tactical, the English linking naturalisation with legal union, and then pointing to the Scots reservation on discussion of legal union as an argument against present 'concession' of naturalisation. De Beaumont at least was convinced that the English wanted no legal union; and there was no serious attempt by James, his English ministers or other English Commissioners to have the subject discussed. Cecil's 'Certayne Clauses' significantly alludes to a perfect union in laws as part of the king's design — but as a long-term aim, not something for immediate achievement. This distinction between short-term and long-term aims is fundamental to our understanding of James's attitude to the Commission. His letter to Cecil (November 22) expressed satisfaction with the Commission's limited scope — as a first step in a gradual unification process:

> Am I fully resolved that the smallest beginning of this happy errand at this time with the hearty applause of all parties will imprint such a general apprehension in the hearts of all the people, who are more ruled with shadows than substance, that the Union is already made . . . for being once made friends and homely together they will no more stick upon such punctilios which as otherwise strangers they might have stood upon.[75]

The king therefore required only limited action now, but a great show of unity, brotherhood and determination among the Commissioners — fuelling the engine of gradual unification. In the same letter, he asked Cecil to include in the Instrument 'such a pretty reference for the full accomplishment of all other points which fault of leisure could not now permit you to end as it may appear that working in this errant shall never be left off till it is fully accomplished, I mean specially by the uniting of both laws and parliaments of both the nations.'

It was this 'pretty reference' which occasioned the only real difference in opinion between James and his Commission — over the form of the Preamble. This split was partly his own fault. After initially intending to attend every meeting of the Commission, James allowed himself to be distracted to the hunting lodge at Royston.[76] His knowledge of the Commission came therefore secondhand, in letters that spoke much of the Commissioners' hearty accord but papered over more general feelings of unease regarding the wider union. These feelings, analysed cogently by de Beaumont, prevented the Preamble being as whole-heartedly unionist in tone as James required. Bacon's enthusiastic draft was thus rejected for one produced by Cecil and Fyvie.[77] At first, James seemed satisfied with the latter, merely cutting out 'some superfluity in it'.[78] Shortly afterwards, however, he hurried to London demanding substantial alterations.[79] The nature of these changes can be seen in a letter to Cecil, wrongly calendared under 1606,[80] stronger references to divine providence and to the accomplishment of future union being the main themes: 'What great expectation can ye have that there shall ever be a perfect union when ye say no more but that ye most heartily desire it . . . were it not as easily said till God by time and his Majesty's travels bring it to that perfection which all honest men long for?' James also demanded omission of a reference to 'mutual consent', lest some Commissioners protest later that they had been overruled, and the inclusion of a hope that parliament would approve their proceedings.

James's demands caused consternation, the Scots through Balmerino urging him to accept the Preamble as it stood.[81] The delay of alteration, the jealousies it would cause and the danger of opposition in the next English parliament were all stressed. Nevertheless, the Preface *was* changed to suit James, and to present the Instrument as a major step forward in the gradual process of unification. The Commissioners, however, were unhappy about the latter, some anticipating with equanimity opposition in ensuing parliamentary sessions.[82]

NOTES

1. B.L.Add.MSS 30640 fol. 421 (Oct 22, 1604) *et passim*.
2. B.L.Add.MSS 30641 fol. 15v.
3. See B.L.Add.MSS 30640 fols. 157ff and 432r for use of the Albany Company. The king's verdict is in his letter of Nov. 19. Henry's caution did not however prevent him from sounding out visiting Scots on the union: *HMC. Salis.MSS* XVI 367 and S.P.14/10/83.
4. B.L.Add.MSS 30640 fols. 126ff and 421v: *Cal.S.P. (Ven) 1603-7*, 190-1. For Huntly's protestations of loyalty and counter-accusations, see N.L.S.Adv.MSS 33.1.1. No. 16. Angus's letter of Nov. 20 in the same volume confirms Molin regarding James's displeasure with Moray and the Scots parliament.
5. B.L.Harl.MSS 1305 Cap. 31 contain's Savile's strictures. The 'Discourse of Naturalisation' is in S.P.14/10/16 & 17.
6. *Larkin & Hughes*, 94-8. The Scots proclamation was read at the Mercat Croce in Edinburgh on Nov. 15: *Reg.PCSc*. VII, 16-17.
7. *Larkin & Hughes*, 7 and 99-103.
8. Lythe, 'Union of the Crowns', 221.
9. S.P.14/10A/19 & 20.
10. An exhaustive list is in Robertson, *Coinage of Scotland*, 87-90.
11. See Sir Thomas Wilson's paper, S.P.14/10A/22.
12. This explicitly reflected provisions for a British coinage in the proclamation on the royal style: Tanner, *Constitutional Documents*, 34.
13. S.P.14/10A/21.
14. Tanner, *Constitutional Documents*, 32-5.
15. *Reg.PCSc*. VII, 27 and Balfour, *Annals* II, 5.
16. B.L.Stowe MSS 856. See also Harrison, *Journal*, 164.
17. Spedding, *Bacon* III, 217-57. See also the intermediary digest (?) at B.L.Harl.MSS 292.63.
18. Tanner, *Constitutional Documents*, 35.
19. See B.L.Harl.MSS 292:62, 'What his Ma[ty] may do w[th]out parliament', and above, Chapter 2.
20. Bindoff, 'Stuart Style', 212-13.
21. S.P.14/9/82.
22. B.L.Add.MSS 30641 fol. 12v (Nov. 15, 1604) and S.P.14/10/83. See also S.P.14/216/18 for the existence of a 'pasquil' written against the style.

23. *Larkin & Hughes*, 92-3.

24. *Cal.S.P.(Ven) 1603-7*, Ext. 278: Winwood, *Memorials*, 32: Maidment, *Melrose Papers*, 5.

25. B.L.Add.MSS 30640 fol. 421.

26. A full list of Commissioners is in S.P.14/8/101.

27. *HMC. Salis.MSS* XVI, 314.

28. S.P.14/9/35, 'Reminder of His Majesty's Thoughts to be Debated'. Sept. 16, 1604.

29. S.P.14/9/36, 'Certayne Clauses wch may fall into the draught of bills touching the Union, being the matters of greatest difficulty'.

30. B.L.Harl.MSS 292:61, 'Certaine Lawes of England offensive and repugnant to the Union'.

31. For a list of Scots Commissioners, see *Rg.PCSc.* VII, 5n-6n. The English delegation included 14 nobles, 2 Privy Councillors, 2 ambassadors, an archbishop, 4 common and 2 civil lawyers, 4 merchants and 16 gentry. The Scots had 12 nobles, 4 clerics, 2 civil lawyers, 4 merchants and 9 gentry.

32. *Reg.PCSc.* VI, 597.

33. *Cal.S.P.(Ven) 1603-7*, 155.

34. Spedding, *Bacon* III, 240. The basic account of the Commission is its Journal: B.L.Add.MSS 26635 fols. 1-29.

35. Craig, *De Unione*, 277-8; Winwood, *Memorials* II, 38.

36. B.L.Add.MSS 26635, 31; Spedding, *Bacon* III, 242-4; Balfour, *Annals* II, 2. Note also the tenor of Northampton's address to the Scots: B.L.Cott.MSS Tit.C.VI fols. 429-30 and 433-4.

37. B.L.Add.MSS 30641 fol. 13v (Nov. 15). For Fyvie's cooperation with Cecil, see *HMC. Salis.MSS* XVI, 345 and 357, and S.P.14/10/39.

38. B.L.Harl.MSS 1314, fol. 47. The volume is described as 'A Paper Booke . . . from the papers of some eminent member of the House of Commons who in Parliament AD 1606 was against uniting with the Scots'.

39. N.L.S.Adv.MSS 33.1.1. No. 21.

40. See e.g. Winwood, *Memorials* II, 38.

41. B.L.Add.MSS 26635, fols. 5-7 contains a list of the laws for abolition.

42. Tough, *Last Years of a Frontier*, 147-71 and 95-134. See also Rae, *Scottish Frontier*, 47-60 and Watts & Watts, *From Border to Middle Shire, passim*. I am grateful to Dr Rae for our conversation on this subject.

43. Such orders make up over 20% of the Council's business in *Reg.PCSc.* VI.

44. B.L.Add.MSS 26635, fol. 6.

45. These institutions existed in theory, but were bypassed. See Tough, *Last Years of a Frontier*, and Coulomb, *Administration of the English Borders during the Reign of Elizabeth*, New York, 1911.

46. Tanner, *Constitutional Documents*, 34; B.L.Harl.MSS 292:61.

47. S.P.14/9/36. See also the reference to dispensing hostile laws by prerogative, in B.L.Harl.MSS 292:62.

48. S.P.14/10/39. The same letter advised settlement of outstanding Border Causes by liaison of the two Privy Councils.

49. B.L.Harl.MSS 292:61.

50. B.L.Harl.MSS 1314, fols. 140 and 146-50, 'Touching the matter of cautions that English Goods shipped for Scotland shall not be abused'.

51. Ibid., 148. See also Spelman's 'De Unione' (B. L. Sloane MSS 3521 fol. 9r) and the 'Discourse of Naturalisation' (S.P.14/10/17 fol. 45r).

52. Riley, *Union of England and Scotland*, 4.

53. HMC. Salis.MSS XVI, 359.

54. B.L.Add.MSS 30641, fol. 13.

55. S.P.14/10/55.

56. B.L.Add.MSS 26635, p. 8.

57. S.P.14/9/36, fol. 80. Cecil's policy also appears in a letter from Fyvie on Nov. 3 (*HMC. Salis.MSS* XVI, 345), answering Cranborne's contention that customs continued between Castile and Aragon after union.

58. Winwood, *Memorials* II, 38.

59. S.P.14/10/15. See also B.L.Harl.MSS 292:61 and Bacon's 'Certain Articles' (Spedding, *Bacon* III, 217-47).

60. S.P.14/10/18.

61. B.L.Harl.MSS 1314, fols. 45-6.

62. Winwood, *Memorials* II, 38.

63. S.P.14/10/15.

64. See the letters from James and Worcester to Cecil on Nov. 22: *HMC. Salis.MSS* XVI, 363-4.

65. S.P.14/10/40. See also James's comments to the Commissioners at the end of their deliberations: 'Inequality of privileges is not the way to effect the union I desire; capacity of offices ought to be equall to both people; but the moderation of that equality must be left to me, neither you to suspect that I will offer any manner of grievance to either of the Countreys' (*Spottiswoode*, 486).

66. Fyvie in a letter to Cecil on Nov. 27 refers to it as the king's own amendment: *HMC.Salis.MSS* XVI, 369.

67. *CJ* I, 323.

68. Craig, *De Unione*, 329-35 gives a full treatment to the events during mid-November.

69. *Ibid.*, 335ff. The cases cited by Craig and are self-seeking, and can also be found in polemics for the suzerainty of England. Craig is therefore forced to assert an ancient naturalisation of the Scots as a reward for their services against the Vikings!

70. B.L.Add.MSS 30641 fol. 24r.

71. See James's policy statement in *HMC.Salis.MSS* XV, 405 and the perceptive comments in Watts & Watts, *From Border to Middle Shire*, 134.

72. *Cal.S.P.(Ven) 1603-7*, 200-1: B.L.Add.MSS 30641, fol. 21ff.

73. E.g. in S.P.14/9/35-6.

74. Omond, *Scottish Union Question*, 70.

75. *HMC.Salis.MSS* XVI, 363-4.

76. See *Cal.S.P.(Ven) 1603-7*, 182-3 and 192-3.

77. Spedding, *Bacon* III, 242-4.

78. *HMC.Salis.MSS* XVI, 366-7.

79. Nichols, *Progresses of James I*, I, 468; Harrison, *Journal*, 168.

80. *HMC.Salis.MSS* XVIII, 373-4.

81. N.L.S.Adv.MSS 33.1.1. No. 18.

82. B.L.Add.MSS 30641 fol. 24r.

5
The Project Outside Parliament:
January 1605-December 1606

1. Deferment of Parliamentary Consideration

The Commission dissolved under the assumption of immediate action. An English parliament was scheduled for February 1605, to discuss the Instrument. It was however November 1606 before Union was actually considered in detail by either national parliament.

This delay reflected two deferments of debate. The first was the prorogation of parliament in England from February to November 1605. Some contemporary observers considered this inexplicable.[1] Historians have occasionally invoked the influence of Salisbury, in explanation. It was indeed the Secretary who announced deferment to the Council. Predicting opposition to government proposals for union, subsidy and provisioning of the Household, Salisbury emphasised the need for extra preparations.[2] Carleton similarly glossed the delay as 'giving time to the great Union-Makers to play upon the bit'.[3] This is a more credible explanation for deferment than covert opposition by the Secretary. Prorogation could not have happened without royal agreement. The later stages of the Commission were marked by reluctance in both national camps, English Commissioners threatening parliamentary non-confirmation. Deferment therefore reflected James's requirement not merely for union, but union by open and public consent. It qualifies the picture of James as a man dazzled by a private vision, hastening towards union in disregard of his subjects' caution.

The same gradualism appears also in the second deferment. This followed the discovery of the Gunpowder Plot. It is unnecessary to enter into the controversies about the Plot.[4] Some historians follow the official version: a genuine Catholic conspiracy foiled at the last by a chance letter. Others insist that the 'Plot' was not only known to government at an early stage, but encouraged — even launched — by Cecil to justify new measures against recusancy, obscuring James's earlier half-promises of toleration. It is perhaps improbable that such a major campaign would have been launched, without provocation, while government attention was so heavily given over to Union; nor is it necessary to see parliamentary prorogation as part of the build-up to a sensational discovery.[5] Salisbury may however have infiltrated the conspiracy early in 1605, and decided to exploit it for propaganda purposes.[6] This decision would have been easier given the continued bitterness between England and Scotland, and the opposition to Union expected in the English Parliament. There is certainly evidence for national hostility early in 1605. Two particular incidents stand out: the English execution of Thomas Douglas, despite Scots protestations;[7] and the harsh treatment of Marston, Jonson and Chapman for some fairly mild anti-Scottish sentiments in 'Eastward Hoe'.[8] The three playwrights were imprisoned, Jonson and Chapman finding rescue through their Court patrons.[9] The administration's sensitivity to public expressions of prejudice is indicative of the existing tension. This appears strongly in the Plot itself. The conspirators intended to exploit national prejudices, with a 'proclamation' against Union and the King's Scots courtiers.[10] Birch expanded this to an intention 'to have them blown back into Scotland'.[11] The stress laid by the conspirators on their independence from foreign influences confirms this 'Little Englander' aspect of the Plot; but despite this, a deathlist of Scots allegedly found in their chambers, and tantalising references to discussions between Percy and Northumberland about the Instrument, the anti-Unionist element appears of secondary significance.[12] Tension after November 5 resulted in street brawls in London between Englishmen and Scots.[13] Relations between the Councils were also embittered, the English resenting Scots offers to protect James.[14] Even in a crisis, differences were not forgotten.

This background hostility may have persuaded James even before November to delay parliamentary consideration of union. This was certainly the prophecy of the Venetian ambassador on October 12:

> The question of the Union will, I am assured, be dropped; for his Majesty is now well aware that nothing can be effected, both sides displaying such obstinacy that an accommodation is impossible; and so his Majesty is resolved to abandon the question for the present, in the hope that time may consume the ill-humours.[15]

In Parliament, the new anti-recusant campaign was given (understandable) priority. It began in January 1606 with a Commons committee under Doddridge. Fuller's report on February 1 made sixteen recommendations, including a new oath to distinguish 'loyal' from 'Jesuitised' Catholics. The same distinction was emphasised in the trials, particularly of Garnet. Other recommendations included confirmation of the non-attendance fee, penalties for husbands of recusant wives, exclusion of recusants from official positions, and the Protestant education of recusants' children. English regiments in the Netherlands under Stanley were considered a potential Catholic invasion force. These prospects dominated discussion in the Commons during Spring 1606, the recusancy bill not passing until May. Salisbury alleged deliberate procrastination, creating extra time for discussion of grievances.

Notestein regards the discussion of grievances as proof of the Common's populist, reforming concerns. There were bills on impositions, patents of monopoly and privilege, Typper's investigation of defective titles, and the church. Debate was however greatest on purveyancing, which we have already seen as part of Cecil's programme for the session. As Munden has shown, Cecil wanted to replace purveyancing with a regular composition. The Commons reacted geographically; Household provisioning affected mainly the south-east, where reform was most strongly advocated. Two methods of reform were possible. Composition, affecting all shires proportionately, had little support from the north and west. They supported Hare's plans for enforcement of existing statutes limiting the scale and arbitrariness of purveyancing. Dispute lay not in the need for reform, but the appropriate method. The Commons' decision to support Hare, against clear warnings from the Upper House, marked its endorsement of fiscal feudalism against the progressive administration proposal of composition.

Notestein's connection between grievances and the subsidy has more force. Despite Russell's dismissal of the 'revenue weapon' in early Stuart parliaments,[16] the Commons did withhold grant of subsidy until their position on purveyancing had been placed before James. They decided on May 9 not to pass the subsidy bill until their petition of grievances had been presented.

Amid this general activity, Union was passed over. There was some initial hope of debate on the Instrument. First consideration came as early as January 21, with 'a long unnecessarie weake speach' by Sir William Morrice answering objections to the new royal title.[17] More relevant was Salisbury's letter to James in February, reviewing proposed legislation. Union 'must not longer lie asleep than mere necessity required'.[18] As late as March 9, he anticipated a quick end to the tangle over purveyancing, 'then have on to our union'.[19] Further delays eliminated this possibility. By April, deferment was inevitable. The Lords advised deferment in their message on the tenth, and in conference two days later.[20] This created some discussion in the Commons, with an exchange between Fuller and Wingfield.[21] The House was however almost suspiciously content to accept delay. A bill was framed by the Lord Chief Justice, judges and certain learned counsel, given three readings by the Lords in four days, and despatched to the Commons on Mayday. It was quickly committed, returning to the House with minor amendments on May 9 and passing back to the Lords the same day. The amended bill became law on May 12. Commending 'the long and worthy labours of the Commissioners . . . in all Particulars fully and effectually pursued', it related deferment to the conspiracy and pressure of other legislation.[22]

Some predicted early discussion of Union in Scotland. 1604 had set a precedent for prior debate in London, but there was no theoretical reason why the Scots parliament of July 1606 should not have considered the Instrument before its English counterpart. De la Boderie expected such consideration, urging Paris to move quickly 'pour empêcher ladite union' by informal contacts between himself and leading Scots.[23] This advice was rejected, to avoid alienating James. Villeroy ordered the ambassador to maintain his contacts, and emphasise France's desire to preserve the Auld Alliance, but James was to be assured of French support for Union, and offered sympathy over the short-sightedness of its parliamentary opponents. In fact, the Scots session was asked merely to recognise the Instrument, leaving England to debate substantive issues first.[24] This is unsurprising; the Scots had other questions to discuss, and would not welcome passage of measures that were known to face opposition and amendment at Westminster.[25]

2. Executive Measures: Coinage, Seals, Flags and Commerce

In the absence of parliamentary discussion, progress on the Union came through executive measures by the two governments. James sought to advance his project by further unification in the public symbolism of England and Scotland. This reflected continued emphasis in Court culture on Union, the revival of Britain and the personal mission of the king.[26]

One measure has been mentioned in Chapter 4: the extension of the Unite coinage to Scotland, by proclamation on March 4. This Proclamation was however premature. It was not until June that the Scots acknowledged receipt of pylles, tursells and puncheons for manufacture of the coins.[27] Action was simultaneously taken to issue Scots seals reflecting James's new, British title. The warrant was issued on March 28, the form being decided by Dunfermline and deputy Treasurer Arnott. The old seals were not however replaced until June.[28]

The most important and controversial of these minor measures was the union on the national flags. The early history of the Union Jack was in some ways a microcosm of the overall project. It was launched as part of James's gradualist approach to a union of hearts and minds. It involved questions of superiority and equality. It created disagreement between the nations, spilling over into public and political relations, and proved an eventual failure.

The circumstances of James's decision to unite the flags are uncertain. The proclamations establishing the 'Union Flag' on April 12, 1606 spoke of differences 'between our Subjects of South and North Britain, Travelling by Sea, about the bearing of their flags'.[29] The ships of both nations should therefore carry on their maintops 'the flags of St Andrew and St George . . . interlaced, and thesse of North Britain in their stern that of St Andrew and thesse of South Britain that of St George'. But it is difficult to see what spontaneous disagreement could arise between the two mercantile marines. After 1603, each carried its existing national plumage; in the rare joint ventures, the matter could be settled by individual agreements, as before. Unification therefore almost certainly reflected James's own concern with symbolism.

The central problem lay in design. The flag was intended to suggest a fraternal, equal union, but demonstrable equality was an unattainable goal. It was theoretically possible to achieve equality, by adopting an indifferent, overall design symbolic of 'Great Britain'. No such identifiably British symbol existed, however, while a new design was unlikely to command public acceptance. All designs therefore concentrated on the unification of existing symbols — the vertical red St George's cross on a white field for England, and a diagonal white St Andrew's cross on a blue field for Scotland. Unfortunately, their mutual placement on the flag carried inevitable implications of precedence. 'Heraldry knows no way of making two places on a flag of equal value. The position next the staff is more honourable than the corresponding position in the fly; in the same way the upper part of the flag is more honourable than the lower.'[30] Several possibilities were considered, notably a group of six designs submitted to Admiral Nottingham by the heralds (see inserted colour plates). Their variation is as notable as their underlying unity. In all but one, the St George's cross occupied the centrepiece, cutting the flag into four parts. The St Andrew's cross was then fitted in. In Options One and Six, it occupied the position of honour in the top, left canton. Honour was 'balanced': St Andrew had the point of honour, but had not displaced St George, and was smaller. But it could be argued that since the St George's cross quartered the flag, its field (albeit superimposed by the St Andrew's cross) extended to the prime position. In Options Two and Four, St Andrew was fitted into the centre of the flag. Option Four reduced it to a diminutive white symbol within St George's crosspiece. Option Two superimposed the whole Scots flag over the crosspiece and part of the arms. The idea is clear: England has the bulk of the flag and the point of honour, 'balanced' by the superimposition of St Andrew. Despite its central position, however, the St Andrew's cross was again conceding precedence to England. The two remaining designs were equally ingenious. In Option Three, St George's cross was bounded by four Scots flags, in the cantons. This was visually the most equal design. Option Five, preferred by Nottingham as 'the most fittest for this is the man and wyfe wthout blemish on the other', is blatantly Anglocentric. Although the St Andrew's cross has displaced St George from the centrepiece, it occupies an inferior position on the fly.

None of these designs was approved. The manuscript bearing them also carries a rough contemporary sketch, perhaps by the recipient, of a seventh possibility: St George's cross having the cantons of greatest and least honour, St Andrew occupying the intermediate positions (see inserted colour plates, Number One). In strict heraldic theory, this still left England supreme. But then, the same could be argued about the eventual choice, Number Two. The first Union Jack is a remarkable device. Both crosses occupy the same physical area, the whole ground of the flag. The Scots flag is superimposed on the English white field, and might be considered to have first claim upon the point of honour. But St George is not displaced from the centre, and its own field presumably extends under the superimposition to the corners of the flag. As a centrepiece, it cuts the St Andrew's cross. Perrin believes that no inequality was intended here, citing an Elizabethan precedent.[31] The use of centrepiece and superimposition as balancing factors in other designs however makes this improbable. At any rate, the visual prominence of the St George's cross elicited immediate complaints of inequality from Scots merchants, relayed to James by his Council in Edinburgh. They prophesied 'heit and miscontentment betwix your Majesteis subjectis', and enclosed 'two new drauchtis', indifferent to either nation, for presentation by Mar.[32]

These 'indifferent' designs were not accepted, and are now lost. The Council's prophecies proved accurate, however. In 1607, there were disputes between English and Scots masters in Portugal, about the flag. Scots masters were using their own design, in which the St Andrew's cross superimposed St George.[33] The Union Jack remained unpopular in both nations throughout the reign of James. Charles I discontinued its carriage, the flag being unused for twenty years. It returned to favour under Cromwell, after 1654. After a brief experiment in which the union of England, Scotland and Ireland was represented by quartering (St George having the top left and bottom right cantons, and St Andrew the top right, with an Irish harp in the bottom left), the Protectorate reintroduced the Union Jack with a central Irish harp. The flag continued after 1660 without the harp, reaching its present form in 1801 on reunion with Ireland, with the red diagonal 'Cross of St Patrick' (the heraldic device of the Fitzgeralds) taking a place within the white cross of St Andrew.

The wrangle about flags boded ill for the commercial union proposed by the Commission, which James now sought partly to carry into effect. At Christmas 1604, James exempted Scots and English from the payment of Alien's Custom.[34] The situation regarding ordinary custom is uncertain. Lythe believes that the relaxation of custom on internal trade established in 1603 continued; but the circumstances for free trade quoted by him appear rather to reflect an Act passed in 1607. There is evidence for the continuation of ordinary custom.[35] Most noteworthy is the Scots Act of July 11, 1606, 'Anent the Customes betuix Scotland and England'.[36] This required customers to keep records of all goods passing over the Border, regularly exchanged with their English counterparts as a check on falsification. While possibly intended to provide background information for parliamentary debates on trade, as Bruce believed,[37] this implies that customs were still being taken. It followed orders by the Scots Privy Council in February 1606 tightening procedures on the Border, with goods being required to go through the customs posts, receive a 'cokquet' and be inventoried.

Relaxation of Alien's Custom apart, the principal commercial measure of 1605-6 was the despatch of the mercantile sub-commission to France, to compare trading privileges. This followed a letter from the English Council in July 1605, and a special meeting of the Scottish Convention of Burghs. The Scots considered a visit to France unnecessary, authorising the payment of 2000 merks for the purpose only under protest.[38]

3. The Middle Shires

Border administration in 1605-6 is the first of two major areas where it is difficult to separate action taken to advance the Union from the simple continuation of longstanding policy. James's purpose towards the 'Middle Shires' was twofold. Ultimately, he intended to remove formal differences between them and other areas, for example by the imposition of ordinary justice. Immediately, however, the priority was pacification. Without order, institutional changes would be meaningless. Without such changes, Border policy would not be really 'unionist'; after all, pacification had concerned both governments before 1603, and reflected James's emphasis on the extension of centralised authority throughout his dominions. Nevertheless, the vigorous pursuit of peace in this period did undoubtedly reflect James's concern with unity.[39] It was also directly connected with the united sovereignty achieved by James's accession in 1603. A single monarch now commanded both nations, allowing unprecedentedly close cooperation between English and Scots authorities. After the Commission, James considered how to exploit this opportunity. His chief adviser was Home, made Earl of Dunbar in January 1605. Dunbar was James's leading Scots counsellor in London: granted large estates in Durham and Middle March, and an English peerage, raised onto the English Privy Council and naturalised by Act of Parliament. As Lieutenant of all three Marches in 1604, and member of the Northumberland Commission of Peace, he had great experience to offer. 'This quiet, ruthlessly efficient man had more influence in shaping policy towards Northumberland and the Middle Shires than did any other single councillor of state with the possible exception of Sir Robert Cecil.'[40]

The result of James's early consultations was a joint Border Commission, with five members from either nation. It was established in February 1605, with powers of oyer, terminer and gaol delivery in the English counties of Northumberland, Cumberland, Westmorland and part of Durham, and the Scottish counties of Roxburgh, Selkirk, Peebles, Dumfries, Kirkcudbright and Annandale. Two troops of horse were raised, under Sir Henry Leigh and Sir William Cranston.[41] The Scots Commissioners were Sir William Seton, Sir William Home, Patrick Chirnside, Robert Charteris and Gideon Murray. Their English counterparts, saving Joseph Pennington, represented major factions. Sir William Selby and Sir Wilfrid Lawson were connected respectively to Salisbury and the Earl of Northumberland. Edward Grey was the agent of Lord William Howard, who exercised great unofficial influence on the Borders despite his Catholicism.[42] Sir Robert Delaval represented local Protestant gentry. The Commission's activities led to an unprecedentedly high number of convictions and summary executions.[43] Courts were held regularly, while Cranston received an Act of Indemnity. By late 1606, the campaign had 'fully reduced the . . . inhabitants to the obedience of hes Maiesties lawes'. This is of course an exaggeration.[44] Williams has demonstrated both the continuation of petty thievery on the Border, and the occasional breakdowns in close cooperation between English and Scottish Commissioners.[45] Nevertheless, the overall picture of success is clear. The procedures of the Commission reflected the Instrument of Union, in detail and spirit. The stress was on the use of ordinary, common law justice, and on extradition of fugitive offenders to trial in the country of offence. Remand and extradition were decided at the Commission's first meeting, on royal instructions. They contradicted the common law maxim limiting capital crimes to trial in the defendant's shire. They were opposed by Selby, absent from the meeting. Selby obtained an invitation to observe a Scottish court in Roxburgh, in August 1605, and protested strongly thereafter at the harsh treatment meted out there.[46] He later negotiated an agreement with the Scots allowing English Commissioners to attend Scottish courts regularly, as observers.

Selby resisted remand, but keenly promoted ordinary justice by J.P.s in Northumberland. He held the first petty session there, appointing high and petty constables, and other officials. The Commissioner confidently predicted ordinary justice throughout the Borders, within a year.

This prospect was dashed by the Gunpowder Plot. Percy's involvement created a campaign against northern Catholics. The greatest casualty was the Earl of Northumberland, imprisoned in the Tower until 1621. Agents and protégés suffered accordingly. Recusancy in the north was considered threatening enough to warrant extraordinary measures. Sir Henry Widdrington was authorised to interrogate everyone who had or might have had contacts with Percy. The Commission was required to assist this witch-hunt. It did so with ill grace, Selby particularly resenting Widdrington's overriding authority and use of extraordinary justice. Their feud created friction at Court, and dissatisfaction among Commissioners and London administrators alike,[47] culminating in a public reprimand in 1606 to the Commission, for trying cases from before 1603 — as the Instrument had recommended! Finally, Dunbar was appointed extraordinary adviser and 'assistant' to the Commission, for the apprehension of fugitive malefactors.[48]

4. Union and the Kirk

Border administration is one area where it is difficult to separate 'unionist' measures from simple continuation of existing policies, undertaken for other reasons. These difficulties are even greater with policy towards the Kirk, in 1605-6. This period saw new efforts to increase royal and episcopal authority over the Kirk, at the expense of presbyterian government. In one sense, these merely continued James's policy of gradual introduction of episcopal authority, visible before 1603. The creation of titular 'bishops' after 1601, holding parliamentary seats but without special ecclesiastical status, was followed by the grant of administrative functions to these 'bishops' within their 'dioceses'. After 1604, James began to tamper with the times and places of General Assemblies, despite the 1592 Act establishing that they should be annual. The prorogation of the 1604 Assembly was an opening shot in the campaign. James was adept at selecting as 'bishops' moderate and experienced presbyterian ministers, establishing a credible alternative party to the Melvilleans. His immediate aims were to secure a position for bishops within the presbyterian system, as Constant Moderators of Presbyteries and Synods.

It could be argued that this programme was irrelevant to union. It predated 1603. It was accompanied by royal promises in 1603-4, and again in 1605, not to seek reconciliation of the national churches.[49] The restrictions placed on the Anglo-Scots Commission by parliament, forbidding discussion of ecclesiastical union, had been obeyed. Bancroft's proposal asserting the primacy of Canterbury was passed over. The tracts, especially those closest to James, emphasised the practical identity of Anglo-Scots doctrine, implying that no further union was required. The changes proposed would not establish an Anglican episcopacy in Scotland, although they did entail some advance in the position of Scots bishops.

There are reasons, however, why discussion of the Kirk is necessary here. Many Scottish historians are adamant that ecclesiastical policy reflected the union.[50] Some contemporaries suggested the link. We have already seen the apprehensions roused by the union project among Scots presbyterians, in 1604. The introduction of new proposals was widely regarded in Scotland as part of union, despite royal denials.[51] Giustinian, the Venetian ambassador, agreed.[52] Bancroft openly spoke to John Melville and other Scots ministers about 'his Royal endeavour to unite us together in one Church and Policie'.[53] James's express desires for 'una Grex' and 'one Worship to God' are also relevant.[54]

State papers and letters from the period are no more conclusive than the partisan ecclesiastical histories regarding the links between union and ecclesiastical policy.[55] The question concerns royal intent, and is, in the absence of any direct comment from James himself, unanswerable. It is *prima facie* probable that James did want union to extend to the government and discipline of the two churches. It is equally likely that he would have sought to return bishops to the Kirk had there been no union project. This was an area where general policy and the union coincided in purpose — and where action was pursued with consequent vigour.

The campaign accelerated after James's indefinite prorogation of the July 1605 Aberdeen Assembly — despite protests from Synods about the freedom of the church.[56] Nineteen ministers, encouraged by hints of support from Dunfermline, resolved to meet in Aberdeen at the appointed hour, establish an 'Assembly', but dissolve immediately on receipt of an official demand.[57] The meeting duly occurred. When charged by Ecclesiastical Commissioner Lawreston to disperse, they did so — but appointed another meeting for the following September.[58] Ten other ministers, arriving late, associated themselves with these proceedings.

The gathering was a direct challenge to James's assumption of power to call, prorogue and veto General Assemblies, and it was immediately punished: fourteen ministers were warded, in Blackness, and proclamations were issued against recognition of the 'Assembly'.[59] Pressure was exerted on the ministers to recant — with some success. Six recalcitrants, led by Forbes, remained warded throughout 1605, appearing regularly for examination before the Council. Their case gained widespread public support, including prayers in many churches for their deliverance.[60] The ministers were eventually tried early in 1606, before an assize in Edinburgh. A narrow majority verdict was recorded against them, after much pressurisation of the jury, on charges of treasonously denying the ecclesiastical authority of the Crown. The ministers, theoretically open to death sentences, were remitted to James's will and pleasure.[61] Their incarceration produced new protestations and ill-feeling in Scotland.[62] Eventually, in September 1606, they were exiled.[63]

This trial was the start of concerted royal efforts in 1606. In February, simultaneous Synods were convened to discuss a number of royal propositions: that the next Assembly should not consider the position of the 'bishops'; that James's authority to call and prorogue Assemblies be recognised; and that the 'bishops' should be elected as Constant Moderators of Presbyteries and Synods.[64] These proposals were largely rejected, or referred to the next Assembly for discussion. Failure merely increased James's resolve. In May, he established a conference in London on the future of the Kirk, summoning eight leading presbyterian ministers (including both Melvilles) and a similar number of episcopalians.[65] The presbyterian delegation were naturally suspicious, protesting beforehand that they could not represent the Kirk. They were soothed by Dunbar, who presented the conference as an opportunity for reformation.[66]

At first sight, the prospect of conference appears distinctly unionist. The strongest hints of a royal purpose to reconcile the churches certainly appear from this period. Bancroft's comments were paralleled by sermons read before the conference members by leading English divines, justifying the Anglican settlement,[67] but the chief purpose of the conference was more limited — namely, to obtain an acknowledgement of James's general authority over the Kirk, and particularly over the meetings of the General Assembly. This entailed implicit condemnation of the Aberdeen 'Assembly' and the warded ministers. English sermons were addressed specifically to episcopacy and royal supremacy. Doctrinal and ritual matters were not considered.

It was never likely that James could secure the acknowledgement demanded. The bishops and episcopalian ministers of course gave this freely, on September 23.[68] The presbyterians began by prevaricating. Lengthy cross-examination by James himself soon broke this cover, Andrew Melville in particular defending the warded ministers and the rights of the Kirk to free assembly. A petition on the ministers' behalf was submitted, and the presbyterians admitted to having prayed for their warded compatriots.

This led to virtual imprisonment in England. The ministers were free to travel and congregate, within London, but not to return to Scotland without royal permission, which was not forthcoming. Increasingly, the conference appeared to have two covert purposes. The first was punishment, notably of the Melvilles, for previous opposition. Andrew Melville's behaviour made this easier. Besides composing scurrilous epigrams on the rites of the English church, at least as practised in the Chapel Royal, Melville openly condemned Bancroft for wearing 'Romish rags' and profaning the Sabbath.[69] The English Privy Council considered this almost treasonable. The Melvilles' reply was to appeal to the independence and liberty of Scotland — an interesting reaction, confirming Scottish resentment of absentee rule.[70] This deterioration in relations led to the imprisonment of Andrew Melville in the Tower, and warding of other ministers 'for instruction' in the town houses of English bishops.

This continued into early 1607, before release. Andrew Melville was confined to the Tower until 1611, and James was exiled to Newcastle, confirming the

APPENDIX
The Union Jack

Part I: Original Designs (N.L.S. MSS 2517, fols. 67-8)

(1)

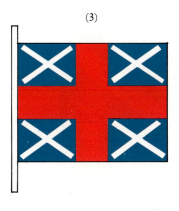

(2)

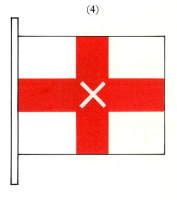

(3)

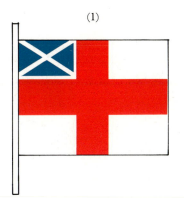

(4)

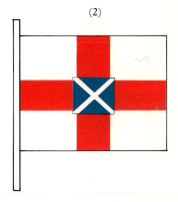

(5)

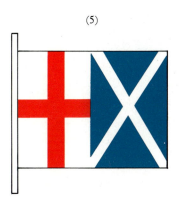

(6)

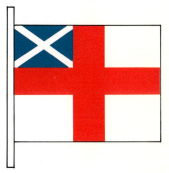

Part II: Other Designs

(1)

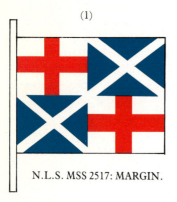

N.L.S. MSS 2517: MARGIN.

(3)

UNION FLAG WITH SCOTS
CROSS DOMINANT.

(2)

UNION FLAG: 1606-1801.

general belief that the second and main purpose of conference was to remove likely leaders of opposition before a new campaign in Scotland.[71]

This campaign was pursued in the July 1606 session of the Scots parliament, and in a special ecclesiastical assembly called in Linlithgow that December. Great care was taken to ensure passage of a bill introduced into parliament, restoring the temporal estates (but not ecclesiastical status) of the bishops. The session was called in Perth, rather than presbyterian Edinburgh.[72] The support of nobles was gained by confirmation of lands previously seized from the church, and the erection of seventeen new temporal lordships from prelacies. The bill greatly enhanced the civil and financial position of the bishops, and so indirectly increased their power within the Kirk. It was coupled with an acknowledgement of royal supremacy over the Kirk and its Assemblies.

The Linlithgow 'Assembly' marked another important stage in the elevation of bishops. Its status was questionable. No elections were held; presbyteries were asked to send specified ministers as their delegates instead.[73] Many considered it to be a preparatory convention rather than a General Assembly. Its proceedings however carefully observed the legal technicalities of an Assembly. Much initial time was spent on measures with which no presbyterian could quarrel — notably, the suppression of papists and plantation of new churches. Royal propaganda presented bishops as necessary 'shock troops' for anti-papist campaigns. Only later did James's supporters introduce the proposal for which the 'Assembly' was called: namely, that presbyteries should have permanent or Constant Moderators, for effective action between sessions — and that bishops, where these existed, should be the Moderators.[74]

Presbyterians made much of the 'travelling expenses' doled out by Dunbar to compliant ministers, but the proposal was accepted only after much discussion, and with severe limitations. Moderators should have no unusual jurisdiction or power, might not act without advice and consent of their brethren, and must be subject to trial and censure by the synod. The majority of the Moderators selected were common ministers. It was nevertheless an opening that James could exploit. Judicious alteration of records turned the gathering into a full-blown Assembly, and its approval of Constant Moderators was extended to synods as well as presbyteries.[75] 1607 saw a major campaign to secure acceptance of this scheme from presbyteries and synods, without much success.[76] Nevertheless, the 'Assembly' and other measures in 1605-6 continued the progress in Scotland towards a compromise settlement, retaining the presbyterian hierarchy under 'moderation' by *de facto* diocesan bishops. This was not unity with England, or even uniformity, but it did mark a step in the general direction of English government and discipline.

G

NOTES

1. Chamberlain was one: Nichols, *Progresses of James I*, I, 491.

2. 'For the Union, howsoever I conceive upon this time to be able to give reasons for mine own counsel, yet I assure your lordships many things are so far out of my exact remembrance . . . that hap had [someone] nothing else to do but study the same, [he] may quickly put me such a book case in a public meeting as I shall be loth to reply.' *HMC.Salis.MSS* XVI, 425-6.

3. Nichols, *Progresses of James I*, I, 76.

4. The main academic works on the Plot are: D. Jardine, *A Narrative of the Gunpowder Plot* (London, 1857); M. A. S. Hume, *Treason and Plot* (London, 1901); Williamson, *Gunpowder Plot*. The conspiracy has of course attracted a wealth of popular historical interest: L. Winstock, *Gunpowder Treason and Plot* (London, 1976); F. Edwards, *Guy Fawkes: The Real Story of the Gunpowder Plot?* (London, 1969); C. N. Parkinson, *Gunpowder Treason and Plot* (London, 1977), etc.

5. This is implied by Williamson, *Gunpowder Plot*, 123ff.

6. The best brief account of its propaganda use is in a popular work: *Parkinson, op. cit.*, 116ff.

7. *Cal.S.P.(Ven.) 1603-7*, 258.

8. Talking of a Scots settlement in Virginia, the playwrights wished 'a hundred thousand of them were there, for we are all one Countreymen now, yee know; and wee should finde ten times more comfort of them there, then we doo heere'. Act III, Scene II, lines 1380-7.

9. *DNB*: Jonson — Vol. X, 1071. For their letters and contacts, see editions of the play by J. M. Harris (New Haven, 1926), xxvi ff. and by G. Petter (London, 1973), 125-33.

10. S.P.14/216/37. The MS reference is crossed out, but legible.

11. Birch, *James I*, I, 37. The reference comes in a letter from Hoby to Edmondes, on Nov. 19.

12. The references to discussion are in S.P.14/7/39 and 14/216/137, and concern a mealtime's conversation. The deathlist is mentioned in *Cal.S.P.(Ven.) 1603-7*, 303-4.

13. Wilson, *History of GB*, 28ff.

14. *Cal.S.P.(Ven.) 1603-7*, 293, 303-4.

15. *Ibid.*, 280. See also 270 for royal worries about 'turbulent and seditious spirits, who right willingly thwart all his Majesty's schemes'. An example of consultation between M.P.s before the session appears in a letter of 20 September 1605: *HMC.Cowper MSS* I, 57.

16. See e.g. Russell, 'Parliamentary History in Perspective', 12.

17. Bowyer, 1 and 1n (Clerk of Commons' oblated note).

18. B. L. Stowe MSS 4161, fols. 260-1.

19. S.P.14/19/27.

20. *Bowyer*, 116-17.

21. *CJ* I, 297.

22. *Statutes of the Realm* IV, Part II, 1070-1. For royal pressure to hasten the bill, see *HMC.Salis.MSS* XVIII, 129-30.

23. *De la Boderie* I, 77. The same letter makes it clear that the ambassador had already established these contacts.

24. *Acts, Sc.Parl.*, 280 (July 3rd).

25. For a (biassed) assessment of Scotland's alienation, see S.P.14/22/17.

26. See e.g. the masque by Anthony Munday, *The Triumphs of Re-United Britannia* (London, 1605). Marriage masques at court habitually included encomia on national as sexual union, some like Ben Jonson's *Hymen* amounting to extended allegory. See Nichols, *Progresses of James I*, I, 576 and II, 105; Axton, *Two Bodies*, 131-2 and 136-7.

27. *Reg.PCSc.* VII, 54 and N.L.S. Adv.MSS 34.2.2. Vol. II, fol. 345. For the proclamation, see Balfour, *Annals* II, 5.

28. N.L.S. Adv.MSS 34.2.2. Vol. II, fols. 335, 345; *Reg.PCSc.* VII, 27.

29. W. G. Perrin, *British Flags* (Cambridge, 1922), 55. The two proclamations were issued on the same day: *Larkin & Hughes*, 135-6; Balfour, *Annals* II, 13.

30. Carr, *Flags of the World*, 33.

31. 'Elizabeth had granted the Levant Company, by her Charters of 1581 and 1592, the right to wear as a flag "the Armes of England with the redde crosse in white over the same" [royal arms]. We may be quite sure that in consenting to such an arrangement Elizabeth had no thought of giving the national flag precedence over the royal standard, but merely wished to signify their intimate union.' Perrin, *British Flags*, 57.

32. *Ibid.*, 57; *Reg.PCSc.* VII, 499.

33. *HMC.Salis.MSS* XIX, 72.

34. Lythe, *Economy of Scotland*, 202 and 'Union of the Crowns', 221.

35. Keith, *Commercial Relations*, 16.

36. *Acts, Sc.Parl.* IV, 285. A parallel order was made to English customers: S.P. 14/26/50.

37. Bruce, *Report on the Union*, 115.

38. *Reg.PCSc.* VII, 473.

39. The connection between the Borders and fraternity is clearly drawn in several official statements: see for example the Scots Order-in-Council on the Debateable Lands of 18 July 1605: *Reg.PCSc.* VII, 81-2.

40. Watts & Watts, *From Border to Middle Shire*, 138.

41. *Cal.S.P.(Dom.)* 1604-10, 198 (Docquet) and S.P.14/3/4.

42. See Reinmuth, 'Border Society in Transition', in his *Early Stuart Studies*, 231-50 (and esp. 236-45). I am grateful to Dr Reinmuth and to Carlisle Record Office for our discussions on Border administration under James VI and I.

43. 'Never before had the Borders for two years together been under such ruthless discipline': Masson, *Reg.PCSc.* VII, lxxi.

44. Balfour, *Annals* II, 16-17.

45. Williams, 'Northern Borderland', 9-10.

46. 'Albeit in strict law such men may with us peradventure be forcibly dealt withal, yet force would be charitably used and never but in cases of extreme extremity.' *HMC.Salis.MSS* XVII, 400, 410.

47. See e.g. S.P.14/21/9 & 10.

48. S.P.14/24/18 & 19.

49. *Calderwood*, 498; *Spottiswoode*, 488.

50. Masson thus calls it 'his more secret and delicate enterprise', reserved for himself. See *Reg.PCSc.* VII, xlv and VIII, xviii. Williamson's treatment of the Apocalyptic Vision makes the same assumption.

51. *Spottiswoode*, 487-8.

52. *Cal.S.P.(Ven.)* 1603-7, 401 and 411.

53. 'We both hold and keep the ground of true Religion, and are Brethren in Christ . . . We only differ in the forme of Government of the Church, and some Ceremonies'. *Calderwood*, 564. See also Row, *History*, 233; Melville, *Diary*, 699.

54. *CJ* I, 171 and 367.

55. There is nothing, for example, in Laing, *Ecclesiastical Letters*.

56. *Calderwood*, 490.

57. For Dunfermline's part in this, see Forbes, *Certaine Records*, xxxix ff; Lee, 'Government of Scotland', 44-5.

58. Details of the 'Assembly' are given in *Calderwood*, 491-4; *Forbes*, 388-400; Thomson, *Acts of Kirk*, 1013-17; Melville, *Diary*, 570-6; Scot, *Apologetical Narratioun*, 132-6; *Row*, 227ff. These all emphasise its loyalty and obedience to royal wishes. For a hostile account, see *Spottiswoode*, 486.

59. For the proclamation, see *Acts of the Kirk*, 1018-19 and *Melville*, 580-1.

60. *Scot*, 136-48; *Forbes*, 401-53; *Melville*, 581ff; *Row*, 230; *Calderwood*, 494-507.

61. *Calderwood*, 508-16; *Melville*, 618-26; *Scot*, 148-55; *Forbes*, 453-97.

62. For Dunfermline's demi-defence of the ministers at this time, see his letters to Salisbury on 8 and 21 January, 1606: S.P.14/8/8 & 31. *Forbes*, 514-18, cites a second proclamation against sermons, fasts etc. on their behalf.

63. *Forbes*, 557-8; *Melville*, 668-72.

64. *Calderwood*, 516ff; *Scot*, 156.

65. For the summons, see *Scot*, 165-6; *Calderwood*, 518-19; *Melville*, 634-6; *Spottiswoode*, 496-7.

66. *Melville*, 645; *Calderwood*, 519.

67. *Row*, 231ff; *Spottiswoode*, 497ff; *Calderwood*, 537-42 *passim*.

68. Laing, *Ecclesiastical Letters*, 62ff. See also *Calderwood*, 537-49; *Row*, 231-8; *Scot*, 166-78; and above all, *Melville*, 654-88.

69. *Calderwood*, 548. The epigrams are reproduced in *Row*, 234-6, and mentioned in *Spottiswoode*, 500.

70. James Melville called himself 'a free subject of the kingdome of Scotland, which hath lawes and priviledges of their owne, as free as any kingdome in the world, to which I will stand': *Scot*, 170. For Andrew Melville's outburst, see *Row*, 237.

71. *Melville*, 675; *Row*, 239. See also the reports of *de la Boderie* on 11 Oct., 21 Nov., 2 Dec. 1606: I, 379-86, 419-26, 432-7.

72. For the parliament, see *Melville*, 636ff; *Scot*, 157ff; *Calderwood*, 520-32. The last includes a supplication by the warded ministers, and protests from the Commissioners of Presbyteries to the Lords of the Articles against restitution of episcopal estates.

73. An example of the summons is in *Acts of the Kirk*, 1020-1. See also *Calderwood*, 550-1;
Row, 240-1.

74. For details of the discussion, see *Acts of the Kirk*, 1022-38; *Spottiswoode*, 500-1; *Calderwood*, 552-60; *Row*, 240-2.

75. *Row*, 243-4.

76. *Scot*, 185-8 and 196-7; *Melville*, 715-20 and 731-5; *Calderwood*, 565ff.

6
The Project Inside Parliament:
November 1606-July 1607

Introduction

The 1606-7 English Parliamentary session is undoubtedly the centrepiece of the union project. Even more than the 1604 session, it has dominated the attention of historians, at the expense of other parts of the programme. It has also been used to reinforce traditional, 'whig' ideas of an assertive, coordinated party in the Lower House, protesting grievances and parliamentary authority against the pretensions of divine right monarchy. The 'defeat' of James VI's project in the session thus becomes proof of the existence — and strength — of this party, and of the methods by which they operated. The elaboration of committee structure, and the growth of the Committee of Whole House to bypass the Speaker, are stressed here. In this, the actual issues at stake, and reasons for 'opposition', are frequently mistaken, sometimes absurdly so.[1]

The Parliament was called not to approve 'union' as a whole, but a specific set of proposals outlined in the Instrument of December 1604. Details of these are given in Chapter 4. In his Introductory speech on November 18, James took care to give reasons favouring each of the main propositions.[2] He also sought to answer the most popular objections of 1604 against the union: that union would enrich Scotland at English expense, that James had shown undue favour to Scots, and that there was no necessity for a union. Only in passing did James allude to the longer-term prospects of general union, for example in the laws. These allusions however were important, particularly in later debate, for their references to 'perfect Union' and laying Scotland 'subject to the [presumably English] Laws'.

James's speech is the earliest record extant for the session. There is no indication of particular preparation by the government, embroiled as it was in the Scots church campaign, or by any of the major parliamentarians — 'Crown' or 'Country'! An extensive debate would not, on the face of it, seem to have been anticipated by either 'side'. Nevertheless, as we shall see, such a debate did result, over many months. Besides playing a vital part in the 'progress' of the union project, and providing many useful insights on the nature of parliament/ crown relations, it also saw the elaboration of previous themes and arguments about union, helping to explain opposition to the project.

The debate on the union was enormous. For convenience, it is considered here in three parts: before February, from February to April, and from May to June.

Part One: Discussions before February 1607

1. Discussions on Discussion: November 20-December 2

The ensuing fortnight saw neither rapid progress towards agreement of the Instrument, as James had hoped, nor the kind of blanket opposition that might suggest prior organisation. Parliament instead discussed the correct procedure for debating the Instrument — with a few speeches obviously against the Instrument, and many more showing great caution and doubts. In this preliminary discussion, several features are noteworthy. The first is the energetic, concerted prosecution of the project by the Lords, under the direction of Ellesmere and Salisbury.[1] This patently reflected royal wishes. In the Commons, the government case was pressed by a handful of leading parliamentarians, Bacon again being the principal. These consistently supported the propositions of the Lords, adding their own reasons for immediate, substantive debate. There was little unity in attitude elsewhere in the Lower Chamber. The future leaders of the opposition on commerce and naturalisation — Sandys, Fuller, Martin, Hyde — favoured different and in some cases diametrically opposed schemes for debate.

· This day-by-day discussion on procedure is relatively well-documented.[2] The opening days demonstrate very clearly the contrast between an active Upper and uncertain Lower House. The Instrument was formally produced for the first time in the Lords, by Chancellor Ellesmere on November 20. It was read, and sent to the Commons 'that they may be well-informed of the contents, before any further Proceeding'.[3] Examination in the Commons was deferred because of the late hour,[4] and the Instrument was given its first reading on the following day. No attempt was made, however, to debate its contents then or on the day after — although the irrepressible Sir William Morrice did introduce a motion on November 22 to declare James 'Emperor of Great Britain'.[5] The Instrument was copied, and the original returned to the Lords on the 24th with a message relating the Commons' willingness to await the pleasure of the peers. Their reply was to demand a conference between committees of both Houses.

'This word conference made some staggering because we had nothing to confer of':[6] that is, because the Commons had devoted no time to discussing the Instrument. Fuller quickly pointed out the risks of a conference for which they were unprepared but the Lords well advised and consulted. Before conferring, they should have full debate, with every member freely stating his mind. A conference was eventually agreed — but only to hear the Lords' arguments, without reply or debate.[7] This unusual ploy was excused by reference to the small number of persons present in the Commons.[8] The Upper House was disconcerted. The conference of November 25 was large, comprising forty Lords and eighty M.P.s, and was clearly seen by the Lords as the powerhouse of the project. Ellesmere objected that 'silence in Consultation effected nothing',[9] and required a speaking brief as well for future conferences. Salisbury and the Chancellor alike stressed the Commons' liberty to discuss issues, but asked for 'minds of indifferency and equality, to weigh all things and to forbear all terms of bitterness'.[10]

Montagu's report to the Commons on November 26, asking for full and open conference on either side, sparked off a further lengthy debate on procedure. Bacon inevitably supported the proposal. The first objection came from Martin, who proposed a division in the treatment of the Instrument. Naturalisation and Border laws should be left to the Lords, the Commons considering commerce and hostile laws. This division is interesting, firstly in its assumption that hostile and Border laws could be treated separately, and secondly in its attitude to naturalisation. This had caused the greatest controversy during the Commission,[11] and was to do the same again in 1607. Abandoning such an important issue to the Lords probably reflected the overriding commercial interests of Martin himself — a leading figure in the 1604 Merchant Adventurers debate, and closely associated with the London trading community.[12] Martin's proposal gained immediate support from Poole, Johnson and Stroud, George Moore's compromise suggestion of a committee of consideration followed by conference being rejected out of hand.[13] On the 27th, Fuller attempted to give the debates a more definite anti-unionist tenor by questioning Hoby on his reasons for not subscribing the Instrument. The reply was enigmatic:

> During the Commission I both saw and heard many things, which then I could not savor, nor can now deliver by reason of the weaknesse of my Memory . . . the Zeale of the House comendit me, and the desire of a true Unity so as it may be with the good of the Mother Crowne of England . . . I ever shall submitt myself when I shall heare better reasons, and stronger Arguments than at that time I did . . . I never delighted in the singularity of my Witt, although I have been taxed in that kinde, and yet I could have wished to have had Fellowes.[14]

Hoby successfully requested leave of the House not to divulge his reasons further. This tactic allowing him to evade the question, discussion returned to the two proposals on the table — for immediate conference by select committee, and for a split in subjects between the Houses. Bond spoke for the former, citing historical precedents for the proposals (including the offers of Protector Somerset), and urging action to complete before Christmas. Brooke and Alford however objected, arguing that the Commons were not ready for conference. Sandys and Fuller agreed — in both cases urging an immediate debate on naturalisation as a matter of greatest moment. Fuller and Dannett also desired consultation of merchants as part of these preparations for conference. Hoby's wish to leave commercial union to the Lords went almost unheard.

Of three possibilities before the Commons on November 27 — an immediate conference, a request for several days' grace to debate all issues, and a split in the subjects — the Commons interestingly adopted the third. Again, this was opposed by the Upper House, Ellesmere repeating the Lords' demand for conference and opposing a split on several grounds.[15] Under this pressure, the Commons partially relented, agreeing to conference on the Instrument as a whole, but demanding time for proper debate beforehand. This was granted — effectively giving victory to Sandys and Fuller.

Agreement on procedure had therefore occupied a confused week of debate and messages. Nor was it to end discussion of the subject. On November 29, the Commons gave the Instrument its second reading and established a committee to consider it further. This was a sizeable body, almost a prototype of the 1607 Committee of the Whole House: 'All the Commissioners, All the Burgesses of Porte Townes, All the Knights and Burgesses of Cumberland, Northumberland and Westmoreland, and the Bishopricke of Durham . . . and all the House to be present, and have free speech'.[16] No lawyer in the Commons was to depart the city without permission.[17] The Grand Committee was therefore an amalgam of Borderers, lawyers and those with commercial interests, plus other active members. The Lords, also faced with the complexities of the Instrument, followed a parallel course. On December 1, they abandoned their usual rules of debate (for example that one man might speak only once on each reading of a bill) for a more open format 'after the Manner of a Committee, and with the same Liberty of Speech'.[18] The judges were summoned to their meetings, as legal advisers.

Theoretically, the procedure was now agreed and in operation. Discussions in committee would precede a Grand Conference between select committees of either House, examining the proposals in the Instrument as a whole. In fact, debates on trade in the Commons Committee were so delayed that naturalisation was never discussed before the conference. Examination of the other issues — hostile and Border laws — was partial, and sidetracked into the question of escuage. Given this confusion in debate before the conference, it is convenient to examine progress by subject rather than chronologically.

2. Hostile and Border Laws, Escuage

The provisions for hostile and Border laws in the Instrument were outlined in Chapter 4. Proposals included abolition of archaic statutes expressing hostility between England and Scotland, replacement of March Treasons and special Border courts by the operation of common law and ordinary justice, settlement of outstanding causes by some means left open to the parliament for decision, and the trial of fugitive offenders by a mixture of extradition and reciprocal jurisdiction. The abrogation of clauses of hostility in borough constitutions was also proposed.

The Commons Grand Committee began with consideration of hostile and Border laws, yet made relatively little progress. Their first step was to review the list of hostile statutes contained in the Instrument. The principle of abolition met with little overt opposition, although the anonymous author of Harleian MSS 1314 — the 'Paper Booke' — did attempt to justify their retention as old weapons to be kept in chests, ready for any renewed hostility between the countries. Abolition would in his view encourage James in his plans for gradual unification: 'Every parl^t will be laboured to yield some stones or other matter out of the Quarrie of England to make the Scottish frame of building equall'.[19]

Ironically, the main controversy during committee concerned a statute passed under Richard II against passage out of the realm into Scotland — and arose by government initiative. 'It was proposed by one of the kinges Counsell to repeale so much only as concerned the law of hostillitie, and not the point of State. But it was overruled by the Committyes.'[20] Various other statutes were picked out for possible retention, by M.P.s clearly unsympathetic to the Scots: Acts of 23 Henry VIII and 1 Elizabeth I for selling horses, 7 Richard II for transportation of victuals and horses, 2 and 3 Philip and Mary and 13 Elizabeth I for letting lands. However, the objections to their repeal were overruled. The same committee also looked at Border laws. They decided that clauses of hostility in borough constitutions should be left for repeal by Berwick and Carlisle themselves, and that outstanding Border causes since 1597 should be settled by arrangements similar to those prevailing before the union of the crowns, not under common law. Borough constitutions were widely discussed on December 3, when the Commons heard Hyde's report from Committee on hostile laws. At length, 'It was left to be reasoned with the Lords, whether it should be enacted, That no Scottish man should be made Bayliffe etc of any Town Corporate or Citty'.[21]

That same day of debate raised another issue — escuage — which was to divert discussion of hostile and Border laws. Fuller had already sought discussion of escuage, on November 27; and this time he met with greater success, escuage occupying most of the next three days of debate.

Escuage was a variety of land tenure on the Borders, equivalent to medieval scutage. The tenant held land on condition that in any war with Scotland he would be available for forty days' military service by land or sea, at his own expense. This tenure had outlived military feudal holdings elsewhere because of the continued hostilities along the Borders. In the years of peace after 1550, however, escuage had become a privileged form of tenure, involving little outlay of rent, and the years after 1603 saw a costly campaign by local landlords to eliminate this customary tenure.[22] Fuller therefore had the support of northern knights, in his claim that escuage (as a form of tenure commemorating previous hostility with Scotland) should be abolished. But his reasoning went deeper. Escuage involved the feudal obligations to the Crown of marriage, relief — and wardship. By this, the Crown retained the right of guardianship (including estate administration) during minority tenancies: a source of revenue for royal servants and of spoliation of the estate for immediate profit. On December 4, Fuller 'pulled off his maske and said playnly that it tended to taking away of wards'.[23] Bacon and other royal supporters defended escuage, claiming rather lamely that it existed for general military service, not merely against the Scots. Initial feeling in the House ran strongly for abolition, as Wilson makes clear. Papers were hurriedly prepared on both sides to consider the question, Cotton in particular discussing its historical origins.[24] There was some rumour of the abolitionists receiving support from Salisbury, as Master of the Wards; but Wilson's report of the debate suggests that this was rather improbable.[25]

After two full days of debate (December 5–6) the issue gradually subsided.

On December 13, it was agreed to submit the question to the opinion of the Lords. At the great conference between Lords' and Commons' committees, four days later, the judges ended the controversy with a single, terse sentence: 'that though the service ceaseth, the King's profit [i.e. through feudal dues] must continue'.[26] The conference also established broad areas of general agreement on hostile and Border laws. Hostile statutes should be repealed, along with Border laws, customs and treaties. A new law should be passed to re-enact the royal veto on passage out of the realm contained in the Act of Richard II, and a commission established to settle outstanding Border causes. Hostile clauses in borough constitutions would be left to Berwick and Carlisle themselves. This closely reflected the proposals of the Grand Committee, but did not cover the most contentious issue of all — extradition and reciprocal jurisdiction. That was left for future debate.

These provisions were reported to parliament after the Christmas recess (December 18 — February 10),[27] but were not debated because of the storm surrounding the conference's 'agreement' on commercial union.

3. Commerce

The commercial provisions of the Instrument are again reviewed in Chapter 4. Mutual access to the commercial Companies was proposed. Imports and exports prohibited by statute would pass freely between the nations, Anglo-Scots trade generally to be custom-free on goods intended for domestic use. The main exceptions were raw materials, needed to maintain the manufacturing and clothing industries of England and Scotland. Bonds would be introduced to avoid abuse of free trade. Strangers' Custom would no longer be charged on natives of either kingdom. The main outstanding question concerned Scots trading privileges in France. The principle was agreed: if Scots paid less by any privilege in France, they would face a corresponding surcharge for French goods in England. The Bordeaux wine trade had been examined by the Commission, and was thought to show no difference in privileges. The special sub-commission of Scots and English merchants established by the Commission had since reported broadly the same verdict for other parts of France — implying that no surcharge would be necessary.[28]

Discussion of commercial proposals in the Commons and Grand Committee continued alongside that of hostile laws, in preparation for the same conference on December 17. Many of the same figures were involved in both discussions, Martin being predictably active in examination of the commercial issue.

The Grand Committee was established amid calls for consultation of London merchants; and its first report, on December 4, related the start of that consultation. The merchants, a powerful part of the London lobby,[29] had requested a copy of the commercial proposals, for further study. They alleged that the sub-commission had been rigged, the French being bribed by the Scots (Speir and Fischer) to conceal Scots immunities. The Commons agreed to let the committee hear further evidence from the merchants, shipwrights and the

Master of Trinity House. Martin reported the results on December 8. The committee was in confusion, following objections by the traders and by Trinity House that enactment of the Instrument would give all trade to the Scots. Clearly, feeling in committee and Commons was turning further against the commercial provisions. The Lords' intervention on the 10th, demanding conference on commerce and hostile laws, was therefore from one viewpoint timely. The Commons, however, were clearly unprepared for conference without further examination of the merchants' case. A conference agreed for December 13 was consequently postponed a further four days. During that time, consideration of trade was given to a select committee that would also form the Commons' deputation for conference. The leading spokesmen were Bacon, Hobart, Doddridge, Montague, Hyde and Martin — the last two being particularly concerned with trade.

The conference included a major debate on trade, and much contemporary material has survived. The principal surviving documents are: the objections of the London merchants;[30] notes by Salisbury and Ellesmere upon those objections;[31] answers to them, recorded by Cotton but probably given originally by the Chancellor;[32] memorials of the conference, and a draft Act (again, possibly by Ellesmere) embodying its results;[33] and lastly, answers to the objections by Scots merchants.[34] The last are particularly interesting, implying either the presence of a Scots deputation, or a pre-conference list of English objections submitted to the Scots for comment. A great deal of other material survives from November and December 1606, rather harder to date or place in context — the objections of Trinity House,[35] laid down for the Grand Committee of December 5-8, being an exception. This material includes a speech on commercial union,[36] a tract on the subject,[37] thirty-three pages in the Paper Booke,[38] and various notes on differences in privileges and customs in France.[39]

This wealth of sources indicates the homogeneity of discussion. The themes used at the conference are consistently found in earlier papers on the subject from Autumn 1606. Indeed, this cohesive body of argument can be traced back directly to themes used during the Commission of 1604, and sometimes to tracts (like Spelman and 'A Discourse of Naturalisation') written before its first meeting. To analyse the controversy therefore repeats some ground covered in Chapter 4, as well as in the work of Lythe and Keith.[40] Lythe's account of the debate is rather less important than his analysis of Scots trade at the turn of the seventeenth century. As he and Keith have shown, trade between England and Scotland was comparatively unimportant to the commercial systems of either country. As a market for Scots goods and purchases, England ranked behind France, Spain, Holland and Scandinavia. The English objectors to commercial union were quick to point out that Scotland had few commodities not readily obtainable domestically.[41] The same was true of English goods and Scotland. The two economies were parallel, competing rather than complementary. This lack of commercial incentive to union appears in the merchants' objections of December 17:

> We see no furtherance that can come unto our nation by this community of
> commerce, considering alsoe that the kingdome of Scotland noe way affordeth
> commodyties in any reciprocal course with England for trade and merchandising,
> we being already more English merchants than can live by trade, embolden our
> selves to declare, that it cannot otherwise prove to be but impoverishment . . . we
> humbly pray this honourable assembly . . . that we may enioy all ymmunities,
> priviledge and advauntage of trade as we have done hitherto, and that the Scottish
> nation may likewise enioy theirs without any community of comerce.[42]

Merchants and their associated M.P.s were concerned mainly with two
possibilities. One was the possibility of using the union to benefit England, by
non-reciprocal trading arrangements. The best example is the Paper Booke's
proposal, echoed in the objections of the merchants, for Scotland unilaterally
to drop her prohibition on export of wool, sheep, hides and leather to England.
By contemporary protectionist theory, this was greatly to English advantage,
giving her access to Scotland's raw materials and boosting her clothing industry.
The second possibility was rather a fear, that commercial union would tilt the
normal balance of trade towards the Scots. The arguments here emphasised the
low trading costs of the Scots. Their merchants traded after 'a meane sort and
condition'.[43] Their seamen lived cheaply, off salt fish rather than beef, accepting low wages in return for the transportation and bartering of their own goods.
Scotland was close to the flocks and markets of northern England, and might
come to dominate the trade in northern goods. The Scots merchants in reply
pointed to the parlous state of indigenous ports like Hull and Newcastle. Above
all, the English stressed the Scots' use of small ships. The English put to sea in
large vessels, ready for war. The small Scots ships, able to trade in smaller
cargoes, unfitted for war and amenable to any wind, had an advantage. This
curious inversion of economies of scale was advanced solemnly, but probably
without real credence. The Paper Booke thus feared the beaching of the English
merchantmen through the competition of the small Scots vessels — and then
continued the scenario with prophecies of the Scots purchasing the uneconomi-
cal monsters! As Ellesmere and the Scots alike pointed out, many Englishmen
owned and used small ships — these generally being the poor and despised out-
port merchants, dominated by the great entrepreneurs in London. This lack of
basic economic consistency may be traced in other objections to community of
commerce. Thus free trade was thought to involve a dearth of English corn and
raw materials, monopolised by Scots purchases,[44] and a glut of English and
Scots ships chasing a limited amount of available trade.[45]

The specific objections raised against particular parts of the commercial
proposals again repeated arguments of 1604. Again, the exemption of Scots
from Alien's Custom, and the abolition of ordinary custom on goods travelling
between the countries for domestic use, was rightly held to involve loss of royal
revenue. The three main themes were, however: the possibilities of deception,
lower Scots customs, and Scots privileges in France. Each affected more than
one area of trade. If Scotland was incapable of managing its trade without
evasion of customs, community in commerce would be deleterious in different

ways. Prohibited exports travelling to Scotland could be smuggled abroad. Permitted exports, travelling custom-free for domestic use, would be smuggled or openly re-exported (at lower custom) as Scots produce. Bonds against re-export needed only falsification, a corrupt Scots customer or isolated Scots harbour for evasion. Enforcement of the provisions on a small Scots trader distant from Aberdeen, let alone London, would prove impossible. French and other continental goods might be brought in Scots ships to England as 'Scottish ware', exempt from duty: a danger which the Scots self-deprecatingly dismissed by reference to the higher quality of continental produce! Foreign manufacturers might enter England via Scotland, having already paid the lower import dues at the Scots port. Again, an element of deception was entailed, but one easily credited by English merchants and M.P.s. Thus lower customs threatened the prospect of Scots merchants undercutting their English counterparts at home and abroad. As the Scots pointed out, these calculations ignored the extra transportation costs involved in a three-way trip. They further argued, self-seekingly, that the coarser nature of Scots cloth made Scots customs rates at least equal to those in England. English demands before and after conference for equal rates as the price of commercial community would have had a disastrous effect on the small Scots manufacturing sector, and so indirectly on her mercantile marine.[46] One must remember the enormous quantitative difference between the nations in shipping and trade. The entire commercial volume of Scotland was only equal to that of the five northernmost English ports — a fraction of the annual trade passing through London. Comparison of the sophisticated, large-scale undertakings in the English capital with the few professional merchants in Leith and Aberdeen indicates this gulf. In practice, only some large and definite body of privilege extended to Scots by a foreign country could begin to redress the advantage in organisation and capital possessed by the protesting English traders.

This was of course the place of the alleged Scots privileges in France. Scots trade with her old ally was mainly directed to Bordeaux, for wine, and to Normandy. The former area had already been dismissed by the Commission as indifferent between English and Scots in privilege. Some Englishmen, notably the author of Harleian 1314, disagreed. After lengthy 'calculations', he concluded that there was a very considerable difference in the dues paid; and that even if this financial advantage were discounted, the Scots had two major advantages. Firstly, their naturalisation in France let them buy direct from the vineyards, while Englishmen waited in Bordeaux for the middleman to take his share. Secondly, the French affinity with Scotland would allow for more bargains to be struck. No mention was made of the shorter Scots sailing season, or the greater travelling distance. In Normandy, the mercantile sub-commission had again discounted the differences between the privileges of the two nations.[47] Certain advantages to the Scots could be accepted. These principally reflected the naturalisation of the Scots in France since the marriage of Francis and Mary in 1558, confirmed by Henry IV in 1599.[48] Scots might buy and sell goods from their houses or ships, and store goods rather than place them on immediate sale.

Englishmen *purchasing* the same rights of burgess-ship automatically became aliens in England. Scots naturalisation moreover exempted them from the payment of the French version of Stranger's or Alien's Custom. However, these privileges applied only to trade directly with Scotland; a certificate system similar to the Bond proposed by the Commission ensured that privileged goods leaving France entered Scotland for domestic use, not prejudicing French trade with other nations. A Scot transporting a French commodity into England via Scotland would therefore be liable to four payments of custom: at the French port, the Scots harbours of landing and departure, and the English destination. 'If he bring anie French comodities into England out of Scotland, theis customs cost him more than the French privileges can advantage him. If he come directly for England he must pay English custome.'

Despite this analysis, 'Scots privileges' became with lower customs rates a catch-all reason to oppose the commercial provisions of the Instrument. Again, it was seen as a decisive advantage, enabling Scots directly or indirectly to undercut the English in domestic and continental markets. It was even suggested that community in commerce should be used as a lever, to end Scotland's Auld Alliance with France.[49]

These were the principal lines of argument used in the conference of December 17. The merchants also threatened the loss of Company privileges (for example in Poland) through mutual access, and that community in trade would enable private Scots merchants to indulge in commerce between England and overseas markets where the Companies had a monopoly. The first was readily dismissed by the Scots: their privileges in Poland were just as great as the English, while extra trade would encourage such countries to expand rather than contract their reciprocal trading arrangements. The last objection had more force, in that Scots merchants operating from Scotland could trade with Muscovy and other areas monopolised by the English Companies. In practice, however, the absence of Scots commerce with these markets rendered the question academic; while Scots merchants in England would be covered by existing laws and prohibitions. One author rather caustically remarked that Scots interference in closed markets like Muscovy could only be to the advantage of the people, by helping to break the Companies' stranglehold.[50]

Lythe quite rightly called the discussions of commercial union 'a controversy in which economic principles were hopelessly submerged in the flood of national prejudice'.[51] English fears of competition, measured against the actual state of the two systems of commerce, seem almost ludicrous. This was a charge made by the Scots themselves in their submission to the conference. 'It appears that their heads are so directly repugnant to the effort of the Unyon that they rather conteyne one generall reacting of that most godlie profittable and necessary communication nor any particular reasons against the same.'[52] Scots attitudes are also questionable. Commercial community would, as we have seen, have threatened the infant Scots economy.[53] The enthusiasm of her representatives reflected perhaps the connotations of equality in commercial union, rather than its dubious economic advantages.

The conference debate on trade was stormy, with the merchants' objections receiving vociferous support from M.P.s.[54] The notes made by Salisbury show how close he was to accepting many of the merchants' propositions, notably the need for equality in the rates of custom. Ellesmere, too, though roundly dismissing many objections, accepted the need to strengthen the protective clauses in the Instrument. The remembrances of the conference, taken by Montague and Hobart, were rather a series of restrictions than advancements on union.[55] Alien's Custom would be charged on Scots as long as they retained 'privileges' in France; Scots would not be permitted to import even native prohibited goods, and would pay double custom when selling English goods to aliens. Equality in customs was desired; otherwise, continental goods entering England from the north would likewise be liable to double custom. The only proposals emerging unscathed were mutual exchange of permitted native commodities, and access to the Companies. The former only survived with draconian measures against re-export, involving punishment of owner and customer as well as the merchant.

Despite these restrictions, the conference was itself regarded with hostility by the English Commons. The report on February 10 occasioned great opposition, many members denying that the above articles had been accepted as the basis for a bill. The Commons clearly objected to any commercial union; rejecting Montague's articles, they resolved to 'leave it to the Lords to draw such Bill or Bills, that then this House will afterwards have further consideration'.[56] This decision effectively ended the discussions on trade. This was not immediately clear. Several Commons speakers during ensuing months spoke of the need to return commercial union to debate. In practice, the subject was swallowed up by the even greater controversy on naturalisation. The only substantive moves on trade were by the government. Arrangements were made by the Scots Council for payment of Speir and Fischer, in January 1607.[57] The two merchants themselves were returned to England in February and detained there until late April, in the hope that discussions on commerce would resume.[58] On March 31, the King informed the Commons that the merchants would be examined on the charges of corruption. This examination was clearly in their favour, since they were returned to Scotland by April 28 with a commendation from Salisbury — and formally exonerated by the Scots Council a fortnight later.[59] The same Council had also commanded on April 9 that while no custom should be taken on goods transported over the Border, the merchants should be asked to 'find caution for payment of the said custome in cais the said treaty [i.e. the Instrument of Union] tak not effect'[60] — of which more in our next chapter.

Part Two. The Naturalisation Debates: February-April 1607

1. Introduction and Background

The naturalisation question was introduced in the new sitting by a message from the Lords on February 14. Contrasting the 'progress' on hostile laws and commerce — 'handled but not perfected' — with the lack of discussion on naturalisation, the Lords demanded conference as a preliminary to the drafting of legislation.[1] The Commons predictably demanded time for consideration, before conference.[2] The relevant articles in the Instrument were then read. These recommended two acts. The first would merely declare that under existing law, Scots born after James's accession to the English throne — the *Post-Nati* — were already *de iure* English subjects. The second would extend subject status to those born before the union of the crowns — the *Ante-Nati*. English offices should be protected by a (non-binding) declaration of royal intent not to prefer Scots to such positions until legal and political union had been achieved.

These provisions had occasioned the greatest controversy in the Commission, with English and Scots alike (for very different reasons) disliking the compromise. Some English Commissioners had predicted opposition in parliament.[3] The same distaste appears in letters written early in the session — and in the Paper Booke.[4] The latter questioned the legal status of the *Post-Nati*, described James's saving as effectively an extension of the prerogative, and considered naturalisation of the *Ante-Nati* 'the waightyest case that ever came into the parliament . . . or can come'. Parliament should proceed deliberately, with leaden feet, examining whether naturalisation was equally honourable, profitable and pleasing to either nation, and considering the necessity for limitations. The author particularly feared the entry of Scots into legal offices and the English parliament. His arguments were a mixture of commonsense and prejudice. A Scots judge in England would thus not only lack experience in common law, but be unable fairly to judge a case between an Englishman and a Scot (could an Englishman?). The Scots temperament — 'hasty and giddy-headed, impatient of delays in that they desire, or in hearing that they desire not' — would be as disruptive in parliament as their peers' claims to antiquity and precedency in the Lords. The Booke threatened a flood of Scots into England after naturalisation. Places at court and clerical livings would be monopolised by them, and bullion drained away to Scotland.

These arguments recurred frequently in February-April 1607. The Booke's mixture of fear and superiority towards the Scots characterised the early debates on naturalisation. On February 13, Sir Christopher Piggott, M.P. for Bucks., spoke in the Commons on the report from the December 17 conference:

> Pretending, at first, to deliver some reasons why he pressed the reading of the Remembrances, generally; he afterwards entered into a bye-Matter of invective against the Scots and Scottish nation; using many words of obloquy, ill-beseeming such an audience, and not pertinent to the matter in hand . . . 'They have not suffered above two kings to die in their beds, these two hundred years. Our king hath hardly escaped them.'[5]

The Commons greeted this outburst in silence; but it could not long be overlooked. News of the speech reached James through Ramsay, one of the

Scots Gentlemen of the Bedchamber. De la Boderie describes James's reaction.[6] Salisbury and the Council were harangued; James told them that he was a Scot, loved the Scots, and commanded Prince Henry to do likewise. A royal message to the Commons followed, on the 16th, upbraiding them for their silence and demanding instantaneous punishment. Piggott was expelled from the Commons and incarcerated in the Tower.[7] A plaintive letter survives from the luckless knight, excusing his conduct to Cecil.[8]

This episode made an unfortunate start to the naturalisation debates. Henceforward, James was highly sensitive to any comments made in the Commons about Scotland — and with good reason, given the outrage that Piggott's speech caused in Edinburgh. The Scots Council on March 3 wrote to James thanking him for the punishment of Piggott, and advancing into a long and emotional defence of the Scots nation.[9] James's reply on the 17th attempted to 'cast water upon ye fire in Scotland',[10] repeating Piggott's disclaimers and absolving the Commons. James's private opinions were perhaps less charitable. Under pressure from both nations, he certainly came to suspect the collusion of peers, if not Councillors, in the opposition of the Lower House.[11] The speech similarly crystallised feeling in the Commons. Piggott had merely voiced what many privately thought.[12] His punishment, while deserved, threatened freedom of speech, and may have stiffened the stubborn resolve of those objecting to union.[13] It certainly revealed how fragile the relationship of cooperation and trust was between King and Councillors, Government and Commons, England and Scotland.

2. Early Days of Debate: The Point of Law

The first speeches in the Commons after Piggott and the Lords' message showed immediate resistance to the naturalisation articles in the Instrument. Fuller in particular condemned naturalisation on the 14th, using the same emotive arguments about a flood of Scots into England's rich pastures as the Paper Booke. His tone was sombre, even apocalyptic.[14] His 'derogatory flings' at Scotland 'and the notorious poverty and quarrelsomeness of its people'[15] were answered by Bacon on the 17th. Bacon's 'defence' of naturalisation consisted, however, only in refuting the charges of Piggott and Fuller, and thanklessly exonerating the Scots: 'a people ingenious, in labour industrious, in courage valiant, in body hard, active and comely . . . if they have been noted to be a people not so tractable in government, we cannot . . . free ourselves altogether from that fault, being indeed a thing incident to all martiall people'.[16] He saw no possibility of mass immigration, since the trickle of Scots over the Border since 1603 had been easily absorbed by an under-populated England. Naturalisation would bring closer union, and thereby greater strength; its denial threatened renewed conflict, with bitter Scots resentments fanned by foreign and domestic enemies.

These speeches apart, there was little debate on the *principle* of naturalisation.

On the 18th, Owen trenchantly asserted England's suzerainty, demanding Scots submission to English laws and worship as part of the price of naturalisation — the remainder being the end of the Auld Alliance, and an acknowledgement of England's 'precedency and preferment'.[17] 'The fear that Scotland might gain an advantage over England was seldom absent from their minds.'[18] As early as February 17, this was manifested not in men arguing the 'inconveniency' of naturalisation, but in questioning the position *de iure* — challenging the contention of the Instrument that the *Post-Nati* were already naturalised under common law. The tactical advantages were obvious. Opposition to the principle of naturalisation threatened an immediate confrontation with James. No argument against the principle not involving opposition to the Scots themselves had yet been deduced. By contrast, questioning the point of law could delay, possibly avoid, naturalisation, without implying hostility to the principle or the Scots. This would minimise the danger of acrimony. Moreover, the Commons were partly a judicial institution, called on to make a declaration about the nature of the law on the *Post-Nati*. Questioning the point of law was therefore their duty.

The main difficulty was finding an avenue through which *de iure* naturalisation could be challenged. There was universal agreement in 1604 about the legal status of the *Post-Nati*. Even those like Spelman opposed to other parts of the union project had accepted them as natural subjects, with full powers of inheritance, bequest, ownership and office. The accepted legal position was summarised by Bacon's speech on February 17, separating people into four legal categories. The first two were alien enemies, with no rights at all, and alien friends, protected by the law in persons and moveable goods while peace persisted between the nations. The third category was the denizen, a resident former alien granted indenizenation by royal letters patent. The denizen forfeited subject status in his former nation, receiving in exchange the right to purchase and possess lands, and to hold any crown office in England.[19] Many Scots were indenizenated in 1603-4, while resident at court. Finally, there were natural subjects. Naturalised aliens apart, these were persons born under the king's allegiance, who might be rebels but could never be *or have been* enemies. This retrospective application explained the distinction in law between *Ante-* and *Post-Nati*. The latter owed allegiance to James, and could never have been an enemy at any time. They were therefore natural.

The Commons' main recourse after February 17 was to question the object of allegiance by invoking the 'Two-Body' theory of monarchy. The popularisation of this idea in Elizabethan tracts and plays has been amply traced by Kantorowicz, Maitland and more recently by Axton.[20] Its links with Bodinist thought abroad have also been stressed. Polemicists for the Stuart succession had been active in its use, and James's accession had correspondingly enhanced its claims to legitimacy. The common lawyers in the House now applied the theory in a new manner, tracing allegiance not to the body natural of the king, but the body politic: not to James, but the crown and laws of England. There were old, but unfortunate, precedents for this argument. Hugh de Spencer had used it to justify the deposition of Edward II; and the inclusion of de Spencer's speech in Hayward's *History of Henry III* had been a major prosecution theme in the unfortunate historian's trial. Its use in 1607 therefore laboured under treasonous overtones. Nevertheless, the thesis was consistent and tenable. It was confirmed by one branch of the civil law tradition.[21] Its implications of a direct personal relationship between the subject and the law, and of an unchanging law as master over the changing body natural, appealed to the English immemorialist tradition. Finally, the thesis followed logically from the 'historical philosophy of union' contained in the tracts of 1604. Their blunt contrast between unions in the person of the king only and unions in law, offices, privileges etc. implied a link between naturalisation and the body politic.

The theory was above all convenient as the basis for opposition. James, as king of two nations, had one body natural but two bodies politic, and two allegiances. Scots were not subject to him as King of England, and could not under common law have privileges or office in England. This argument appeared in the Paper Booke, very briefly,[22] but its first use in the Commons was by Wentworth, on February 17, during 'a long and learned dispute . . . touching Naturalization . . . the whole labour of this Day'.[23] 'They acknowledge no Crown, no King, no Sovereignty, but that of Scotland; we none, but that of England — A Difference between the Person Natural and Royal . . . Not Rex Angliae et Scotiae; but, Rex Angliae, et Rex Scotiae . . . Subject to him *that is* King of England; but not subject to the King of England.' Wentworth was particularly at pains to argue *against* the popular belief in English suzerainty over Scotland — because this would, as he explained very clearly to the House, effectively concede naturalisation. Scotland *was* by rights an inferior dominion; but she had not given homage since the thirteenth century, and was therefore ineligible for naturalisation.

It was to this speech that Bacon's exposition was addressed, in the hope of returning debate to the point of conveniency. He was unsuccessful. Owen's statements of precedency gave way to speeches by Holt, Hedley and Carew stressing the theory of allegiance to the body politic.[24] Each emphasised the contrast between subordinate unions (conquests and consolidations) and equal unions of sovereign states seen in the tracts. Holt and Carew dismissed examples of *de iure* naturalisations in Ireland, Gascony etc. as inapt, while Hedley more interestingly urged James to unite the bodies politic, declaring Scotland a conquered or consolidated dominion. Each spoke of the dangers they faced by speaking, and the need for free speech.

The House now came under further pressure from the Lords for conference, and agreed on the 20th to speed debates towards that end.[25] This was followed by urgent discussion on procedure. Supporters of the Instrument again tried to turn debate to the principle of naturalisation. The majority however urged a decision on the point of law as the first priority. Strode and Twysden pressed for an immediate decision by vote of the full House, Wingfield for consultation with the Lords and judges, Cotton for consultation with the civil lawyers. Eventually, a committee was established to ripen the issue in law and report back — as Martin had already urged on the 19th.[26] The antiquarians Cotton and Tate were instructed to prepare a paper on the legal question.[27]

On February 23, Brock reported the committee's expected decision against *de iure* naturalisation; and the Commons correspondingly informed the Lords of their agreement to consider that point only. The conference was appointed for the 25th.

Both Houses prepared diligently. The Lords submitted the question to the judges, for an opinion. The Commons established in committee on February 24 a scheme for argument, with an impressive list of propounders including seven common lawyers, five civil lawyers and a dozen or so 'Gentlemen of Other Quality'. Leading members were assigned specific points of argument, with others briefed simply 'to give their best Assistance, upon Occasions offered'.[28]

3. Conference

The Great Conference on naturalisation duly assembled on February 25 in the Painted Chamber. Its deliberations covered two days, Moore's report occupying twelve pages in *Somers Tracts*.[29] Only an outline can be included here. The format was less that of a discussion, with exchanges of views and interjections, than of a trial. It began with a lengthy presentation by the Commons, introduced by Bacon. Bacon rejected the reference in the proclamation changing the royal style to the *ipso facto* expiry of diverse laws as an opinion given only by those 'skilfull in laws' rather than actual judges sitting *in camera*.[30] He then divided the presentation into two categories, Inducement and Proof. The former comprised background arguments from common reason, the 'law of nations', historical precedent and the civil law; the latter examined common law itself.

The Inducement was presented by Sandys, Owen and Bennett. Sandys drew seven reasons from the law of nations against *de iure* naturalisation. The first was a general assertion that while subjection 'may remain in the general to one head . . . the manner of it is locally circumscribed to the places whereof they are brought forth, and those of one place do not, nor should partake of the discipline, privileges and birthright of the other'.[31] Other countries naturalised not by general law but individual charters; while the Romans had four degrees of naturalisation, granting all of which would be 'over-liberal'. He alleged that Scots law did not allow for automatic naturalisation of English *Post-Nati* and that Scots *Post-Nati* would by naturalisation have citizenship without payment of English impositions or taxes. The case might provide a precedent for other unions where commonalty of privileges would disrupt settled government. Finally, all reasons for naturalisation of the *Post-Nati* (security, strength, safety) applied also to the *Ante-Nati*; since the latter were not *de iure* naturalised, the former too must be aliens. Sandys hints at compromise, Scots being neither accounted as aliens nor fully as English subjects.

Owen then examined continental precedents, pointing to the Roman naturalisation by charters,[32] and the naturalisation by parliamentary act in

France and Scotland under Francis II and Mary Stuart. The only precedent for *de iure* naturalisation, Castile and Aragon, was dismissed as a reunion, and therefore inapplicable. The civil lawyer, Sir John Bennett, cited two points. The first was the civil law maxim, 'cum duo jura concurrunt in una persona aequum est ac si essent in diversis'. Two deaneries held by the same dean remained separate estates. The Duke of Brabant and Holland, holding the earldoms of Flanders and Artois from France, might legally conclude alliance between his duchy and England. The second point was the civil law doctrine of conquest right — demonstrating the civil law basis of the 'historical philosophy of union'. Bennett distinguished between conquests and consolidations, involving a communication of privileges, and peaceful unions between sovereign states.

The Lords answered this 'Inducement' dismissively. Ellesmere quoted references in the proclamation on the style and the Act of Recognition to 'one imperial crown'.[33] Any doubt should therefore be resolved in favour of naturalisation. Northampton gave a lengthy, far-flown analogy of union with the human body, James being the soul. One body could not have two souls. Salisbury considered 'Inducement' to be irrelevant, the question concerning only the common law. This returned the initiative to the five common lawyers from the Lower House, assigned to 'Proofs'.

Their argument again asserted the theme of allegiance to the body politic. Stress was laid upon the statute of 25 Edward III known as *De Natis Ultra Mare*. This act, regulating the royal succession and the inheritance rights of those born overseas or beyond English allegiance, had been debated in the 1590s over James's title to England. It also defined a 'subject'. To quote Cowell, it provided that 'A man born out of the land, so as it be within the limits of the King's obedience, beyond the sease, or of English parents out of the King's obedience . . . is no alien in account, but a subject to the King'.[34] The Common lawyers pointed to its use of phrase, 'out of the legeance of England' — linking allegiance to the body politic. They also argued: that since Scots *Post-Nati* were not subject to English laws, they should not benefit from the same; that English laws did not extend to Scotland, and therefore could not naturalise Scots; that the Great Seal, by which law was conveyed, had no force in Scotland, and therefore that Scots could not own English lands or be answerable to the Seal. Carew rejected precedents for *de iure* naturalisation — notably a Gascon, Prior Shels, in the time of Edward III — as inappropriate: Gascony, like Ireland, Aquitaine and Angois, being then a subordinate dominion, subject to English laws and the Great Seal.[35] The last three arguments used were the 'inconveniences' of naturalisation, the impossibility of obeying two ligeances or two laws, and a statute (14 Edward III) declaring that while Edward was also King of France, Englishmen were subject to him only as King of England.

The Commons' presentation occupied the 25th, the Judges retiring, as it were to consider their 'verdict' for the morrow. In fact, an opinion favouring *de iure* naturalisation had already been given to the Lords, on the 24th.[36] The Commons probably knew of this: certainly they had briefed their representatives only to listen to the Judge's, and not dispute.

Of the dozen judges present, only one was known to favour the Commons' Case.[37] Three — Popham, Fleming and Coke — monopolised the talking.[38] Their opinion contradicted the Commons. Allegiance followed the body natural, not the body politic. Laws did not govern allegiance; the sovereignty of the king, itself an expression of allegiance, instead underlay the establishment of law. Allegiance was owed where there was no law, where the crown was usurped, or where the king vacated his realm (for example on campaign) with certain of his subjects. A king with several kingdoms might call on any subject to defend any of his lands. Allegiance was thus before, after, and beyond the law.

The judges followed this constitutional theme by individually refuting the Commons' 'Proofs'. Statutes were cited relating allegiance to the king himself rather than to the body politic. The other parts of *De Natis Ultra Mare* were examined, and dismissed as inapplicable. Gascony and Ireland were considered 'free and divided states in their law and government'.[39] Precedents for *de iure* naturalisation from these lands, such as Prior Shiels' Case, therefore stood. Other examples were added, for example of men of Calais inheriting English lands in Edward III's reign. Methods of pleading were also invoked: those disabling a man in court: as alien must not only prove he was born 'extra obedientiam domini regis' but 'assign a place where he was born infra obedientiam of some other king'. The Great Seal might convey law (by writs), or command persons. If the former was bounded by legal jurisdictions, the preceptory powers extended to the person and not the place of the recipient. The civil law maxim 'cum duo jura etc.' of Bennett applied in common law only to matters of real property, not personal privilege. Scots owning estates in England would be subject to English laws and taxes for those possessions. Finally, they dismissed the distinction between allegiance *quatenus* King of Scotland and King of England as 'never heard of in the books of our law'.[40]

4. Search for New Arguments: Emergence of the 'Perfect Union'

Gardiner believed that the Commons had had the best of the allegiance debate, Sandys making broad statements of principle and the Lords replying only with 'technical arguments'. In fact and practice, the judges' opinion made opposition to naturalisation very much more difficult, and dangerous. There were few options. The Commons might accept the natural status of the *Post-Nati*, and pass the declaratory act — or accept, and turn their opposition to the point of conveniency. They could pass a bill de-naturalising the *Post-Nati* — but this was most unlikely to receive royal approval! If they rejected the judges' opinion, they had only two options: to delay the issue by argument, in the hope of securing limitations on Scots privileges in England, or pass their own judicial opinion against the *Post-Nati*. Such an opinion might carry weight in a court of law, should the crown seek to prove the point in a test case.

The Commons juggled these opinions for several days after conference. With

Bacon absent a day through sickness, it was March 2 before he was able to complete his long report to the House.[41] Their mood was uncertain. Wingfield wrote to Salisbury on March 4 believing that the Commons would give way both on the point of law and the principle of naturalisation — in return for 'reservations of some natural, needful conditions, and these but for a time'.[42] The Lords certainly pressed their advantage, asking for renewed conference on 'naturalisation in general'. The Commons baulked, promising only consideration and the earliest answer possible.[43] Various emergency motions were advanced. Fuller correctly argued that the judges' opinion, *ex camera*, had no legal force. He urged the Commons, as a superior 'judicial' institution, to declare in writing its own opinion.[44] Hyde, by contrast, regarded the legal point as lost, and pressed for a disabling (de-naturalising) act. At length, it was decided to reject the judges' opinion, but accept conference only on the conveniency of naturalising *Ante-* and *Post-Nati* alike. Three days of discussion ensued, tactical messages being exchanged with the Lords on the terms of the next conference. On March 3, the Lower House submitted consideration of terms to a sub-committee, informing the Lords that they would confer on 'naturalisation in general' only as the House understood the phrase — 'touching Naturalization of the *Ante-Nati* and the *Post-Nati*, and of the Conveniency of it, and for such Limitations and Restraints as might be fit for both'.[45] The Lords replied urging speed, and repeating their intention to discuss *all* the issues raised by the Instrument and Conference. Matters became even more complicated on the 4th, with a second message to the Lords through Hoby. This followed renewed pressure from Poole and others for a declaration on the point of law, diverted by Recorder Montague.[46] The Lords found this second message extremely suspicious. It contained an explicit refusal to confer on the point of law, and restatement of their opinion against *de iure* naturalisation. It asked the Lords to make the first move; and it included references to the Commons as a 'court', containing 'barons'. The Lords immediately picked up these points. They demanded assurance that the Commons would confer as well as listen — reiterating that the conference would bind neither Chamber. They condemned the quasi-judicial aspirations of the Commons, expressed in 'court' and 'barons'. The Lower House had no barons, the Lords argued, and formed only the lesser half of the single High Court of Parliament.[47]

How seriously these aspirations were meant is questionable. Wingfield interpreted the message as a reference to the barons of the Cinque Ports, and the House's accepted function as a Court of Record. The Lords' reaction is more interesting, indicating their fears of a legal declaration by the Commons. Such a declaration would have entailed a major constitutional crisis, which the Lower House was unlikely to win. In the event, the Commons were content with inconclusive debate about 'barons', on March 5, and a message accepting conference on the Lords' terms for March 7. The Commons' Great Committee, which had already met on the 4th, reconvened two days later to prepare the Commons case.

It was on the morning of March 7 that the committee reported to the

Commons the arguments proposed for that afternoon's conference. The reporter was Sandys — and it was he who took the lead over the next week in pressing the new theme.

This theme was the 'perfect union', and its central argument was the inequity of naturalising any Scots before a legal union. This argument had been advanced sporadically in February, notably by Owen (February 18), Hedley (19th) and the civil lawyer Frances James (23rd). Bacon had considered it dangerous enough for answer in his February 17 speech.[48] Only on March 7, however, did it emerge in full form. Naturalisation would admit Scots to the benefits of English law, yet Scotland would remain under an alien legal system. The Commons had no wish to resist union. They had always desired an absolute unity involving the institutions of government as well as the laws. This would eliminate the inconveniences of the 'imperfect union' proposed in the Instrument — a union which gave privileges to the Scots without attendant responsibilities. Extending these benefits now would remove the incentive from the Scots for further union; they should rather impose restraints on the holding of real possessions, offices and preferments, to keep up the Scots' appetite. A new Union Commission was needed, with the perfect political and legal union as its brief. Finally, the failure to achieve perfect union was blamed upon the Scots Act of Commission, preventing discussion of the fundamental laws or free institutions of Scotland.[49]

The perfect union formed the mainstay of Commons resistance during the remainder of the naturalisation debates. It would be premature to consider the theme in depth, at this stage. Nevertheless, several points stand out. The first is its convenience to anybody opposed to naturalisation. They might appear better unionists than the Commission, equal in ardour to James himself. The speeches of James and Bacon were thrown back in their faces. This made the line difficult for the government to counter, and cut down the apparent potentiality for acrimonious confrontation. The perfect union equally entailed delay in all short-term moves towards unity. The Scots 'blame' for lack of progress could be used to justify the expressions of prejudice and hostility in the speeches of many M.P.s. To many government supporters, this convenience was proof positive of ill-intent — the project being but 'a stratagem, to evade and do nothing'.[50] Certainly, the support of men like Fuller for the perfect union, after years of consistent opposition to the most minimal unionist proposal, raised grave doubts about the sincerity of the project.[51]

Nevertheless, the perfect union fitted consistently into the line taken by the Commons on allegiance and naturalisation. If allegiance lay to the body politic as the Commons had decided, legal union would automatically bring united allegiances, and *de iure* naturalisation — without a specific enabling act. The perfect union similarly connected logically with the 'historical philosophy of union' — which Sandys indeed used in his report. Sandys distinguished two types of union: one where the kingdoms remained separate under one head, with no union in offices, laws or government, the other an absolute consolidation. No compromise was possible. The 'perfect union', while not justifiable normally in a peaceful union of sovereign states, was the only alternative allowing naturalisation. Finally, the reverence of early Jacobeans for the law, as the unchanging soul of the body politic governing all aspects of public and private behaviour, can be seen in action in the connection drawn by M.P.s between the privilege of naturalisation and subjection to the law. We must also remember Savile's reference to common lawyers demanding legal union as a *sine qua non* of reconciliation between the nations.[52] To some, 'perfect union' was undoubtedly a pretext for resistance. To others, it was the only justifiable form of union.

Whether the limitations proposed by the Commons on March 7 were the cause or effect of the perfect union project, their extent was considerable. One major target was the Auld Alliance, with renewed calls to end Scots commercial privileges and naturalisation in France. This attack was led by Nevill.[53] The Alliance was called 'the back door to let in what poison their French sweetheart list spit upon us', and there was much dark comment about Gentlemen of James's Bedchamber in the French king's 'Scots Guard'.[54] The other main exercise detailed statutory limitations proposed on Scots possession of real property, offices, ecclesiastical preferments etc. For real possessions, Scots might inherit and purchase all goods, lands etc., but must not enrich Scotland at England's expense by transporting bullion home to Scotland. Scots owning lands and goods in England must pay the same taxes as the English, and be personally liable under English law as if resident in the country.[55] Francis Moore was particularly concerned about Scots holding wardships of English minors, insisting on their education in England.[56] Stringent conditions were demanded by Bennett in respect of Scots holding ecclesiastical places. Higher positions (for example bishoprics) and offices like chancellors and commissaries exercising canon law should be closed entirely; a Scot would need an M.A. (in an English university) to be liable for any benefice, a B.Div. for a canonry or deanery. No more than a tenth of England's benefices must be in the hands of Scots, at any one time. The restrictions on civil offices were the most extreme, Sir George Moore and Sir Anthony Cope pressed for J.P.s, sheriffs, under-sheriffs, coroners and escheators to be reserved, as 'offices of Iudicature'. There also survives a much more comprehensive list of reserved posts.[57] These cover an enormous range: temporal offices of state and government (Privy Councillor, Secretary of State, Clerk of Council, High and Under-Treasurer, Receivers, tellers), of judicature (Chancellor, judges of either bench, barons of Exchequer, justices of assize and the Court of Wards), of attendance at court (Chamberlain, Comptroller, Treasurer, Marshall) and so on. The clear intention was to eliminate *all* Scots office-holding in England, 'until the perfect union'. To prevent the king dispensing with the law by *Non Obstante*, a prohibition would be laid on the person receiving the preferment!

All this was reported to the Commons in the morning and related at the conference.[58] The Lords were bemused. Salisbury, Northampton and Ellesmere talked of the union's honour generally, for safety and defence.[59] They then 'arose, giving at that time no Answere, or Resolution, nor Opinion in any part'. Holles interpreted this as keeping 'themselves within their trenches and strength, out of which they will not sally without assured advantage'.[60] In fact, the bold assertion of the perfect union and the severe restrictions proposed until its achievement had left the Commons temporarily with the upper hand. After agreeing to a conference on March 11, the Lords were forced to request deferment to the 14th while they discussed the situation. The debates in the Commons, notably on the 12th, simply reiterated existing themes. For conference, they would listen to the Lords' response, 'but not . . . yield to them'.[61]

The conference of March 14 shows how far the Lords would go to accommodate the Commons — or perhaps, how far they were motivated covertly by the same fears and desires.[62] 'To a casual observer . . . it would seem that the Lords were making an effort to meet the Commons halfway.'[63] Salisbury agreed the reservations on ecclesiastical preferments (except for the one-tenth limit, which violated the royal prerogative), on wardships, and on J.P.s. He also accepted the need for some restraint on bullion. This advance towards a settlement was however ended precipitately by a speech from Sandys. At first sight, this termination is curious. Sandys simply rehearsed the themes of March 7 and 12, including reference to the special trust of the Commons as a representative assembly, the dangers of wholesale naturalisation, and the need for a perfect union. The real point of breach was however his insistence that 'if your Lordships will not give us leave to handle the *Ante-Nati* and the *Post-Nati* both alike, we will humbly give your Lordships Audience, but not any answers'.[64]

Notestein considered this 'the boldest refusal to cooperate with the Upper House that the Commons of that generation had ever made'.[65] This is an exaggeration. The Commons position had been clear since February. Nevertheless, it was this 'refusal' which led Salisbury to break off the conference, demanding a wider commission from the Commons.[66] On reflection, there is an obvious explanation. Salisbury would continue discussion as long as the likely result went further towards naturalisation than was already conceded under common law. Sandys's insistence on making the reservations a permanent, statutory feature, applying to the *Post-Nati* as well as the *Ante-Nati*, thereby offering less than the former already had by right, made continuation of the conference meaningless.

5. 'Gradual Union' v. 'Perfect Union'

The conference was followed by a fortnight in which there was no parliamentary discussion of union, except for Salisbury's report to the Lords on March 19. The reason for this interval lay in the absence of the Speaker, through illness; without him, the Commons did not sit. However, this initially genuine illness was artificially extended by a letter from Salisbury. The Secretary informed Phellips of a move in the Commons 'to get some such definitive sentence pass[ed] . . . of the invalidity of the Judges' Resolution, as may make them daynty herafter to judge the question, or make the judgement less acceptable'.[67] It is clear from the letter that the initiative for the delay came from James, reflecting royal fears — and that Salisbury was doubtful whether any such resolution was really contemplated. The growing royal anxiety and exasperation this implies is confirmed by diplomatic sources. By this time, James's initial 'determination'[68] had waned considerably: 'The King complains bitterly that his advisers, by representing the achievement of the Union as an easy affair, have committed him to a labyrinth, in which his honour is involved'.[69] James's complaints were made after the resumption of the English session. The renewed debates contained hints of a legal declaration, not carried into action, while the Lords' message of March 27 pressing for a full and liberal conference met immediate resistance.[70] The message demanded separate discussion of the *Ante-* and *Post-Nati*, implying submission to the judges' opinion on the point of law. Debate correspondingly ran high on whether to agree to a conference, and upon what terms.[71] On the 27th, Hyde spoke powerfully against a separation, proposing instead a new commission to perfect the union. 'I do assure myself, that the King's desire and Ours is all one, namely, to worke the Perfect Union . . . by a Subiection to the same lawes'.[72] Hyde insisted on an end to Scots private jurisdictions and powers of pardon, and more generally implied the submission of Scots to English common law in the 'perfect union'. The speech is typical in its attitudes. Overwhelmingly, the proponents of the 'perfect union' saw it in Anglocentric terms, of Scotland accepting English laws and institutions. This can be seen in its earliest expressions, such as Owen's speech of February 18 — and can of course be linked with consolidation, English 'suzerainty' over Scotland and general assumptions of superiority. Levack distinguishes between the Anglocentric union proposed by Sandys or Hyde, and the synthetic or compromise union supported by civil law supporters of the perfect union, such as James.[73] There is no evidence, however, that James shared the enthusiasm of Albericus Gentilis or Cowell for a synthetic union.[74] The predominant attitude of Members towards Scots law would seem to be one of dismissal — as one would have expected.[75]

Hyde's speech was followed by two days of uninterrupted debate about conference. Carleton, Barkley and Wingfield pressed for conference — the first accepting the separation between *Ante-* and *Post-Nati*, the others not. Owen, Duncombe and Crofts opposed conference, Crofts in particular presenting the perfect union as a venture easy to achieve. His proposal for further debate in effect meant delaying conference indefinitely — since the Easter Recess was impending. Owen's suggested approach to the king, protesting the sincerity of the perfect union, had the same practical implications. Debate continued on March 30, with an increasing number of speakers urging deferment.

Of the speeches for conference, the most able was by Bacon, on March 28,[76] providing the 'government' answer to the perfect union Bacon mentioned in his longstanding support for a legal union, a fine and heroical work requiring digestion of both English and Scots law. But such unity was not essential for naturalisation; many other countries combined one allegiance and sovereignty with separate legal systems. The perfect union would take time to achieve, during which English and Scots would become habituated to separation. By contrast, naturalisation was a step forwards, towards perfect union. In short, Bacon countered 'perfect union' with James's own project for 'gradual union', working steadily towards political and legal integration with the full consent of both peoples at each stage.

This introduced James's own speech on March 31, adjourning parliament.[77] In a long audience, the king answered every major objection to the Instrument, and defined his attitude to the perfect union. This had provided many quotations for political historians. To those who alleged either Scots resistance to or gross eagerness for the union, he replied at length:

> This I must say for Scotland, and I may truly vaunt it; here I sit, and govern it with my Pen; I write, and it is done; and by a Clerk of the Council I govern Scotland now, which others could not do by the Sword. And for their Averseness in their Heart against the Union; it is true indeed . . . they did never crave this Union of me, nor sought it, either in private, or the State, by Letters, not even did one of that Nation press me forward, or wish me to accelerate that Business; but on the other part, they offered always to obey me, when it should come to them . . . I know there are many Piggots amongset them, I mean a Number of seditious and discontented particular Persons . . . but no Scottshmen ever spake dishonourable of England in Parliament. For here must I note unto you the Difference of the Two Parliaments in the Two Kingdoms: For there they must not speak without the Chancellor's Leave.

This picture of a subservient Scots parliament was not calculated to increase desire for union among English M.P.s, especially given James's opinion that a mean between the parliaments would do well![78] In other respects, James went far to meet English fears and demands. He denied allegations of partiality, pointing out that he had not generally preferred Scots to civil or ecclesiastical positions. He promised an end after union to the Auld Alliance,[79] cited reasons against a 'flood of Scots', and praised the peace, security and love brought by union to the Middle Shires. His treatment of the perfect union was very gentle. After referring to the length of time taken in the session — with 'many Crosses, long Disputations, strange Questions, and nothing done' — he declared himself not only in favour of local union, but of one reflecting predominantly English practices.[80] English law would 'conquer' Scotland, and a united parliament would make Scots law conform to English statute. England was the greater part of the new kingdom, the husband to Scotland's wife. The royal residence, court, seat of justice and government would all lie in England. Having thus laid bare his long-term union strategy in terms very flattering to the English sense of precedency, James made it equally clear that perfect union must be achieved gradually, and by mutual consent.[81] If union was a marriage, it did not start by throwing the couple together into bed! By sounding these notes of caution, James secured the honour of Scotland as well as his own position. He further emphasised the rights of Scotland by stating that a perfect union must nevertheless leave her 'those particular privileges that may stand as well with this union as in England many particular customs in particular shires'.

It was an admirable speech, as even Gardiner sourly admitted.[82] French and Venetian ambassadors alike commented favourably, de la Boderie believing that a proposal submitted with the speech might have been easily passed. The oration, suitably amended by the inclusion of ideas from Bacon's speech,[83] was hurried out in pamphlet form, during the recess, as propaganda.[84]

James's gentle treatment of the Commons probably reflected hope, almost against hope, of the sincerity of the perfect union project. For four years he had sought gradual advance towards just such a goal. The time was not ripe for a giant leap towards perfect union — especially if this meant foregoing the immediate progress that could be made by enactment of the Instrument. The passage of such acts, accompanied by a further commission for the perfect union, might be a major step forward, however, and worth fostering.

It was his last attempt to secure naturalisation through parliament. Despite the speech, James's patience was wearing thin; he was openly alleging collusion between the Houses, blaming his counsellors for misrepresenting the achievement of union as an easy matter, and threatening to implement the project by prerogative powers.[85]

6. The Final Days

Parliament re-assembled on April 27. By May 2, the naturalisation debates had come to an abrupt end. The intervening days had seen rapid deterioration in the relations between King and Commons, and increasing animosity within the Lower House. The central feature was the continuation of pressure for the perfect union, and refusal to concede naturalisation as an interim measure. Consideration of the union was moved on the 27th by Sir Francis Barrington — at the instigation of the Speaker, who was urgently seeking directions from Salisbury about forthcoming debates.[86] The initiative however passed quickly to the opponents of naturalisation, with a speech by Sandys on the 28th. This rejected the possibility of conference, proposing instead a bill to establish a new commission. This would consider the perfect union: one parliament, one criminal law, uniformity in the administration of justice, one Great Seal, one Chancellor, etc. The motion to introduce this bill astonished Phellips, who called for debate to be limited to the question of conference. The Speaker was overruled. Croft defended Sandys, firmly rejecting allegations that the perfect union was a diversionary tactic.[87] His assertion of candour was repeated by other speakers on April 29-30. As a proof of sincerity, there were offers to draft bills for restricted naturalisation, to become void in four years if no perfect union was forthcoming.[88] But the 'restrictions' were not made clear. These proposals split the 'Sandysian' ranks. Wentworth openly opposed the idea of parliamentary union. Yelverton too opposed Hyde's plan, seeing abolition of hostile laws as the only step possible this session. Fuller was happier speaking *against* the immediate extension of privileges to the Scots even by restricted naturalisation than *for* the perfect union commission. His speech was typically apocalyptic, opposing both conference and a bill for restricted naturalisation: 'When the Parliament is done, the Judges . . . will they not also tell us that our Law for Restrictions will not binde the Prerogative?'[89] Brooke on the 30th showed similar fear of the judges, that they might give a verdict leaving the *Post-Nati* naturalised without limitations. Several speakers insisted that the perfect union could not be offensive to James, being his project. Owen was particularly effective here, reciting the slogans of the 'Unite' coinage back at the king. Like Holt and others, he presented perfect union as an easy venture, entailing no dishonour to the Lords or to the Commissioners of 1604.

Speeches for the perfect union do little to resolve the question of its sincerity. Many eloquently defended their motives. Others, like Wentworth, Yelverton and Fuller seem to have adopted the idea to delay naturalisation. In the middle lies the ambivalence of supporters like Alford: 'Although by Union wee shall reape no Profitt, nor have no Quid pro quo, yet if they come to our lawes, they become ourselves, and wee give to men of ourselves, which wilbe an answer to the Countrey and satisfaction to our Consciences'.[90] This statement reveals perfectly the Anglocentric assumptions of its proponents, and their conservative view of law and its links with personal life.

Government supporters were quick to demonstrate the contradictions within the 'Sandysian' ranks. Marten commented acerbically on the changes in Fuller's position on the union. Carleton questioned the feasibility of the project, as a whole. 'I wish not the perfect Union, first because it is not likely to be effected . . . The Commissioners you say shall be provided against these Inconveniences, I ask you How? Why, it must be by Restrictions, and then it is not perfect.'[91] Innumerable precedents were cited for imperfect unions. Perfect union would take time, action was needed *now*. Bacon asked if 'all this time be spent to repeale a dead law or renew a commission?' Hobart agreed: 'If in these three yeares wee have done nothing in the Imperfect Union, surely in three tymes three yeares wee shall doe nothing in the perfect'.[92] Wingfield, Montague and Doddridge each emphasised the need to advance gradually, by steps — the Instrument being but one of the stages. Doddridge urged bills for hostile laws and commerce, and for naturalisation of *Ante-* and *Post-Nati* alike with 'suitable' restrictions.[93] All those favouring conference saw the perfect union as a digression, several implicitly questioning the professed good intentions of the propounders. Wingfield simply condemned 'The speaking of a general Union now . . . [as] the only way to hinder a general Union for ever'.

No progress in any direction seemed likely in the House. On April 29, a motion for conference was rejected in favour of further discussion; yet on the 30th and 1st, support for the perfect union waned before strong 'government' pressure. Eventually, a message was received from James announcing his intention of making a second speech.

James's speech of May 2 was not so much 'petulant'[94] as extremely angry. The Commons was infertile ground, 'barren by preconceived Opinions'.[95]

Perfect union was a long-term goal, to be achieved gradually. 'I would not have you think on that to be done To-day, that is to be done To-morrow.' His initial wish had indeed been for 'unus Rex, unus Grex, una Lex'. The restrictions on the last appeared in the English as well as Scots Acts of Commission, and reflected the demands of the English Commons.[96] He had decided to take the matter into his own hands, by prerogative powers. The speech ended bitterly:

> I am your King; I am placed to govern you, and shall answer for your Errors: I am a Man of Flesh and Blood, and have my Passions and Affections as other Men: I pray you, do not too far move me to do that which my Power may tempt me unto . . . make not all you have done, frustrate.

The spectacle of James angrily condemning the Commons for supporting the perfect union is bizarre. Even more disturbing to any neat analysis of the session is James's apparent determination to pursue a 'no-win' objective. By abruptly ending discussion in this way, James effectively ended any chance of commercial union or naturalisation being achieved through parliament. He also killed the idea of a new commission to examine the perfect union. The speech played into the hands of those who objected to union *per se*. Two factors operated here. The first is clear: after his open, conciliatory speech on March 31, James regarded continued support for an 'immediate' perfect union as proof of bad faith, and a desire to frustrate naturalisation. In this, he was at least partly justified.

The second factor was Scotland. As usual, documentary evidence for Scots attitudes and activities during the naturalisation debates is poor, almost non-existent. The historian can only rely on the Council's letter of March 3, and ambassadorial reports. It is nevertheless clear that, as in 1604, the debates in the English Commons had created resentment towards England and opposition to union in Scotland. The Council's letter had included long sections disavowing enthusiasm for union. Only their own vigilance had prevented expressions of Piggotry in Scotland, and suppressed anxieties about the project. They therefore asked James to abandon union, and naturalise the Scots by prerogative power. This letter clearly influenced James's speech of March 31.[97] Both ambassadors refer to the alienation of the Scots, Giustinian rightly believing that the Scots were being encouraged in their attitudes by the French.[98] English allegations blaming the Scots for lack of progress on union combined with the Anglocentrism of the 'perfect union' to increase resentment. This was conveyed to James by a further resolution of the Scots Council, despatched on March 24 via Balmerino.[99] It was therefore extremely unlikely that the Scots would willingly have authorised a new commission, to discuss the perfect union. Since James's strategy relied on consent, gradually cementing relations between the two countries, Sandys's project could not be realised. Once the Lower House's refusal to pass naturalisation as a first step had been demonstrated beyond possible doubt, the time had come to call a halt — before M.P.s like Fuller and Yelverton had further opportunities to poison Anglo-Scots relations.

Part Three. May-June 1607: Hostile and Border Laws

1. Introduction

James's speech marked a transition point in the 1606-7 session. It ended the prolonged and acrimonious debates about naturalisation, allegiances and the 'perfect union'. James, despairing of the open and frank display of fraternity for which he had originally sought, abandoned the naturalisation bills for a collusive court case to establish the legal status of the *Post-Nati*. The *Ante-Nati* were quietly forgotten.

However, this was by no means the end of parliamentary debate on the union in 1607 — although many historians have cursorily dismissed the following two months as a sideshow.[1] This underestimates the importance of a long, intricate and revealing debate on the abolition of hostile and Border laws. As we have seen, discussions on this part of the Instrument before Christmas 1606 had led to an agreement, reported to the Commons on February 10. This broadly accepted the Commission's proposals, approving the repeal of hostile statutes, the replacement of March Treasons and Border-Law courts by common law and ordinary justice, and a commission to settle outstanding causes. The only substantial change had been the decision to leave the alteration of hostile clauses in borough constitutions to the boroughs themselves.

A draft bill embodying this agreement was introduced to the Commons by Speaker Phellips, on May 4.[2] It was given its first reading on the same day, and its second on the 6th. Discussion was delayed by the general crisis of confidence between King and Commons. The Lower House spent much time debating the royal speech, the circumstances behind it, and their most suitable reaction. May 6 was spent examining 'how his M. was pleased . . . to tax and blame the Judgement, Discretion and good Meaning of sundry Members of the House', notably Yelverton.[3] Three demands were made: an opportunity for disfavoured Members to clear themselves, confirmation of the right to free speech, and an end to the communication of private information to the King about proceedings in the Lower House. James satisfied the second demand before any formal approach, with a message on the 7th. This did not however prevent lengthy debate about informers, Wingfield in particular being mistrusted for his support of private information.[4]

2. Early Discussions: Title, Preamble and General Clause

Initial discussions on the bill therefore proceeded against a background of mutual distrust. The debate on May 7 was notable both for its general suspicion of the bill, and for certain specific arguments. Yelverton, having made a ritual obeisance and apology to the king, roundly condemned the clause establishing a Border commission of ten Englishmen and ten Scots to clear outstanding causes.[5] Fuller attacked the title of the bill, 'for the Continewance and

Preservacon of the blessed Union', arguing that there was no union to continue. He also took exception to a reference in the bill to English and Scots being 'under one allegiance', repeating what Sir Thomas Wilson called 'that old point' of allegiance being to the crown and laws, not the king's person. Fuller feared that the phraseology of the bill was designed to prejudice the legal position in any court case on the *Post-Nati*. Yelverton went further, arguing that the bill covertly encompassed naturalisation, and even commercial union.[6]

The bill was eventually committed to the Whole House, on a motion by Brock. Initial debate in committee concentrated on the title, and the reference in the bill to abolition of other hostile laws not specifically named. Fuller's fears regarding the former gained sufficient credence for a move to make him chairman of the committee — a position eventually conceded to Bacon. General concern immediately demonstrated itself. 'They fell to mincing of the title and the preamble . . . it seemed they thought the word "Union" a spirit, for they shunned the very shadow and name of it.'[7] The title was amended to 'An Act for the utter abolition of all memory of hostility' etc., while the florid unionist phraseology of the preamble was reduced to a single reference, 'for the furtherance and advancement of the happy Union already begun in his Majesty's Royal Person'.[8] Even this required pressure from Bacon, citing references to union in previous acts and proclamations as reassurance that it would not have unwanted legal significance. The other section of the bill excised by the committee on May 8 was the clause abolishing other, unspecified hostile statutes.[9] This was considered to leave too much discretion to the judges — the unspoken implication being that they would use it to further the union.[10]

These dilutions of the Act produced a predictable reaction from James, on May 9. In the first of several messages monitoring the progress of the bill, the king accepted the excisions in general but requested compromise on certain points. On the preamble, he desired a strengthening of 'already begun' by the inclusion of the words 'settled', 'grounded' or 'inherent', emphasising his personal involvement in the project. This received detailed consideration by the committee, Poole in particular resisting the change. Eventually, it was deferred to consideration of the Commons, as a matter of great consequence. James also urged a substitute clause on abolition of other hostile statutes, indicating 'a resolucion to repeale all such lawes when they apeered unto us'. This gave control over future abolition to parliament, with no judicial discretion. Even here, James's desires were not fully met. The clause eventually agreed was retrospective, not committing future parliaments even morally to such abolition.[11] The May 11 meeting of the committee also saw a wide-ranging but rather confused debate on other aspects of the bill. Time was spent on the exact delineation of the Borders, and on the nature of 'Border law' and 'custom'. A proposal to submit the latter to a special sub-committee was only headed off as delaying an issue which the committee could itself manage. The objections to the phrase 'under one allegiance', as comprehending legally both naturalisation and commercial union, were again raised. The last part of Clause Two in the bill was correspondingly altered, English and Scots being only 'under the government of his Majesty, as under one parent and head'.[12] Even the proposal to abolish the name of the Borders was suspected.[13]

3. Remand

Despite the suspicions voiced on these clauses by the Commons, their minor alterations occasioned no great controversy with the king. The committee therefore moved on to more substantive issues, of judicial arrangements on the Borders. Attention turned particularly to the clause allowing for remand and extradition from their native country of fugitive offenders, to stand trial in the place of offence.[14] Extradition had been accepted by the English Commissioners in 1604 without enthusiasm, while its implementation during 1605-6 had led to allegations against Scots courts of excessive severity. These claims were now revived, notably over the case of the Lord of Barrow. Barrow, extradited to face fifteen charges of horse-stealing, had refused to recognise a Scots court, and accused the Scots of bias against him. James, clearly worried that such charges would reflect badly on his Border Commission, and endanger the remand clause, asked the Commons on May 17 to hear a report on the case by Sir William Seaton. This report 'gave the House good satisfaction'[15] — but only reinforced a growing belief among M.P.s that Englishmen standing trial in Scotland would be convicted out of hand. A major figure in the campaign against remanding was the Northumberland M.P., Sir Henry Widdrington, who feared that his arch-rival Selby would use remand to extradite him and his supporters to Scotland, to face almost certain death.[16] Widdrington had taken the lead very early in the month, introducing a bill against remand, allowing defendants counsel and sworn witnesses. His influence is shadowy. It is wrong to see him as the leader of a large parliamentary party of friends and clients, opposing extradition purely for factional reasons. Rather, his appeal to the rights of Englishmen and the wrongs of Scots justice had influence because of their timeliness, and because he was able to interest more important figures than himself, such as Sandys and Fuller.

On May 20, in the middle of this ongoing debate, Phellips 'came early to the house before the companie was in anie sort full and adiourned the court untill that day senight'.[17] This dramatic act caused general speculation about the king's motives. There were persistent rumours that James intended to pack the House on its return, and carry the issue on remand.[18] This was denied in a message on May 27, when the House re-assembled; James alluded to the small number of M.P.s present at previous meetings, and a bill was introduced to penalise unnecessary absences. The adjournment however remains mysterious — unless designed to hammer out a government policy on remand and extradition, before the debate in the House. Discussion came on May 28, after a report by Bacon on the bill's progress in committee. The report[19] contained an admirable summary of the arguments for and against remand. Those favouring extradition had urged the greater example that execution in the place of offence would carry, and the use of remand by the Border Commission in 1605-6. They also pointed out that only seven extraditions in four years had ended in capital sentences. This was clearly in answer to the opposition, which emphasised the severity, inequity and corruption of Scots justice. Majority juries, the trial of accessories before principals, the private hearing of prosecutor and evidence by the jury were cited, and 'the easie procuring of witnesses in Scotland'. As for example, there was more in executing the guilty amongst his family and friends. Various compromises had been suggested, permitting remand in cases of hot pursuit or after a judicial examination. One speaker had suggested joint juries of English and Scots. Bacon concluded his report with a call for conference with the Lords. The debate in the House however turned rapidly against remand, Owen especially repeating further arguments used in committee against extradition, alleging that it was no part of any existing law, and pointing to differences in the definition of felonies in the two countries. Notwithstanding eloquent persuasion by Phellips, Sandys secured a motion requiring the committee to examine a form of justice not involving remand. This the committee did — despite a petition for extradition on May 29 launched by Selby, Widdrington's rival, and involving such important figures as the Earl of Cumberland and the Bishop of Durham. Remand was definitely rejected, in committee on June 1. Yelverton protested that remand might still be established, by royal dispensation of the Act under *Non Obstante*. The committee therefore inserted a clause making it a felony to remand and extradite an offender.

By this time, Yelverton's presence seems to have been regarded by James as a personal affront. Certainly, the king lost no time in expressing his displeasure at the new clause, despatching a message through the Speaker on June 2.[20] This admitted a desire to keep remand, but accepted the Commons' decision against extradition and promised not to dispense with the prohibition clause. He regarded the provision for punishment of remanders as heinous, however, showing jealousy and mistrust of the king. If the new provision were not removed, he *would* dispense with it by *Non Obstante*, and continue remand through the Commission. He further threatened that continued opposition would bring retribution after the end of parliament.

The concessions in this message were marked by patent ill-temper — the work of a weary and rather disillusioned man, which is certainly the verdict of the French and Venetian ambassadors: 'The King is now forced to desire the Union not only because it is useful, but also for his own reputation . . . some of the popular leaders show such hardness that everyone wishes his Majesty had kept out of it, as it is evident that this business breeds temper in the King and in both nations'.[21] However, the aim of the message has been much misunderstood. Watts and Watts regard it as an attempt to preserve remand, so alienating the Commons as to make the prohibition on extradition a certainty. This is inaccurate. The case for remand was already lost. James addressed his message to the penalties clause only, and was successful in having this removed from the bill.

4. Witnesses

By early June, the Commons were moving onto other aspects of judicial procedure on the Borders. This provided the last major area of controversy before passage of the bill. Discussion began in committee on May 29.[22] Several minor matters were first debated, involving some practical reconciliation of English and Scots procedures. It was agreed that English accessories to crimes committed in Scotland would be tried as principals, since the main culprits might be over the Border. (Common law would not allow trial of the accessory before the principal.) Cases in England involving offences in Scotland would contain no benefit of clergy, limited peremptory challenge of jurors (five rather than the usual twenty), and limited penalties (loss of life and goods, but not corruption of blood or forfeiture of estates). Sandys moved for Scots tried in England to have advocates and counsel, as they would in their own courts. 'He wold wish that liberty permitted all over England.' This was condemned by Attorney-General Hobart as too radical, and deferred until union in Scots and English law had been achieved. Sandys's motion followed the line in Widdrington's draft; and on June 3, Fuller likewise echoed the draft bill in pressing successfully for defendants in Border cases to be allowed witnesses, on oath, whom juries might not disregard. Sandys and Hobart were alike dubious here, the former advancing some qualifications to the clause.

Apart from some time on June 4 debating (and rejecting) James's earlier demand for a strengthening in the preamble, and confirming the committee's amended title for the bill, the House now turned wholly to the question of witnesses.[23] This reflected another royal message, condemning Fuller's clause as an encouragement to malefactors. James also denied that sworn witnesses were a part of existing Scots law. The king's message came initially to the committee, sparking off a debate in which Fuller and Jones defended the witnesses clause vigorously. Fuller pointed out that witnesses for the prosecution would frequently be sworn enemies of the defendant, or worse still Scots. The issue was eventually referred to the House, and debated at length on June 5.[24] Supporters of the clauses argued that the laws of God allowed witnesses, that sworn witnesses could be justified under existing common law, that they were already admitted in cases of 'Appeal' (where the injured party or relatives instituted proceedings), and that the law allowed witnesses in noncapital cases. To deny sworn defence witnesses meant 'putting the life of an Englishman uppon the Oath of a Scott'.[25] The opponents, led by Queen's Attorney Hitcham and by Montague, protested alteration to the fundamental laws of England, and saw the ban on witnesses as a *quid pro quo* for defence challenge of jurors. Both sides argued that their proposals were more in line with Scots law and procedures, and this was a major factor in debate, the Commons on June 4 examining a detailed paper on Scots criminal procedure.[26] The paper was ambivalent on witnesses, which could only be called at the jury's discretion, rarely exercised.

Various compromises were suggested during debate, including one by Hobart allowing for the exercise of jural discretion, which was rejected, since 'the Law already leaveth to the Jury's discretion the admitting or rejecting of such testimony'.[27] Feeling turned against the royal message, Yelverton even advancing a motion asking James to refrain from future communication with his Commons. Eventually, the move to amend the clause was narrowly lost (139 votes to 106). The bill was now, for the Commons, complete. On June 6, it was engrossed and sent to the Lords.

5. Negotiation and Modification

Some have described the latter days of the session as being a time of great tension and hostility between the two Houses.[28] The four weeks of negotiation and modification between the chambers before the passage of the bill do not really demonstrate any such bitter resentment. It is equally true that Lords and Commons were far from agreed about the measure, the Lords working to achieve a settlement closer to the original draft of May 4. The atmosphere was rather one of guarded respect, and awareness that the issue could create animosity. The 'ample and honourable Testimony . . . of the Gravity and Care of the [Lower] House in their Proceeding' given by the Lords on passage of the bill[29] was much more than a formality, and seems very close to simple truth.

The Lords were quick both to examine the amended bill and discover their differences with the Commons. The bill was read once on June 6, and sent into committee two days later after another reading. On the 7th, their doubts and desires for a conference were communicated to the Commons. Conference was fixed for June 11 — a major gathering, with fifty peers and a select committee of the Commons that included every important figure.[30] Bacon's report to the Commons on the 12th[31] revealed the Lords' doubts. The peers were worried that the bill might affect the trial of their own estate, and be extended to cases of treason. The latter should in their view be tried in the capital, with no defence right to challenge the jury or call witnesses. Salisbury and Northampton had then re-opened the entire question of witnesses, arguing that the clause in the bill would create complexity of evidence and a multitude of defence witnesses. Salisbury urged discretion for juries not to admit witnesses they considered 'unfit'. The Commons debated these three differences on June 13. It was agreed that the trial of peers should not be affected by the bill. Similarly, the Commons were at first unanimous that the bill should not extend to treason cases. On witnesses, however, the Lower House proved intransigent, Yelverton and Brooke bitterly denouncing the Lords' suggestion. Brooke was selected to prepare an answer to the Lords, for the committee's approval.

The events of the next week are difficult to reconstruct, from sparse records in the Commons' Journal and in Bowyer's diary. There was a second conference, on June 15. The Commons' representatives were commissioned to give way on treason, but not witnesses. The result was an unsatisfactory, rambling discussion, spilling over onto other issues like the Spanish Merchants and Jesuits. No agreement was reached. However, the Speaker after debate on the 16th informed Salisbury quietly that the Commons might accept a clause on witnesses, allowing juries discretion not to call them upon oath.[32] This was not, as Watts would have it, a *quid pro quo* for remanding.[33] It was not in fact a covert offer of any kind, but Phellip's private estimation of the Commons' feelings. This opinion was however influential in the preparation of amendments by the Upper Chamber. These were reported to the Lords on June 23 by Ellesmere, approved, and engrossed with the main bill. The whole was then read a third time on June 25, passed, and sent to the Commons for debate.

Some amendments were minor and phraseological, for example on the prohibition of extradition.[34] The main amendments were to exclude treason from the scope of the Act, and to give juries discretion over defence witnesses.[35] Despite previous acceptance of the former, and the Speaker's message, the Commons resisted both proposals. The objection on treason came from Fuller, who believed that its exclusion from the Act might lead to remanding of traitors for extradition. This was elaborated in committee, which eventually decided to include a separate clause specifically prohibiting remand in treason cases. Predictably, there was more controversy over the witnesses question. In the debate on June 26, feeling at first ran against concession. The exercise of discretion would 'trie the truth of a testimony before they heare it', and give too much power in practice to the judges.[36] Only Owen and Bacon spoke for the amendment. Discussion in committee occupied the two following days, with more 'government men', including Hobart, favouring discretion. Gradually, debate turned in favour of the amendment, George Moore and Hoby adding powerful support.[37] Hoby was particularly firm:

> I cannot thincke that anie man speaking against this clause, or for conference on this point, doth love the bill, but doth secretly endeavor under a faire shew to over-through the bill. I was against the Instrument of Union, as it was drawn, but I am for the bill.

The Commons on June 29 accepted jury discretion with a single minor amendment,[38] but resolved to confer with the Lords on their new clause banning remand in treason cases. The Lords readily gave way on this, as a compromise gesture, and finally, on June 30, the 'Act for the utter Abolition of all memory of hostility' became law.

6. Overview

According to Notestein, 'The compromise arrived at in the bill about Hostile Laws did not please his Majesty',[39] but it is not clear from the context which of the various compromises Notestein meant, and equally, there is no hard evidence of royal displeasure. Nevertheless, resistance on this last controversial part of the Instrument was considerable. The unionist phraseology of the title and preamble had been truncated. Extensive alterations had been made in the agreed procedures for Border causes. On remand, extradition arrangements agreed by the Commission and implemented over three years had been replaced with new and untried provisions for reciprocal jurisdiction. Even the commission to settle outstanding causes had been lost — although the date and circumstances of this amendment are obscure.[40] While the two months had not seen major conflict between King and Commons, comparable to that in April, there had been much petty mistrust on either side. Certainly, there had not been the open and wholehearted show of support for the general principle of union that James not only desired, but needed if he was to ensure the amicable cooperation of his two nations in future. James's disillusionment seems practically to have been complete — as Giustinian demonstrated in his report of July 4.[41]

Part Four. Conclusions; The Scots Parliament

1. Overview of the English Session

The English parliament of 1606-7 was an almost unmitigated disaster for James's plans for union of England and Scotland. We will be examining the detailed relations between crown and parliament in Chapter 8; but certain, salient points may be made here, the first of which is to stress the very limited nature of the programme advances in November 1606. In 1604, English M.P.s had taken fright at the prospect of major constitutional or political changes resulting from union. Despite Commons' protestations in 1607, the provisions of the Instrument did not envisage a major upheaval of this kind. They constituted a moderate advance towards unity in trade and citizenship, and attempted to tidy up legal and administrative anachronisms on the Borders and in the statute-book. This was, as James emphasised, one step in a gradual campaign of union, to be achieved by the willing consent of both nations under control of their representative institutions. Repeatedly, supporters of the union stressed the need for greater conformity between the nations — not to fuel visions of British Imperium, but to make secure the divided sovereignty of James and his successors. The proposals advanced were, like the change in style in 1604, intended to be non-controversial. This is even true of naturalisation. The declaratory act for the *Post-Nati* would merely confirm existing law. *Ante-Nati* would be ineligible for office, by the king's own word. James had already naturalised and preferred the Scots he wished to have about his person. Care had similarly been taken to ensure that relaxation of commercial barriers between the nations did not work in favour of either.

The Commons' reaction to the Instrument is not explicable in terms of ordinary political logic, or principle. There is no evidence of consultation between 'opposition' leaders before, or even during, the parliament. Frequently, speakers against the union can be found advocating different positions — either from each other, or from proposals they had themselves advanced at an earlier stage. The development of Fuller from 'anti-unionist' in February to 'perfect unionist' in April is a splendid example. Certain individuals undoubtedly opposed certain parts of the Instrument — for example trade or remand — for specific reasons, but the overall reaction against the proposals was much more general, and deep-rooted. It may partly be described as a belief that Scotland had won a victory in the Commission, which parliament must redress. Individual objections and arguments, however genuinely advanced, became rallying cries for the majority of M.P.s who disliked change, questioned union *per se*, but feared the consequences of open opposition to the principle of unity. This basic, conservative nationalism was complicated by the existence and expression of prejudice against the Scots, concentrating on their inferiority in law, wealth and moral standing. Attempts to achieve a victory on the safe ground of the point of law having failed, the Commons fell back on a line of opposition neatly encapsulating their basic attitudes. 'Perfect union' was Anglocentric, blaming the Scots for the delay in unification and envisaging the incorporation of Scotland into English law and institutions. It also reflected conservative, immemorialist beliefs about the place and function of the law.

The escalation of mistrust within the Commons, between the two Houses of Parliament, and between Commons and King exceeded that even of 1604. To ascribe this to browbeating by James or Cecil, as whig historians have done, is to accept the opposition of the Lower House as justified. This, as we have seen, is at least questionable. The whigs are on much firmer ground in their allegations of mismanagement. Tactical factors like the shortage of Councillors in the Commons, the heavy-handed recourse to conferences and audiences, and the evolution of the Committee of Whole House[1] undoubtedly made resistance more effective. They do not explain the emergence of opposition in the first place.

To James, Cecil and the supporters of the king, the campaign in the Lower House against the union proposals seemed reactionary and short-sighted. It prevented any meaningful step towards unity, by removing the willing consent on which the entire Jacobean strategy was based. James cannot be absolved from allegations of ill-temper, and perhaps occasional faint-heartedness. Nevertheless, his treatment of the Commons had been far more complaisant than anything conceivable under Elizabeth, on a favourite piece of policy. This is especially true during the latter weeks of the session, when the consciousness of years of work lost must have occupied the royal thoughts. Not merely did the session make future Anglo-Scots conflict more likely, and more dangerous; it also saw an immediate and rapid deterioration in relations between the countries — as had the parallel session in 1604.

2. The Scots Parliament

As we have seen, Scots resentment during the naturalisation debates played an appreciable role in conditioning James's response to the Commons. The scanty evidence available for the period after May 2 indicates no diminution in the strength of feeling. There was bickering between the two Councils on jurisdiction, in a case involving the debateable lands between the nations.[2] James was forced to issue an order in Scotland against the travel to England of Scots coming to press suits, 'to the grite reproche and sclander of this natioun' in English eyes.[3] Tension clearly persisted.

The proceedings of the Scots parliament might seem to deny this picture. On August 11, it passed an 'Act Anent the Unioun of Scotland and England', that was in effect a sweeping enactment of all the provisions in the Instrument. It provided for complete naturalisation of English *Post-Nati*, and of *Ante-Nati* with a saving on 'ony office of the Crowne/office of Judicatorie or ony voit/place or office in parliament'.[4] Even this reservation could expressly be avoided, by exercise of the royal prerogative. The commercial proposals were similarly adopted entire. All the hostile laws in the Instrument were abolished, along with Border laws, customs and treaties. The act here is a mirror image of English legislation — and it is here only that its provisions deviate from the Instrument. The Middle Shires were henceforth to be governed by statute and common law. Offences committed by Scots in England would be tried in Scots Border shires, accessories before principals, Englishmen prosecuting to be free from arrest except in cases of treason or murder. Persons acquitted in England might not be tried in Scotland for the same offence; Scottish subjects should not be sent for trial in England; defendants would be allowed witnesses, subject to jural discretion. Even here, the Scots went further than the English, proclaiming that 'whensoever it sall pleis his majestie . . . To appoint commissionaris for taking of ane mair perfyte and constant ordor for mair firmer administratioun of Justice . . . The saidis Estaittis sall omitt na thing upoun thair pairtis tending to the finall perfectioun of the said unioun' — which was nothing more or less than 'their duetie to thair most gratious prince'.

In fact, the Act was a much less spacious document than this outline implies. Hostile and Border laws apart, its provisions were expressly 'suspendit and . . . of na strength force nor effect heireftir Ay and quhill and unto the speciall tyme that the Estaittis of England be thair Acts and statutis in parliament decerne grant and allow the same'. The Scots had therefore in practice gone no further than the English. Their rhetorical gestures towards implementation of the Instrument may be taken in part as a desire to please the king,[5] but it was also intended as a sideswipe at the English Commons. Many clauses, notably in defence of the mercantile sub-commission and the commercial provisions in the Instrument, were scarcely-veiled attacks on the proceedings in the English parliament. The Scots were taking their revenge, putting• the blame for continued lack of union after 1607 firmly back onto English shoulders.

A document even more illustrative of Scots resentment was the Council's second letter to James, in August.[6] This included a lengthy defence of the Scots Act of Commission against the imputations of Sandys. They protested that the references to fundamental laws only reflected parallel passages in the English Act, and applied only to basic laws of state — 'not meaning thairby of our particular Actis or Statutis or uther lawis or customes, whilkis ar and evir aucht to be alterable as the weele of the commonwealth . . . sall require'. In a very important throwaway line, the Council similarly glossed the reference to free monarchy as intended only to prevent Scotland being treated as a colony or subordinate dominion. They pointed to the Scots Act's 'complete' enactment of the Instrument as an indication of their obedience, but reiterated their general indifference to union. As a mark of equality, they urged James not merely to visit Scotland, but to spend half his time in the northern kingdom. The English session had thus again strengthened the feeling in Scotland of inequity and loss — an awareness that, by the union of the crowns, Scotland had *de facto* if not *de iure* become the inferior dominion of an absentee king, ruling from a distant country whose respect for the pride and independence of Scotland was low.

This was, of course, almost precisely the opposite of James's intention in launching the project.

NOTES

Introduction

1. See e.g. Houston, *James 1*, 40-2. Houston implies that parliament was called on to enact a wholesale union in government, laws and the church — none of which were on the agenda!

2. *CJ* I, 315-5.

Part One. Discussions before February 1607

1. 'The Lords were active; they asked for conferences and hoped for proper debate in those conferences': Notestein, *House of Commons*, 215.

2. See esp: Notestein, *House of Commons*; Bowyer, *Parliamentary Diary*; *HMC.Bucc. MSS* III; Spedding, *Bacon* III; Cobbett, *Parl.Hist.* I.

3. *LJ* II, 450.

4. *Bowyer*, 187n.

5. *Ibid.*, 189. *HMC.Bucc.MSS* wrongly dates this to Nov. 24. Morrice was 'a tedious orator from Carnarvonshire' (*Notestein*, 117) with a Celtic interest in British imperium. He was active also in the 1604 and 1610 sessions: see Chapters 2 and 7.

6. *HMC.Bucc.MSS* III, 108.

7. *Ibid*; *Bowyer*, 190-1.

8. *LJ* II, 452.

9. *CJ* I, 1004.

10. *Bowyer*, 191-2.

11. Winwood, *Memorials* II, 38; see also above, Chapter 4.

12. *Notestein*, 116.

13. *Bowyer*, 193.

14. *Ibid.*, 194. Hoby's scholastic pursuits had by 1606 obtained the high favour of James. His embarrassment is thus understandable.

15. *LJ* II, 455. 'Every Member hath an Equality of Interest in every Particular rightly examined . . . their Lordships conceived it a kind of Diminution of Capacity of the Lower House, to think that anything is too great for them or too little for the Lords.'

16. *Bowyer*, 199.

17. *CJ* I, 326.

18. *LJ* II, 457.

19. B.L.Harl.MSS 1314, 54.

20. Lincoln's Inn Maynard MSS 83:5.

21. *Bowyer*, 200.

22. Watts & Watts, *From Border to Middle Shire*, 167.

23. S.P.14/24/13 (report by Wilson to Cecil).

24. S.P.14/24/14; B.L.Cott.MSS Tit.FIV. No. 9, fols. 60-2.

25. One should also note the French ambassador's estimate that escuage brought in 200,000 crowns to James and 100,000 to Salisbury: *De la Boderie*, I, 475.

26. S.P.14/24/23.

27. Lincoln's Inn Maynard MSS 83:7. See also B.L.Cott.MSS Tit.FIV No. 10, fols. 77-8.

28. Their report is not extant; but S.P.14/24/11 may be a copy of part of it.

29. See Ashton, *City and the Court*, 83-120 *passim*.

30. S.P.14/24/3.

31. S.P.14/24/4; Lincoln's Inn Maynard MSS 83:6.

32. B.L.Cott.MSS Tit.FIV No. 10, fols. 65-7.

33. Ibid., fols. 69-74; B.L.Lansd.MSS 486, fols. 173-89.

34. S.P.14/24/5.

35. B.L.Harl.MSS 158, fols. 165-6.

36. S.P.14/24/6.

37. Cam.Caius College MSS 291/274 No. 15, 407-10; B.L.Cott.MSS Tit.FIV, No. 10, fols. 62-5; B.L.Lansd.MSS 486, 153ff; B.L.Harl.MSS 292, fol. 125.

38. B.L.Harl.MSS 1314, fols. 62-95.

39. S.P.14/24/9 & 11; S.P.14/17/98 (*re* naturalisation in France); B.L.Stowe MSS 132, fols. 55-6 and 141-2 (likewise).

40. Lythe, 'Union of the Crowns', 226, and *Economy of Scotland*, 206-9; Keith, *Commercial Relations*, 10-15.

41. S.P.14/24/3.

42. Ibid.

43. Ibid.

44. S.P.14/24/6: Cam.Caius College MSS 291/274 No. 15, 407-10, etc.

45. B.L.Harl.MSS 158, fols. 165-6.

46. 'The countries required different commercial regulations. This was one reason why the union of 1603 could not be complete.' Keith, *Commercial Relations*, 165-6.

47. S.P.14/24/11.

48. B.L.Stowe MSS 132 fols. 55-6, 141-2.

49. B.L.Cott.MSS FIV No. 10, fols. 66-70.

50. Ibid.

51. Lythe, 'Union of the Crowns', 225.

52. S.P.14/24/5.

53. Riley, *Union of England and Scotland*, 4.

54. S.P.14/24/6.

55. B.L.Cott.MSS Tit.FIV, No. 10, fols. 77-8; Lincoln's Inn Maynard MSS 83:5.

56. *Bowyer*, 209: *CJ* I, 333.

57. *Reg.PCSc.* VII, 310.

58. N.L.S.Adv.MSS 33.1.1. Vol. II, No. 10.

59. *HMC.Salis.MSS* XIX, 107-8; *Reg.PCSc.* VII, 377-8.

60. *Ibid.*, 347.

Part Two. The Naturalisation Debates: February-April 1607

1. *LJ* II, 470.

2. *CJ* I, 334.

3. B.L.Add.MSS 30641 fol. 24r.

4. *HMC.Downshire MSS* II, 23; B.L.Harl.MSS 1314, 96-8, 100-30 *passim*.

5. Cobbett, *Parl.Hist.* I, Col. 1097.

6. *De la Boderie*, II, fol. 87ff. (1 March 1607).

7. *HMC.Bucc.MSS* III, 110. Note Montagu's defence of the House: 'by reason of the outrageousness of the speech both in words and actions, they were rather driven to an astonishment than to answer or say anything to it'.

8. *HMC.Salis.MSS* XIX, 59. Piggott pleaded that he did not often speak in the House, and was carried away.

9. *Reg.PCSc.* VII, 512-3; N.L.S.Adv.MSS 33.1.1. Vol. II, No. 15.

10. S.P.14/26/91.

11. *De la Boderie*, II, 89-90.

12. *Ibid.*, 121.

13. See e.g. that much overlooked political document, B.L.Harl.MSS 5191, fols. 17-18: 'Of a Fart that was lett in the Lower House of Parliament 1607'. 'Be advysed quoth another looke to the lott/ If you fart at the Union remember Piggott.'

14. 'We come here not by chance but by gods providence. And the people that by that elecon have layd ther trust uppon us do looke for mercy at our hands . . . as the children of Israel did of Scripture if I should forgett thee O England lett my right hand forgett her left.' B.L.Harl.MSS 6850, fols. 44-5. See also Cobbett, *Parl. Hist. I*, Col. 1082: *CJ* I, 335.

15. Usher, 'Nicholas Fuller', 744.

16. Spedding, *Bacon* III, 315. For an uncharitable assessment of the speech, see Wilson, *History of GB*, 37.

17. *HMC.Bucc.MSS* III, 111.

18. Notestein, *House of Commons*, 224.

19. Cowell, *Interpreter*, under 'Denizen'.

20. Kantorowicz, *The King's Two Bodies* gives the medieval background; Maitland, 'Crown as Corporation'; Axton, *Two Bodies*. 'The king's "two bodies" was never a *fact*, nor did it ever attain the status of orthodoxy; it remained a controversial idea. The idea seemed, for a limited historical span, to express a precarious balance of power between the king and the state. This balance could be re-defined with each fresh application of the theory to a contemporary situation.' Kantorowicz, *op. cit.*, x, Axton, 11-37 are particularly useful for the Elizabethan usage of the theory, e.g. by Plowden and Leslie to support Mary Stuart's succession. For the impetus given to the theory by James's accession, see e.g. Forset, *Comparative Discourse of Bodies Natural and Politique*.

21. Allen, *Political Thought*, 281: 'Two conceptions were found in the Corpus Juris: the conception of a sovereign law-making princeps and the conception of the princeps as the delegate of a sovereign people. The stress might be laid on one or the other'.

22. B.L.Harl.MSS 1314, fol. 106: 'He that is under another law is by the Civil Law alien *a republica*'.

23. *CJ* I, 336.

24. S.P.14/26/54 & 55.

25. *CJ* I, 339; *LJ* II, 475. There is no hint, as Notestein implies (*House of Commons*, 225), of opposition to conference at this stage.

26. *CJ* I, 338-9, 1018-20; *Notestein*, 224-5; Spedding, *Bacon* III, 325-6. Notestein wrongly interprets the reference as a 'speedy committee with instructions to take time to ripen the union' (*House of Commons*, 460).

27. Sharpe, *Sir Robert Cotton*, 153. The paper is in Cam.Caius College MSS 291/274 No. 15, 407-10 and numerous other copies. It did not have the importance that Sharpe ascribes to it.

28. *CJ* I, 340.

29. Scott, *Somers Tracts* II, 132-44. See also Howell, *State Trials* II, Cols. 561-76.

30. Levack has elevated this reference into a major issue of debate, as to whether James had naturalised the *Post-Nati* by his proclamation ('Union of English and Scots Law', 109).

31. Howell, *State Trials* II, Col. 564.

32. B.L.Harl.MSS 6846, fols. 222-3 is an answer to Owen by a Lord or judge; see also B.L.Lansd.MSS 486, fols. 117-29.

33. *Howell*, 566.

34. Cowell, *Interpreter*, 'Alien'. For the 1596 dispute, see B.L.Sloane MSS 2716, fols. 1-38. Cotton's notes on the subject are in B.L.Harl.MSS 6846, fols. 222-3.

35. B.L.Lansd.MSS 486, fols. 117-29.

36. *LJ* II, 476.

37. The judges were Popham, Coke, Fleming, Warburton, Daniel, Yelverton, Fenner, Williams, Tanfield, Snigg, Altham and Walmsley; B.L.Add.MSS 8981, fol. 21. Walmsley was the dissenter: *LJ* II, 476.

38. These were respectively Chief Justice, Chief Baron of the King's Bench and Chief Justice of the Common Pleas. Coke's speech is preserved in S.P.14/26/64.

39. *Howell*, 571.

40. *Ibid.*, 573.

41. *CJ* I, 345; S.P.14/26/66.

42. *Bowyer*, 214n.

43. *CJ* I, 346; *LJ* II, 481.

44. *CJ* I, 1024: 'In this place none betweene us and God'.

45. *LJ* II, 482.

46. S.P.14/26/70 (Wilson to Salisbury).

47. For this almost acrimonious exchange, see Ibid. and *LJ* II, 483.

48. See *CJ* I, 336-7, 1015; Spedding, *Bacon* III, 307-25. The legal point is answered in *Ibid.*, 314-5.

49. *Bowyer*, 219-20. See also *Notestein*, 532; Bod.Rawl.MSS A. 123, fol. 9ff.

50. *Bowyer*, 273: *CJ* I, 1037. The speaker was Hobart. The author of 'Of a Fart' agreed: 'Nay rather saith Edwyn Ile make a digression/And fart them a proiect shall hold them a session'. B.L.Harl.MSS 5191, fols. 17-18.

51. Marten indicated this later, on April 29. 'Mr Fuller will have a union and then no union and then a union. For a perfect union then not for commerce and then for hostile laws.' *Bowyer*, 266n.

52. B.L.Harl.MSS 1305, fol. 20v.

53. *Bowyer*, 220 and 227; Lincoln's Inn Maynard MSS 83:11. These attacks were naturally noticed by the ambassadors: *Cal.S.P.(Ven) 1603-7*, 478-9 and *De la Boderie* II, 121-2 and 129. De la Boderie was given orders to take actions 'soubz main' to ensure its survival. S.P.14/26/87 is relevant. For Neville's antipathy in 1604 to the alliance, see Winwood, *Memorials* II, 28.

54. *HMC.Portland MSS* I, 122-3.

55. *Bowyer*, 222-3; S.P.14/26/73.

56. Bod.Rawl.MSS A. 123, fol. 11.

57. S.P.14/26/75.

58. There are numerous reports of the Conference: see S.P.14/26/72, 73, 78 & 79; B.L.Cott.MSS Jul.FVI, fols. 105-7v: B.L.Harl.MSS 6806, fols. 209-10: B.L.Lansd. MSS 486, fols. 66-7: Bod.Rawl.MSS.A.123, fols. 9v-12.

59. *HMC.Portland MSS* I, 121-3. Northampton's fulsome praise of union survives in B.L.Cott.MSS Tit.CVI, fols. 415-26. Notes on speeches of Ellesmere and Salisbury are at S.P.14/26/76.

60. *HMC.Portland MSS* I, 123; *Bowyer*, 228.

61. Notestein, *House of Commons*, 233.

62. *De la Boderie* II, 136-9: 'sois main le Roi a opinion qu'elles ne sont que trop d'accord'.

63. *Notestein*, 234.

64. *Bowyer*, 239; S.P.14/26/85; B.L.Lansd.MSS 486, fols. 129-31.

65. *Notestein*, 236.

66. *HMC.Bucc.MSS III*, 114. See also S.P.14/26/84 for Wilson's report.

67. S.P.14/26/91. For the limited judicial position of the Commons, see Jones, *Politics and Bench*, 63.

68. *Cal.S.P.(Ven), 1603-7*, 479.

69. *Ibid.*, 485. *De la Boderie*, II, 138 agrees.

70. *LJ* II, 496.

71. *HMC.Portland MSS* I, 111-12 contains an excellent commentary by Holles on these debates. See also *Bowyer*, 243-50.

72. *Bowyer*, 243.

73. Levack, 'Union of English and Scots Law', 110.

74. The latter included strong support for synthetic union in the preface to his *Institutiones*.

75. Levack, 'Union of English and Scots Law', 99-101.

76. Spedding, *Bacon* III, 335-41.

77. *CJ* I, 357-63; Scott, *Somers Tracts* II, 117-32. Tanner, *Constitutional Documents*, 35-7 is a truncated version.

78. Dodd, *Responsible Government*, 10.

79. *CJ* I, 362.

80. S.P.14/27/2 contains his general commendation of a perfect union.

81. Ibid: 'We are now about but an ingres or an entrie to ye great worke. Those who proposed ye perfect union at first had *mel in ore fel in corde*'.

82. Gardiner, *History* I, 336-7. See also Tanner, *Constitutional Documents*, 35 and Spedding, *Bacon* III, 341-2 for their commendations.

83. S.P.14/27/9.

84. Scott, *Somers Tracts* II, 118.

85. *Cal.S.P.(Ven), 1603-7*, 488.

86. HMC.Salis.MSS XIX, 108.

87. *Bowyer*, 262.

88. *Ibid.*, 280. Sandys's speech on the 28th had made a similar offer.

89. *Ibid.*, 265-6.

90. *Ibid.*, 267. See also Lincoln's Inn Maynard MSS 83:12.

91. *Bowyer*, 278.

92. *Ibid.*, 273.

93. Probably similar to the drafted bill at B.L.Cott.MSS.Tit.FIV, fol. 81ff.

94. Gardiner, *History*, I, 337.

95. *CJ* I, 336.

96. This charge was unfair: see above, Chapter 2.

97. See note 77.

98. *Cal.S.P.(Ven) 1603-7*, 385. 'Les Esccssois sont extremement mutines, et plus animes, contre les Anglois': *De la Boderie* II, 147. For French involvement, see *Ibid.*, 139-41 and S.R.O.MSS GD.45/1/8.

99. *Reg.PCSc.* VII, xxxix and 340.

Part 3. May-June 1607: Hostile and Border Laws

1. Notestein openly leaves the remand issue to others: *House of Commons*, 253-4.

2. *CJ* I, 1040; *Bowyer*, 289. A copy of the draft bill is in B.L.Cott.MSS Tit.FIV, No. 10.

3. *CJ* I, 370; *HMC.Bucc.MSS* III, 116.

4. *CJ* I, 371; S.P.14/21/16; *Bowyer*, 377ff.

5. *Bowyer*, 377: 'Ther shold not be in short tyme a man in Northumberland Comberland and Westmoreland worth a shirt on his back'.

6. *Ibid.*, 381.

7. S.P.14/26/17.

8. Tanner, *Constitutional Documents*, 38.

9. 'It maketh voide by Generall words all other Lawes, Statutes and Customes made etc against Scottishmen as enemies.' *Bowyer*, 290.

10. *Ibid.*, 381; *Notestein*, 253. The latter is inaccurate in portraying the committee as diligently searching out laws in order to cut down the judges' scope for interpretation. A comparison of the Instrument with the Act passed on June 30 shows only one addition to the Commissioners' list.

11. *Bowyer*, 382.

12. *Tanner*, 39: 'If there had appeared any other Statute . . . against Scottishmen as enemies, or Scotland as an enemy Country . . . we should . . . have utterly abrogated and annulled the same'. Contrast the original clause at S.P.14/24/2.

13. B.L.Harl.MSS 1314, fol. 60.

14. *Bowyer*, 300n.

15. *Ibid.*, 296n; B.L.Cott.MSS Tit.FIV, fol. 101v.

16. Watts & Watts, *From Border to Middle Shire*, 150.

17. *Bowyer*, 297.

18. *Ibid.*, 298-9; *CJ* I, 1046.

19. *Bowyer*, 300-3; for subsequent debate, 304-5.

20. B.L.Cott.MSS FIV, fols. 79-80.

21. *Cal.S.P.(Ven) 1603-7*, 498.

22. S.P.14/27/30; for the paper on Scots criminal procedures, see S.P.14/27/42.

23. *Bowyer*, 311ff; *CJ* I, 378-9 and 1048-9.

24. S.P.14/27/44 (the record is by Cotton).

25. Ibid., *Bowyer*, 315n.

26. S.P.14/27/42.

27. S.P.14/27/44.

28. Such accounts rely heavily on ambassadorial reports: *Cal.S.P.(Ven) 1607-10*, 2; *De la Boderie*, II, 243-4.

29. *CJ* I, 389.

30. *Ibid.*, 382.

31. *Bowyer*, 325-6.

32. *Ibid.*, 353n.

33. Watts & Watts, *From Border to Middle Shire*, 150.

34. S.P.14/27/60.

35. S.P.14/27/62.

36. *Bowyer*, 353-5.

37. *Ibid.*, 360.

38. By Hyde. This made the use of jury discretion subject to their general oath 'to make trew delivery betweene the King and the prisoner'. *Bowyer*, 362.

39. Notestein, *House of Commons*, 254.

40. It was however presumably related to Yelverton's objections on May 8: see above.

41. *Cal.S.P.(Ven) 1607-10*, 9-10.

Part Four. Conclusions; The Scots Parliament

1. For the full argument, see *Notestein*, 454-74 *passim*, esp. 460-1. The Committee of the Whole House properly developed in March 1607, the committee of December 17th, 1606 being a preview of the same.

2. Maidment, *Melrose Letters*, II, 27-8.

3. *Reg.PCSc*. VII, 381.

4. *Acts. Sc.Parl*. IV, 366-71.

5. This is certainly Masson's view: *Reg.PCSc*. VII, xlii-xliii. The ambassadors concur: *Cal.S.P.(Ven) 1607-10*, 12 and 36; *De la Boderie*, II, Sept. 24.

6. *Reg.PCSc*. VII, 534-8.

7
The Project After Parliament: Union After July 1607

1. Introduction

Most accounts of the Jacobean Union project end with the close of the English parliamentary session — if not with the king's speech of May 2. This ignores not merely the session and Act of Parliament in Scotland, but also a number of developments in either country after the two assemblies had dispersed. At most, historians refer briefly to 'Calvin's Case', and the naturalisation of the *Post-Nati* — overlooking its wider, constitutional implications.[1]

This attitude is partly justified. The union was never as important or contentious a part of public life in either country after July 1607 as during the four preceding years. Its revival during the English parliament of 1610 was brief and peripheral, occupying little debating time in either chamber. There were no widespread general discussions about the present and future state of the union — perfect or imperfect. The actions taken by the king outside Parliament attracted little attention and had little apparent effect — 'Calvin's Case' being the only evident exception. Even that contentious and controversial law case had little immediate political significance. The age of the *Post-Nati* ensured that naturalisation would not be accompanied by any considerable influx of Scots into England, let alone into high offices of church and state. Its effects could therefore not be seen for at least one generation. In practice, the death of James and accession of a king raised in England with English sympathies was to prevent the dire prophecies of Fuller and Spelman from coming to pass. In the same way, the constitutional implications of the arguments and decisions in the case did not lead to alterations in the basic pattern of English government. At most, they changed the continuing long-term perceptions of Englishmen about the balance of power within their nation.

Developments after July 1607 do however have some importance. At the very least, they correct the general impression that James simply abandoned his project at this point, in a fit of personal pique. Besides the enforcement of naturalisation for the *Post-Nati* in 'Calvin's Case', the king used his prerogative powers to advance union in a number of areas: commerce and customs, coinage, weights and measures etc. He continued his campaigns for the reform of the church of Scotland, and for the pacification of the 'Middle Shires'. The latter included new legislation for remand and extradition, secured from the English parliament in 1610. He promoted a conference of English and Scots lawyers to identify areas of difference between the two national systems of law, as a first step towards 'perfect union'. Expressions of hostility and prejudice were suppressed, by legislation and executive action. Before turning our attention to the case in Exchequer-Chamber, therefore, we shall review action in each of these areas.

K

2. Suppression of Opposition

After July 1607, James took action through the Councils to suppress opposition to the union project. This action was partly retributive, punishing M.P.s for their attitudes and statements in the 1606-7 session. The clearest example of opposition to the project in parliament bringing its own subsequent deserts is predictably that of Yelverton. As we have seen, Yelverton's speeches in March-April 1607 had attracted particular displeasure, the Member being covertly condemned by the king in his speech of May 2.[2] Six months later, in December, he was still labouring under extreme disfavour — as a plaintive letter to Northampton begging intercession shows:

> I know either misconstruction of my words or dismembring them from their sense hath ben the occasion yea the foundation of ruinating my name and opinion with his highnes, for had not my speaches fallen in the lower house of parliament among ravening fowles, they had in the relation of them rather discovered my simplicity and plainenes than any acerbity and malice . . . I did never speake but as in a place of counsell to propound not oppose . . . There is no meane man living (my Lord) shalbe so proud to doe his Ma.ties service as I wilbe, nor any that can seeke it with more affection of humility.[3]

Yelverton's disgrace was clearly connected with the union. The fall of Fuller in a few months from parliament to prison is more obscure.[4] The principal cause of his imprisonment was a series of attacks made by the 'puritan' lawyer upon the Court of High Commission, in Spring 1607. In March, he had been threatened with imprisonment by Bancroft, after alleging illegal use of the oath '*ex officio*' by its judges. Two months later he went further, denying the Commission's (statutory) power to imprison, and labelling the Court as 'Popish'. In June, he accused the Commissioners of embezzling their fines, and seeking to extend their jurisdiction to cover the entire corpus of civil and criminal law. The Commission then took him into custody, arranging a trial for July 1607. Fuller secured transfer of the case to King's Bench, by Writ of Prohibition, as he had for innumerable clients during previous years. It was at this point that the case came to the attention of James and Salisbury. James was determined to have Fuller returned to the jurisdiction of the Commission, and roundly punished. This can be explained without invoking union. Fuller's attacks on the Commission implicitly denied the legality of the letters patent by which Elizabeth and James alike had authorised the use of custody by the Court. This could be construed as an attack upon the royal prerogative, as well as upon the ecclesiastical courts. It is however *prima facie* probable that James also regarded Fuller's difficulties as an ideal opportunity to punish him for vocal opposition to the union. The case was prolonged. Fuller's application for *habeas corpus* came before King's Bench in November 1607, and was rejected. Allies promptly published tracts against his 'false imprisonment'; but it was not until Autumn 1608, after hearing in Star Chamber, that Fuller finally secured his own release.

Fuller and Yelverton were only the most spectacular examples of disfavour.

The dismissal of Crofts and Owen from the Commission of the Council of Wales, after much dispute at the Council table, again demonstrated the dangers of opposition to the project by those expected to support royal policy. Other casualties included Sir Henry Widdrington and his brother, for their resistance to remanding. Sir Henry was removed from the Northumberland Commission of the Peace, and confined to Boston in Lincolnshire until the start of the 1610 parliamentary session. His brother fared even worse, being forced into exile in France until the death of Dunbar in 1611.[5]

The heavy hand of royal displeasure was also meted out to lesser figures whose actions threatened to disrupt relations between England and Scotland. This was part of a general campaign to suppress expressions of hostility and prejudice. Immediate casualties included the Reverend Edward Robinson, imprisoned for attacks upon the Scots in a sermon at Paul's Cross on 7 June 1607. Robinson had called the Scots 'a people poor, lying and prone to all manner of treachery', to the outrage of Sir Thomas Craig and his compatriots. Like Yelverton, Robinson is found petitioning for restoration.[6] The king's censure of such slanders was maintained for several years. In April 1608, he ordered Salisbury to prosecute 'the growing common of libelling and detraction', identifying three particular cases. One, Sir Robert Chamberlain, was censured for remarks made in a private letter, despite the author's abject excuses.[7] Another, John Bachler, faced legal proceedings for remarks made about the 'dominant influence' of Scots over the king.[8] This campaign was by no means confined to England. Scots records include 'Ane Act against scandalous speeches and libellis', passed by the Scots parliament on 24 June 1609.[9] The relationship of this to the union was very clearly spelled out. The Act condemned

> fals and calumnious bruttis speches and wryttis craftelie utterit and dispersit be some lawles and faules people of this realme alsweill in privat conferences as in their meittingis at tavernis ailhouss and playis and by thair pasquillis libellis rymis Cokalanies comedies and siclyk occasionis whereby they slander maligne and revile the people estait and countrey of England . . . [leading to] the hindrance of the wished accomplishment of the perfyt union of the saidis kingdomes . . . as he hopes (god willing) in his regne to sie.

Those found guilty would be liable to fines, corporal punishment, banishment or gaol, depending on the gravity of the slander. The reference to a gradual perfect union is particularly interesting, confirming that the project had not yet come to be seen as moribund.

Legislation and prosecution against libels in either kingdom proved relatively unsuccessful in suppressing expressions of hostility. In England, the presence of Scots at court continued to create tension, particularly during the period when Sir Robert Carr held high favour.[10] This tension occasionally surfaced in open conflict. Even a minor incident could create the possibility of violence. When a Scot struck the Earl of Montgomery with his riding-switch at Croydon race-course, 'The English did, upon the incident, draw together, to make it a national quarrel; so far as Mr John Pinchbeck . . . rode about with his dagger in his hand, crying: 'Let us break our fast with them here, and dine with the rest in London'.[11] Similar threats were voiced in 1612 during the trial of Lord Sanquhar, on charges of conspiracy to murder an English fencing-master. The trial inspired a particularly vicious set of verses, 'which were everywhere posted, and did contain as many stories as Lines':[12]

> They Beg our Lands, our Goods, our Lives,
> They Switch our Nobles, and lye with their Wives,
> They Pinch our Gentry, and send for our Benchers,
> They Stab our Sargeants, and pistoll our Fencers.
> Leave off, proud Scots, thus to undo us,
> Lest we make you as poor as when you came to us.[13]

The underlying assumptions of this rhyme are interesting, erecting a stereotype Scot to which all members of the species are expected to belong. This is the language of racial prejudice. An essential element in the stereotype is poverty. The theme could be handled sourly, in an envious and disapproving manner:

> Bonny Scot, we all witness can,
> That England hath made thee a gentleman.[14]

It could also be used humorously, as in Sir Anthony Weldon's 'Letter out of Scotland'.[15] Weldon, a minor court official, accompanied James on his return to Scotland in 1617. He was not overly impressed: 'The aire might be wholesome, but for the stinking people that inhabit it. The ground might be fruitfull, had they wit to manure it'.[16] There was much 'fowl' and 'deer': foul houses, foul linen, dear lodgings and tobacco. Their court was so barren that they begged James to leave the hangings he had brought. Edinburgh was a parish rather than a city. The Kirk was fanatical and hyprocritical — 'Their Sabbaths exercise, is a preaching in the Forenoon, and a persecuting in the Afternoon'.[17] Scots women were hideously ugly, and their men (needlessly) jealous. Scotland had no trees, no grass, little wealth except coal: 'I wonder, that so brave a Prince as King James, should be born in so stinking a Town as Edenburg, in Lousy Scotland'.[18]

Weldon's letter, a private satire written with a view to publication, won him instant dismissal from his post.[19] He was by no means the only casualty of royal sensitivity at the end of the decade. The case of Thomas Ross, a native of Perthshire who nailed a series of anti-Scots theses to the door of the University Church in Oxford, during 1618, also merits attention. This prank led to conviction and punishment by the Justice-General in Edinburgh.[20]

The significance of these incidents should not be overstressed. They did not imply any immediate, serious danger to the union of the crowns; nor was their hostility carried over into relations between the English and Scots Councils. Diplomatic relations remained generally cooperative, and polite. Their significance is primarily negative. They mark the failure of James's strategy to secure a union in the sympathies of the two peoples. The suppression of prejudice was both part of this strategy, and a reaction to its failure.

3. Economic and Commercial Measures

Government action to promote 'racial harmony' was paralleled by activity in the commercial and economic spheres. Some of these measures simply kept executive programmes in operation during 1604-6. Ships thus continued to carry the Union Jack, into the reign of Charles.[21] The two countries continued the quest for a common currency, and for standard weights and measures. A second issue of the 'Unite' coinage was made; while in December 1609, Scots treasurer-depute Arnott received a 'standard' and three mint-condition English coins (the 10s, 15s and 30s pieces) 'for the bettir declaration of the stampis and inscriptionis of the saidis pieceis' and 'for the tryall of his Majesteis moneyis of fyne gold quhulk heireafter sall be maid in the mynte of Scotland'.[22] Action was taken similarly to put into operation an Act of August 1607, for 'ane universall conformitie of weichtis mettis and measures' throughout Scotland. As Zupko has shown, however, these continued to show baffling diversity within the country, and a multitude of differences from those used in England.[23]

More important than these minor conformities was the continuation of arrangements for internal free trade. The failure of the English Commons to enact the Instrument led the Scots Privy Council in early 1607 to ordain an accounting for goods travelling across the Border, sureties being taken against failure of commercial union.[24] James however decided to forego the revenue brought in by internal customs, with the proviso that such goods should not be re-exported to any foreign country.[25] Customers in Scotland were allowed £10,000 Scots *per annum* in compensation. 'For we had rather chuse yearlie to sustene so much losse then to mak any alteratioun which may be drawne to the constructioun of our falling from our formall resolutioun in any thing concerning the advancement of the unioun'.[26] This exemption however soon ran into difficulties. The Scots mercantile community protested in January 1608 against the ban on transportation of English goods out of Scotland, or their sale to strangers. They petitioned for relief, preferring the previous arrangements of customs on Anglo-Scots trade and permitted re-export.[27] Merchants also complained about bans on shipment of cloth from England to continental markets, and demanded an approach from the Council to James on their behalf. Hamilton's response was uncompromising: there was no possibility of reimposing custom or liberty of export, and English restrictions on cloth export doubtless applied only to countries where the Great Companies had a monopoly.

The basic commercial protectionism of the two nations maintained the pressure for a return to the old restrictions.[28] Eventually, in November 1610, it was decided to levy the same customs on Anglo-Scots as on Anglo-Irish trade. Remaining Scots commercial privileges in England gradually fell away over the following years.[29]

Anglo-Scots commercial relations after 1610 varied greatly. Little progress was made towards commercial union. James attempted to achieve unity in the navigation laws in 1616, extending an English proclamation of 1615 north of the Border; but this soon fell into abeyance.[30] There was only a slight increase in the

relatively low level of commercial exchange, and little investment or establishment by English manufacturers in Scotland. No Scot found his way into any of
the Great Companies until after 1630. Dreams of unified commerce and the
development of Scotland through foreign capital faded away. The English saw
the Scots either as a nuisance, or as a possible area for exploitation. Scots traders
were abused in London, English revenuemen even proposing regular search of
Scots ships going abroad, for prohibited goods. 'In any direction where the
interests of the two countries clashed, England was always anxious to regulate
Scottish affairs to meet her convenience . . . England forgot that Scotland was
neither a conquered country nor a dependency.'[31] After a few years of free trade
in wool before 1622, export of English wool to Scotland was unilaterally banned.
This followed allegations that Scots were re-exporting English *cloth* to Holland;
English merchants then proposed that Scots wool should not only continue to
enter England, but indeed be designated exclusively for English use! This
suggestion was scornfully (and understandably) rejected by the Scots.

'Union' ceased to be a major factor in commercial policy after 1610. The
influence of the *de facto* union in crowns on Anglo-Scots commerce is uncertain.
Scotland may have benefited from the peace and stability brought by union. On
the other hand, union was later to involve Scots merchants in *English* wars,
creating interruptions in Scots trade with France, Spain and Holland. One area
not substantially affected in the short term was the Scots trading privileges in
France. These remained in force throughout the reign of James, and proved
wholly insufficient for the kind of rapid expansion in the Scots mercantile sector
needed to bring it up to English levels.

4. Border Administration and Justice

The administration of justice in the Middle Shires after August 1607 relied not
on the new statute, but on a fresh Commission under Dunbar and the Earl of
Cumberland. Several Northumberland J.P.s who had been holding quarter
sessions were warded, as associates of the disgraced Widringtons. Dunbar's
chief assistant was Selby. The other Commissioners, except *custos rotulorum*
Talbot, were beholden to Dunbar for past favours, or looked to him for future
patronage. They were Sir Ralph Gray, Sir William Bowyer, Edward Charlton,
and Sir William Fenwick. Dunbar's rule during 1607-8 was dictatorial. He
relentlessly purged and pacified the shires, with much success — although
Watts ascribes this as much to the general lessening of cross-Border tension
brought on by the union of the crowns as to the work of the Commission.[32]

Before returning the Middle Shires to the operation of ordinary justice, James
sought and secured a reversal of the 1607 parliamentary decision on extradition.
The uneasy compromise on remand reached in the 1606-7 session had not
pleased the king. He therefore introduced into the 1610 parliament in England a
bill for extradition of fugitive offenders into Scotland, to stand trial at the place
of offence, provided that J.P.s, judges of assize or commissioners of oyer and

terminer in England considered there was 'pregnant proof' of an offence. This was quickly passed.[33] The only scruples came from the Lords, worried lest it should be taken to imply the extradition of peers. The Act was paralleled by reciprocal Scots legislation in October 1612.[34]

The peace and order of 1610 deteriorated temporarily after the death of Dunbar in 1611, as Williams has shown.[35] The continuation of supervision by the Earl of Cumberland alone, a rather less impressive figure, proved a failure, as did a new Anglo-Scots Commission of lesser gentry. This partly reflected the growth of factional rivalry between the Catholics, led by William Howard, and the Protestants under Lord Clifford. Howard was eventually granted wide powers to seek out criminals in the Middle Shires, subject to the overall governance of the Lord President of the North. Detailed regulations were promulgated, covering many subjects including the carriage of guns, bail and surety, and landlords' recognizances for tenants. The situation on the Borders after 1615 was variable. After a considerable assertion of law and order, feuding and raids returned with the disbandment of Cranston's troop in the 1620s. However, the Borders in 1625 were very different from those in 1603: an area of sporadic rather than endemic disorder, and amenable to government measures of control. To that extent, James's policy of pacification and unification can be regarded as a considerable success.

5. The Scots Kirk

In Chapter 5, we examined James's campaign of 1605-7, to elevate royal and episcopal authority in the Kirk at the expense of the General Assembly. This at least was one area where royal policy — however 'unionist' it is considered to be — continued unchecked after the two parliaments of 1607. The major task of 1607-8 was persuading synods to accept constant moderators, episcopal or other. This campaign was generally unsuccessful; and for a time, confrontation between government and kirk seemed inevitable. The immediate prospect was however delayed by the agreement of a conference at Falkland, in June 1608, to recommend a ban on discussion of church government at the Assembly. The Linlithgow General Assembly in July therefore merely established a commission of ministers and bishops to discuss the question, and spent the rest of its time profitably arranging for the persecution of papists.[36] It was generally a well-ordered and amicable gathering. Fears of wholesale Anglicisation were assuaged by English divines accompanying Dunbar on his mission against Highland Papists.[37] The only dispute came with a motion to give bishops *ex officio* power of visitation in their own dioceses. This was disallowed except in the bishoprics of Glasgow and Caithness.

The delay in debate on church government could only habituate the Kirk to episcopacy. Presbyterian writers describe the manipulation of ministerial stipends by bishops, and visits to secure compliant commissioners of pres-byteries.[38] Row at least considers the entire anti-papist campaign a front for promotion of episcopacy — which is excessive; but the two years between Linlithgow and the Glasgow General Assembly of 1610 certainly saw the consolidation of bishops in the church. The commission established at Linlithgow assembled twice in 1609, but without effect.[39] In the meantime, the Scots Parliament in June granted bishops consistorial jurisdiction, to examine and excommunicate Catholics.[40] This supplemented if it did not usurp the jurisdiction of the presybteries. James went further in early 1610, granting Courts of High Commission to Glasgow and St Andrews.[41]

By this time, episcopalians were strong enough to face discussion in General Assembly. Presbyterians like Calderwood have made much of the methods by which the Assembly was called at short notice, the 'godly party' having being disarmed by a previous proclamation of prorogation. Presbyteries were asked to elect specified persons as their representatives. 'Travelling expenses' were used to bring an unprecedented number of northern ministers to Glasgow — and to reward compliant Southern kirkmen.[42] The Assembly itself condemned the gathering at Aberdeen in 1605, implicitly approving the claims of James to sole power over the summoning and prorogation of assemblies. It also established bishops as constant moderators of all synods, with powers of visitation, of presentation and deposition of ministers, and a veto on the ministerial exercise of excommunication or absolution. These powers were however to be exercised within limitations, including censure by the General Assembly.

In October of the same year, three Scots 'bishops' received consecration in Westminster — the first spiritual authorisation given to the new breed. On their return, these three duly consecrated the remaining Scottish episcopacy.[43]

This brief, if not simplified, examination of the Scots Kirk in the three years after 1607 could make it seem very much like a campaign of ecclesiastical union, but it is as impossible in 1607-10 as in 1605-7 to decide how far James's policy reflected a desire for union, or simply episcopalian sympathies. Certain factors suggest that the latter were more important. At no stage during the period did James or any of his followers talk of church union, even privately. The consecration of the bishops took place without Anglican ordination, or the participation of archbishops. The independence of the Kirk was thus secured. Above all, the halfway settlement of 1610, in which bishops moderated a presbyterian church without supplanting any of its assemblies, proved to be James's final word on government. The Kirk of 1610 was undoubtedly closer in government to the English church than that of 1603; the differences between them remained considerable. In this sense, James's own episcopalianism appears qualified. Despite the objections of Calderwood and Melville, the proposals put forward were endorsed and accepted by the majority in the Kirk, without demur. It was, as Donaldson has said, a sensible and operable compromise.[44]

One can therefore say that James sought, not unity, but a measure of uniformity: fitting to his beliefs in gradual union, unity in behaviour, and in hearts and minds. The same impulse lay behind his attempts at liturgical reform in Scotland after 1614. These started with the introduction of Holy Communion at Easter, and moves for the production of a new draft liturgy after 1616. Opposition to such changes crystallised in the General Assembly at St Andrews, in 1617, with the rejection of the Five Articles: kneeling at Holy Communion, the Christian year, private communion and baptism, and confirmation. The approval of these Articles by an engineered 'Assembly' at Perth in 1618 strongly recalls Linlithgow twelve years earlier. In practice the Articles were widely disregarded, even bishops like Spottiswoode turning a blind eye to their disuse. The public pressure in Scotland against the changes, again fuelled by accusations of anglicisation and assertions of national independence, led to a royal retreat. The draft liturgy, never more than a step towards the English Book of Common Prayer, was abandoned; and in 1621, James foreswore all further changes in the Kirk. He kept his word. Successful in increasing the similarity of his two churches, he saw no overriding requirement for uniformity, let alone unity. These dubious goals were left for Charles and Archbishop Laud — with disastrous results.

6. Reconciliation of the Laws

In the administration of Scots justice, James introduced a few English features — J.P.s being the most prominent example. The Venetian ambassador referred to a campaign of anglicisation in Scotland under Dunbar, in 1608[45] — and to long conferences in 1609 between Dunfermline and the king, on legal union.[46] The practical results of this campaign were however very limited. We are told by the same source that the Scots continued to resist unilateral changes in their laws, but it does confirm that, following the English insistence on the 'perfect union', reconciliation in at least the public laws of the two kingdoms was seen by James and his ministers as the most logical and promising next step.

The most ambitious — and abortive — attempt in this field was a conference between English and Scots lawyers in late 1607, to identify differences between the two legal systems and possibilities for reconciliation. The first evidence for this conference came in a series of letters between Salisbury, the Council and the King (or his closest servants) during October. On the 11th, Wilbraham wrote to the Council about consultations that the latter had had with certain of the judges. These advised that 'there should be declared certain principles of the laws of England, especially touching the preservation of his Majesty's person and the government of the kingdom, wherein should be described the form of the trials and the penalties'. These should then be compared with the laws in Scotland, and 'matters would be ripened for a conference' forthwith.[47] James now approved these arrangements, 'because the Lower House objected the division of laws to be the great impediment to the complete union'. This was reinforced by a personal letter from James to Salisbury on the conference, and requiring the English and Scots learned counsel 'whom I have appointed to study the uniformity of the laws' to liaise and cooperate with each other.[48] By December,

preparations for the conference were well advanced. On the 3rd, James gave
Salisbury details of a legal digest prepared in Scotland, and ordered him to
ensure that the English lawyers were similarly prepared for meetings with the
Scots Secretary, President and Lord Advocate.[49] The digest itself was passed to
Salisbury on the 8th.[50] It was to be handed to Attorney-General Hobart, who
had already produced a collection of English laws for royal perusal. The king
had compared this collection with his own memories of Scots law, and found far
more similarities than differences.

Both Hobart's collection and the Scots brief have now been lost. There does
exist one major examination of English law obviously compiled for the
conference, explicitly written for the king's eyes and intended for comparison
with a parallel Scots paper. This is Bacon's 'Preparation Toward the Union of
the Laws of England and Scotland'.[51] This may even have been the official
English document, drafted by Bacon for Hobart. The 'Preparation' is not so
much a legal collection as an incisive analysis of the principles of English law. It
is noteworthy in several respects. It confirms the implications of Wilbraham's
letter, that the conference would examine union in 'public' rather than 'private'
law. The latter was defined as the laws governing private property, and was
considered unnecessary for union.[52] Public law comprised criminal law, causes
affecting the church, magistrates, officers and courts, together with 'certain
special and politic laws . . . that do import the public peace, strength and wealth
of the kingdom'.[53] Most of the paper was devoted to a detailed delineation of
public crimes — definition, punishment, method of trial etc. Offences covered
included high, petit and misprision of treason, felony (including rape,
embezzlement, conjuration, forgery, recusancy etc.), praemunire and heresy —
the last being a matter for the ecclesiastical courts. There was also a long section
examining the place of the royal prerogative in English law, presumably for
comparison with the Scots prerogative. The English prerogative included
powers to summon, adjourn, prorogue, and dissolve parliament, to veto bills, to
create new burgesses or barons, to demand an oath of allegiance from members:
to declare war or peace, conclude leagues and treaties, command military service
or execute martial law; to grant knighthoods, denizenations, pardons, letters of
mart and reprisal; to alter the form and valuation of the currency, at will; to
forbid or place impositions upon the export or import of goods; to deny a person
exit from the country, etc. The tract is less clear on the philosophical definition
of the prerogative, and has therefore been largely ignored by historians like
Wormuth.[54] The intention of the author was, after all, basically pragmatic.

After this impressive degree of preparation, it is more than merely dis-
appointing to find no records of the legal conference. The only evidence for its
meetings comes from a most unlikely source — Craig's *Ius Feudale*, written in
1602. In dedicating the work to James, Craig referred to a conference 'not long
ago . . . between men learned in the law of both nations with instructions to
examine the legal institutions observed in each, and to ascertain how far they
agreed or differed, with the ultimate aim of assimilating them as far as might
be'.[55] This 'Epistle Dedicatory' is calendared among English State Papers under

April 1607.[56] No such bilateral conference had then taken place, at least since the Anglo-Scots Commission of 1604 — whose terms of reference did not include legal union. Craig is therefore almost certainly referring to the conference of 1607/8. His references to *Ius Feudale* as a work inspired by the conference are however disingenuous; it was clearly an older piece updated and submitted for the occasion.[57] Its actual date of submission is dubious. Craig died early in 1608 — implying that the conference took place at the turn of the year. Submission may therefore have been posthumous, in April 1608; the commendations of *Ius Feudale* by the Scots Council at that time, urging royal generosity to Craig's family, support this date.[58]

Craig's dedication is the more important for the insight it provides into the deliberations — and failure — of the conference: 'Not a few of those thus met together were misled into an attempt to persuade the uninitiated that the customs and institutions observed in the two countries are not merely different but diametrically opposed' to each other. This is a tiny base on which to build any definitive statement. Nevertheless, the picture commands *prima facie* belief. The conference was one of the last events before the publication in 1609 of Skene's *Regiam Majestatem*. This included the 'Quoniam Attachiamenta', the 'Leges Quatuor Burgorum', and the 'Statuta Gildae'. The similarities of this material to Glanvill, the constitutions of Northumbrian boroughs and other English codes all excited contemporary comment.[59] In 1607/8, however, the English lawyers still generally saw Scots law as entirely alien, based on Roman and feudal codes. This was even the view of the English civil lawyers, who had pressed so strongly for legal union.[60] Only Craig, in unpublished works, had emphasised the similarities between the two legal systems. Even in his earliest writings, he had insisted on their basic identity.[61] The long section in *De Unione* comparing the two legal systems, defining the crimes, penalties, judicial procedures for different offences reads very much as if taken from Bacon's 'Preparation', and its missing Scots counterpart.[62] If so, this would imply even more substantial updating for the work than that implied above (Chapter 3, n. 24). Craig's main interest lay however in the area of *ius privatum*, tracing the feudal elements in the laws governing private property in either kingdom. His exaggerated descriptions of their feudal origins have attracted much adverse comment from modern historians of Scots law.[63] They were also irrelevant to the concerns of the 1607/8 conference, since that dealt primarily with *ius publicum*. In the absence of evidence for the identity of the two systems here, English lawyers would have had no reason to abandon their previous judgements about Scots law. Equally, the unwillingness of the Scots to agree to alteration of their laws, caused by a combination of natural conservatism and determination to admit no precedency to the English, would have created an uncompromising line from their delegation. Certainly, there was no attempt to use the conference as a springboard to further parliamentary projects for union — clearly James's purpose in its establishment. Only minor alterations in Scots judicial procedures after 1608 show any sign of executive moves in the same direction. Legal union was dead — and, with it, the 'perfect union'.

7. 'Calvin's Case': Overview

Preparations for the conference on the laws proceeded alongside those to test the legal position of the *Post-Nati* through the English courts. The method chosen for this test, famous as 'Calvin's Case', was again decided in October 1607 after consultation between the English Council and the Judges. Wilbraham's letter of October 11 spoke of the judge's approval for a scheme to bring the question before the courts in a test case.[64] The detailed arrangements were explained to the king by Salisbury.[65] An English estate would be conveyed to a Scots child born after 1603. This land would then be forcibly possessed by another, and an action brought by the child's guardians, for recovery. The defendant would assert that the plaintiff was unfit to plead, being an alien. The case would therefore rest on the child's status. A suitable infant had already been identified, by Kinloss. Salisbury's letter described him as 'a grandchild of the Lord Colvyn' — from which has come the English 'Calvin's Case'. In fact, the *Post-Natus* was one Robert Colville, then three years old. His exact identity has been questioned, but there is little doubt that he was the grandson of Lord Colville of Culross, and son of Robert Colville, Master of Culross.[66] The defendant was to be one Bingley, currently holding land forfeited to the king by the treason of its previous owner.

The prearranged case ran into a few initial difficulties. James demanded further clarification how the case would establish the right of a *Post-Natus* to *inherit* landed estates in England.[67] Bingley then succeeded through some bureaucratic tangle in being granted a petition to exchange the land for a different estate. It was however decided to stay despatch of the grant until after the trial.[68] The crucial stage came at the end of October, with the formal grant of the land to 'Robert Calvin'.[69] In fact, two separate estates were made over to the child. One was the area in Bishopsgate, St Buttolph's, held by Bingley and Richard Griffin; the other, Haggard and Aggerston, being in the parish of St Leonard's, Shoreditch, Richard and Nicholas Smith being the defendants.[70] Writs were issued against these by Colville's guardians, John and William Parkinson. The dual grant may demonstrate the government's desire to ensure that no legal avenue was left open to doubt, or to defeat by technicality. Thus the two cases were scheduled for different parts of the legal system — the Smith case coming before the common-law court of King's Bench, the Bingley writ being sued in Chancery. In each, defendants duly pleaded the inadmissibility of the writ, Colville being 'an alien born . . . within the allegiance of the said lord the king of the said kingdom of Scotland, and out of the allegiance of the said lord the king of his kingdom of England'. This squarely identified not only the legal status of the *Post-Nati* as the main issue for decision, but the theme of allegiance to the body politic as the method by which that issue would be argued. Both cases were then adjourned from their respective courts into Exchequer-Chamber. This was a traditional court of reference from King's Bench, Chancery and Common Pleas, for decision on difficult points of law.[71] Its composition was appropriately large: all the King's Bench and Common

Pleas justices, the Exchequer-Barons and the Lord Chancellor. It decided by majority opinion, and its decisions were binding on other courts, as precedents for future cases. This made it almost a Supreme Court — eminently suitable for the king's needs, and apt for a case of political and constitutional importance.

The case was argued at length by counsel, and summarised at equal length by the judges giving their verdict. Besides the importance of the arguments to the history of the union, the case raised many fundamental questions about the English constitution. These we shall examine later. The following is merely a narrative overview, placing the case in its context and showing the main results of its decision.

The case was heard in June 1608. Counsel for Colville were Hobart and Bacon; against them spoke Serjeant Hutton and Laurence Hyde, both active in the parliamentary opposition on naturalisation. There were fourteen judges: Yelverton, Williams, Crooke, Fenner and Chief Justice Fleming of the King's Bench; Coke, Foster, Daniel, Warburton and Walmsley of the Common Pleas; Altham, Snigg and Tanfield of the Exchequer; and finally Lord Chancellor Ellesmere, from Chancery. The verdict was never seriously in doubt. Most of these judges had already gone on record in favour of the *Post-Nati*, in opinions given to parliament in February 1607; and while those opinions were not binding, they implied the likely outcome. By a majority of twelve to two (the dissenting duo being Foster and Walmsley) Exchequer-Chamber considered Colville natural, and ordered the defendants to answer his writ. Ellesmere confirmed this on the return of the Bingley case to Chancery. A week later, on June 14, Bingley and Griffin were ordered to hand over the estate.[72]

Public interest was inevitably raised by 'Calvin's Case'. Many believed that the verdict had been rigged. The historian Arthur Wilson, in retrospect, was explicit. Coke 'was fit metal for any stamp Royal . . . though many strong and valid Arguments were brought against it (such power is in the breath of Kings!) and such soft stuff are Judges made of, that they can vary their precedents, and model them into as many shapes as they please'.[73] Coke had indeed predicted such rumours in his report on the trial, insisting that there had been 'no commandments or message by word or writing . . . from any whatsoever' to influence the decision.[74] He also stressed the near-unanimity of the verdict, and the ample precedents underlying it. Chancellor Ellesmere, in a letter to James on October 10, likewise spoke good-humouredly of the general bruit.[75] This letter concerned the publication of his speech on the case. This was one major part in a government propaganda campaign countering the allegations of bias. The first shot in this campaign was the grant of a licence in August 1608 to Sir William Woodhouse to print and publish reports of the case — notably Coke.[76] James's involvement in the campaign is demonstrated by Ellesmere, in a second letter to the king on November 28. The Chancellor makes it clear that his production of the speech 'out of my scribled and broken papers' was by royal command.[77] It duly appeared in February 1609.[78]

The history of naturalisation after the Summer of 1608 is unusually fragmented and speculative — coming to a complete stop in 1610. There is some evidence that James intended to call a parliament for confirmation of the verdict. The Venetian ambassador referred to this possibility as early as June 1608.[79] Six months later, Chamberlain was confidently predicting a return of parliament for the purpose in February 1609,[80] but this receives no confirmation in state papers or correspondence. The best piece of evidence is the lack of formal notification to the Scots Council of the Exchequer-Chamber decision until February 1609.[81] This curious delay might imply an intention for parliamentary confirmation. If so, it soon waned. No parliament was called. The ambassador explained this away by a campaign for union in Scotland, the English session being delayed until James could convene it with solid progress across the Border and a certainty of success in England. This 'campaign' is conspicuous by its absence from Scots records, the Acts against libels and for J.P.s being the only substantive secular achievements in 1609. Levack has built on these slender foundations a picture of opposition and failure: 'As Dudley Carleton feared, once the Scots received naturalisation without some form of legal union, they could never be persuaded to risk compromising their native legal tradition'.[82] It is more probable, in my view, that no serious attempt was made. The collapse of the legal conference seems to have completed James's considerable disillusionment — if not with union itself, then at least with the chances of obtaining further success through parliament. The pressing financial crisis of the English monarchy may have made the long-term dangers of international friction and separation seem remote. The act on remanding apart, no unionist legislation resulted from the 1610 session, which surprised some who were expecting substantial debates.[83] The only speaker to revive the union as a whole was the man who had spoken also at the very beginning of the parliamentary project, in 1604:

> Parliament in both Houses has sat little. The first man that broke the silence to any purpose was old Sir William Maurice who revived the motion for the proceeding of the Union, dividing his speech into six parts, whereof he only handled two, and spending in that discourse two hours, he forgot to go through with the rest.[84]

Morrice spoke without official sanction — and no doubt without listeners, if they had a choice! The Venetian ambassador merely notes the naturalisation by act of some Scots gentlemen — accompanied by bills to have naturalised persons excluded from parliament.[85] For union itself,

> They intend to leave the matter to ripen by time and to become familiar by the intermarriage of the two races, by a gradual naturalisation through graces, and by the doctrine that all children born after the King's accession to the throne are ipso facto admissible to the privileges of both Kingdoms.

This fell rather short of the 'gradual union' for which James had been working since 1603.

8. 'Calvin's Case': Legal and Constitutional Themes

No examination of the union as a whole would be complete without a consideration of the legal and constitutional implications of 'Calvin's Case'. Here, the historian is hampered not by paucity of sources, but their partiality. The major surviving evidence is the text of Bacon's speech for Colville, of Ellesmere's speech in Chancery confirming the verdict of Exchequer-Chamber, and of Coke's Report;[86] a manuscript reproduction of judge Yelverton's verdict for Colville;[87] and anonymous notes on the speeches and verdicts of all the participants in Exchequer-Chamber.[88] The last does include a brief note of Serjeant Hutton's speech for the defence, and of the verdicts given by the two 'doubting Thomases', Foster and Walmsley. These form the only direct evidence for the defence case. The latter must generally be inferred from the answers to their arguments given by those favouring the *Post-Nati*.

(a) The Defence Case

The nature of the defence case is nevertheless clear. It rested heavily on arguments used by the Commons, particularly in the Conference of February 1607. Its underlying rationale reflected partly the immemorialist attitudes of many Englishmen to their law, and partly the historical philosophy of union. Its central argument was that status followed allegiance, and allegiance was due to the laws, crown, kingdom or 'body politic' of the king, rather than his living, physical or 'natural' body. There was some prevarication about the exact definition of 'body politic', as Bacon was swift to point out.[89] Common law was however seen as a vital element. There was much discussion of leets, where the subject swore allegiance to the king AND laws of England. *De Natis Ultra Mare* was quoted, speaking of the 'allegiance of England'. Also used was the civil law maxim, 'Cum duo jura concurrunt in una persona aequum est ac si essent in diversis'. First voiced by Bennett in the Great Conference, this had been a mainstay of Commons argument on the point of law.

The object of allegiance was not only a major constitutional question itself, but one with a still wider significance. If allegiance was owed to the body politic rather than natural, the latter must be regarded as an inferior or subordinate part of the monarchy. King would not only be inferior to King-in-Parliament but also, by implication, to the common law — even without his coronation oath to maintain the same.[90] The defence coupled this theme with an absolute distinction between (a) unions born of conquest, consolidation of a fief, or the union of a non-sovereign dominion with a foreign sovereign power, and (b) peaceful unions of sovereign states. This reflected the historical philosophy of union laid down by Savile and other authors. The separation between conquests and consolidations, involving reconciliation of laws, offices, privileges etc. and unions by descent having unity only in the monarch's person implied a link between subjecthood/allegiance and the body politic. The defence case extended the first category to include foreign non-sovereign dominions. In all these, the lands were considered to be subject to English law, or the King's Seal, and therefore part of the body politic. This enabled the defence to dismiss precedents for common subjecthood involving Ireland, Wales, Normandy, Gascony and Anjou. The alternative was to assert that the Gascons had in fact remained aliens, as did Foster of the Common Pleas — citing an Act of Parliament against Gascon merchants as aliens, and a petition of Gascons under Henry IV for indenization. Another Act frequently quoted was 14 Edward III, declaring that although he was King of France and England alike, his English subjects owed no allegiance to him for the former crown. Hutton alleged that 'when the King of England was King of France the French men did then take letters of denisacon'.[91] From here, the defence advanced rapidly to its conclusion. Since Scotland rejected subordinate status,[92] this was therefore a peaceful union of sovereign states, involving no union in allegiance.

The third part of the defence case was a recital of legal and political inconveniences entailed by a verdict for Colville. The legal inconveniences were: that English courts could not judge if a man were born outside the jurisdiction of English law; that if Colville had inheritance and privileges by English law, he should be subject to the law; that judgement for Colville would be innovative. Political inconveniences included the prospect of the kingdoms separating at some later date, and the present risk of a flood of Scots. As Walmsley put it, 'If the Scottsmen should be admitted as natural subjects they would come in *sans nombre*', breeding confusion in southern parts. The third inconvenience was the loss of royal profit from letters patent of indenization. Finally, it was fitter for a case of this magnitude to be decided by a new session of parliament, and not by the courts.

(b) The Plaintiff's Case

Hobart's speech for Colville has been entirely lost; but Bacon's survives intact. Bacon made comprehensive constitutional claims for the king's majesty. James's authority was analogous to that of a father, a shepherd, a god ('Rex est persona mixta cum sacerdota').[93] Obedience was akin to reverence. Personal submission went further than mere obedience to the laws. Law was the 'sinews' of the body politic, worth nothing without the 'spirits' — the overriding sovereign power of the king, over and above the law. Law had only two functions: to define succession, and 'make the ordinary power of the king more definite or regular'.[94] Law could not determine that power, given to the sovereign by the law of nature. The king therefore existed before the law, by prescript of superior natural law.

These claims introduced Bacon's presentation. Much of this was devoted to answering defence arguments. Bacon dismissed the maxim 'Cum duo jura' as inapplicable to kings, quoting statutes of 21 and 24 Henry VIII. There was no confusion of two private rights in one person involved in this case. Political inconveniences were unfit for examination by a court of law. On conquest and descent, Bacon flung the historical philosophy back at the defence. The latter had argued that naturalisation followed conquest because the conquered lands were then subject to English laws and body politic. Bacon raised the precedent of Ireland, which had remained for a generation after conquest under its own laws. He also asked if inhabitants of lands henceforth conquered by British arms were to be subjects of both kingdoms, while English and Scots allegiances remained separate. Above all, Bacon returned to the precedents of Gascony, Guienne, and Anjou, united neither by conquest nor consolidation. He quoted the statute *Praerogativa Regis* and Bracton[95] to demonstrate their common subjecthood with Englishmen, dismissing the argument that they were duchies rather than kingdoms as irrelevant. Finally, he denied that these duchies had ever been part of the English body politic; they had not received English law under the Angevins, the English Seal running there only in its mandatory role, to command subjects, not in its remedial capacity as an authority for the issue of writs. Statutes concerning Gascony similarly 'intermeddle with nothing but that that concerneth either the English subjects personally, or the territories of England locally'.[96]

This provided support for the central tenet of Bacon's speech, tracing allegiance to the body natural. Defence precedents were rejected. If *De Natis Ultra Mare* contained references to the allegiance of England, it similarly referred also to the allegiance of the king. The statute of 14 Edward III was an enabling, not a declaratory Act: 'the Common Law had made an union of the crowns in some degree, by virtue of the union in the king's person . . . if this statute had not been made to stop and cross the course of the common law'.[97] In pleading to dismiss a litigant as alien, it must not only be shown that he was born outside the allegiance of one king, but within the allegiance of another, specified king — implying subjection to the body natural. Allegiance was owed where the law had no force. A subject remained bound even when abroad, or on military campaign, or after the deposition of the king. Could a Scot invade England without committing treason against James? It was treason to encompass the death of the king, yet a body politic was immortal. Since treason was always cited as being against the natural allegiance of the subject, this too tied allegiance to the body natural. The Jacobean Act of Recognition was cited, referring to *one*, imperial crown. Bacon's most pregnant argument was one used in his speech of 17 February 1607.[98] English law recognised only four categories of person: alien enemies, alien friends, denizens and natural subjects. Changes in status were brought about by the king in person, by prerogative powers outside the scope of parliament or the common law. By making war or peace, James might turn an alien friend into an enemy, or *vice versa*. By issuing letters patent, he could create a denizen. Status, and therefore allegiance, depended on the body natural — as the banishment of Hugh de Spencer, who had justified resistance to Edward II by a higher allegiance to the body politic, indicated.

All that remains of Hobart's argument is a few notes by our anonymous observer. The Attorney-General made two principal points. He first examined

De Natis Ultra Mare. Enacted (25 Edward III) to settle vexed questions of royal succession and the inheritability of those born overseas, the statute defined a subject as one born in lands within the allegiance of the king, or outside his allegiance to parents who were already natural lieges.[99] This implied allegiance to the body natural. Hobart also dismissed one defence argument, a reference to an act of 13 Henry IV 'naturalising' presumably alien French subjects, by describing the law as declaratory — stating that the Frenchmen were already subjects, under common law.

(c) The Verdicts of the Judges

Of all the judges, only Coke and Ellesmere have received detailed attention from historians. Nevertheless, the other judges did make many interesting and important points in their verdicts. Two supported the defence, dismissing Colville as alien and tracing allegiance to the body politic. The remainder disagreed. Herne, Daniel, Tanfield and Fleming were particularly firm in support of the body natural. Herne rejected Hutton's legal distinction between obedience and allegiance, and saw the changing nature of the law as an argument against allegiance to the body politic. Tanfield similarly dismissed the oath at leets as different from, and inferior to, the full allegiance owed by all subjects from birth. The two kingdoms lay under one protection, and had one allegiance. Fleming[100] condemned the distinction between the two bodies of the king as unprecedented, and supported Bacon's constitutional analysis. 'The liga is to ye king's person not to the law. Comon law is to yield to ye law of nature. The king hath an absolute power . . . above the law by which he may comaund when and where he will.' Other judges similarly repeated arguments used by Bacon, although Crooke's verdict relied on the assertion of Scotland as a special case. He believed that *De Natis Ultra Mare* did block naturalisation, but that Scotland was exempt from its application because not '*ultra mare*'.

Of the 'minor' judges, Yelverton of the King's Bench is the only one whose speech has survived in more than outline. He denied partiality, admitted that the case would have been more suitable for decision in parliament, and did not consider himself bound by his previous opinion in conference for the *Post-Nati*. He had not however altered this opinion. Yelverton regarded the historical philosophy of union as alien to English law, and disregarded differences between unions by conquest, consolidation and descent. Similarly, no statute ruled this case, *De Natis Ultra Mare*'s varying references to allegiance of England and of the king being 'never intended for any difference in matter, nor imagined they should be so applied'. The case relied instead entirely on the common law, which proved Colville to be natural. Allegiance to the body politic was 'a light imaginarie conceit', making aliens of the Irish, and even of the townsfolk of Berwick. Yelverton made much of the case of Prior Shiels, who had claimed restitution of an English priory, successfully countering allegations of alien birth by assertion of his Gascon origin. Since the English king had then held Gascony as part of his Angevin dominions — a separate body politic — the defence case failed. An alien was a man bound by allegiance to the person of another king, as the legal plea of disablement implied. The kings of Scotland and England were the same man, and allegiance was therefore united.

This brief examination of the other judges demonstrates how unexceptional the judgements laid down by Coke and Ellesmere were. The former in particular repeated arguments previously used by others. Coke stressed three themes. The first was the service owed by lieges to the king in circumstances where English law had no authority — for example outside the country, or on campaign. The second lay in the oath of allegiance. How could the subject swear to defend the life of the body politic, that had no life; how could the king in return swear protection upon his soul, which the body politic did not have? The link between treason, allegiance and the body natural made by Bacon was cited here, approvingly. Coke thirdly emphasised another of Bacon's points, that an alien was a person who could be an enemy, and that this was why aliens were forbidden purchase, inheritance etc. of English estates. Scots *Post-Nati* could be traitors, but not enemies. The *Ante-Nati* were not covered by the same distinction, since they could have been enemies at some time before 1603. Coke answered at length the legal inconveniences alleged by the defence. Scots owning property in England would indeed be subject to English laws, impositions, taxes etc. for their estates, just like any Englishman or denizen. English courts could judge the birthplace of persons outside the country. Charges of innovation were answered by the most famous part of Coke's speech — an enormously long passage on the immemoriality and wisdom of the common law, and its ample sufficiency of precedents for this case. He rejected the idea that judgement for the plaintiff would bring about a mixture in the rights, offices and privileges of the two kingdoms; these would remain separate bodies politic, linked by one allegiance.

Ellesmere's principal difference from other judges lay in his explicit rejection of the 'Two-Body' theory of monarchy. Coke had accepted the body politic halfway into English law, regarding it as a philosophical concept enabling kingdoms to overcome royal nonage, death and infirmity. Coronation was in his view the marriage of the bodies politic and natural. The king was however a monarch not by coronation, but natural right. Ellesmere regarded this separation of the bodies as unnecessary, alien to English law, and potentially treasonous.[101] Knafla has shown Ellesmere's later elaboration of the one-body theory, relating it to administrative realities.[102] The Chancellor's other main contribution to discussion was his emphasis on the Act of Commission (with its reference to the countries being 'united in allegeance and loyall subjection in his royall person'), the Instrument, the proclamation changing the royal style and the opinions of the judges in parliament.[103] Ellesmere cited precedents for the last two in particular having the force of law, and for alteration in the law by judicial interpretation. Common law became under this consideration little more than aggregated custom, relying heavily on feudal sources. This attitude fits well with the Chancellor's well-known patronage of civil lawyers.

(d) Constitutional Factors: A Summary

The constitutional and philosophical implications of the arguments used in 'Calvin's Case' could occupy a dissertation in their own right. All that can be done here is to indicate a few of the principal themes.

The case decided that allegiance in England was owed to the king as a natural person rather than a corporate figurehead. This became directly relevant during the English Civil War, when the case briefly returned to public attention in a polemical tract by Austin.[104] This apart, the impact of the case on early seventeenth-century thought was indirect. Wormuth has argued that the acceptance of the Bodinist Two-Body theory of monarchy by Coke and the other judges, while not amounting to absolute judicial approval, nevertheless opened avenues for exploitation by 'parliamentarian' theorists during the ensuing two decades. Certainly, 'royalist' thinkers tended to follow Ellesmere in support of a One-Bodied monarchy — as Knafla shows. Against this must be stated not only the connection of allegiance and obedience to the body natural, but the superiority conceded to the king by many speakers over and above the law. Bacon and Fleming's picture of a monarch owed obedience by natural right, exercising supra-legal powers of prerogative, bound to the laws only by the voluntary oath taken at his coronation fits almost precisely with James's own theories of kingship. The positions taken by Coke and Ellesmere are rather more complicated. Ellesmere too saw all law as positive, being made either by the king (through statutes, proclamations and conciliar acts) or by judges under his appointment. He conceded the power of direct legislation to proclamations, not the predominant view of other judges. If the king did however have the right to create new law, he 'was charged to observe the laws which he and his predecessors had created'.[105] This enabled Ellesmere to combine a basically conservative attitude to the law with a fine line in absolutist theory, pleasing to James. The arguments of Coke are even more interesting. Wheeler sees the judgement as a compromise, permitting *de iure* naturalisation but denying that the king's accession automatically gave him powers to achieve union in English and Scots law.[106] In fact, this point was never seriously at issue — despite the claims of Axton.[107] Coke, like Tanfield and certain of the other judges, made much of the reciprocal duties of king and subject. The subject owed allegiance by the law of nature, the fount of monarchy and a law superior to the municipal or bounded laws of the kingdom. The king owed protection, defence, and (under certain circumstances) maintenance. The implication was that allegiance ended when the king's ability to protect the subject fell away. Wheeler sees this proto-Hobbesian 'compact' as demystifying early Stuart kingship, and an implicit challenge to theories of divine right. Certainly, it amounted to a qualification of allegiance to the body natural, since it was normally the body politic which offered protection. This was perhaps best summarised in Coke's statement that 'Allegiance is to the natural capacitie of the k: as it is accompanied wth the politike capacitie'.[108] The connection likewise anticipated the ideas of a natural compact linking obedience and protection produced by parliamer..arian thinkers in the 1640s. Nevertheless, this did not really enshrine a new principle in English constitutional thought. The references to protection by Coke and others merely repeated the mutual oaths taken by subject and sovereign. They concerned the existing position in law, not the philosophical nature of monarchy.

The most important facet of the case, constitutionally, is undoubtedly the support it gave to the picture of a king ruling by law of nature, over and above common or municipal laws. Historians have allowed Coke's long passage in praise of the common law to obscure this strand even in his own verdict. This was however far from the only constitutional implication. Yelverton, for example, argued the superiority of common to statute law. 'A parliament may make a man to be accompted as naturalised, and conclude every man to say, but that he is so, but it can never make a man to be so indeede'.[109] The speeches made by the judges also said much about the nature of sovereignty in unions by conquest, consolidation and descent. Despite Yelverton, the doctrine of conquest-right was generally approved, and received halfway into English law. This was not without qualification. Coke attempted to make a distinction between Christian and infidel territories acquired by conquest; while laws in the latter were alterable at will, he argued, those in the former might be altered initially at the king's pleasure and subsequently only by the authority of king and parliament. The discussions had far-reaching, if unresolved, implications for the relationship both of Scotland and Ireland to England. Scotland was overwhelmingly accepted by counsel and judges alike as a fully sovereign state. The shadow of suzerainty and consolidation was, temporarily, lifted. The case was less clear in its implications for the sovereignty of Ireland. This is not entirely surprising. An examination of *De Natis Ultra Mare* in 1596 had similarly shown disagreement between lawyers about the legislative independency of Ireland.[110] Bacon, too, in his parliamentary speech of naturalisation, had pointed to Ireland as an example of common subjecthood, but separate bodies politic: 'in the Kingdom of Ireland all our statute laws since Poyning's law are not in force'.[111] This was repeated in his advocacy in Exchequer-Chamber, and taken up by many of the judges, including Yelverton. To this extent, 'Calvin's Case' may be taken as support for the sovereignty of the Irish kingdom; but no definitive statement on this peripheral issue was made.

NOTES

1. Notestein, Gardiner, Houston ignore the Case entirely. The best accounts are in Spedding, *Bacon III* and Howell, *State Trials* II.

2. See above: Chapter 6, Pt.ii. See also S.P.14/21/16 and *CJ* I, 371.

3. B.L.Cott.MSS Tit.CVI, fol. 186.

4. See Usher, 'Nicholas Fuller'; S.P.14/28/51.

5. S.P.14/28/51; Watts & Watts, *From Border to Middle Shire*, 151.

6. *HMC.Salis.MSS* XIX, 458; Craig, *De Unione*, 356.

7. *HMC.Salis.MSS* XX, 138.

8. *Ibid.*, 177.

9. *Acts Sc.Parl.* IV, 436.

10. E.g. *Bowyer*, 154n.

11. Chambers, *Annals* I, 429.

12. Osborne, *Historical Memoires*, 93.

13. Nichols, *Progresses of James I*, II, 449.

14. Chambers, *Annals* I, 429-30.

15. Weldon, Letter out of Scotland: printed in 1659 by Howel as *A Perfect Description* etc.

16. Ibid., 1.

17. Ibid., 14.

18. Ibid., 20.

19. Copies can be found in many public and private MS collections: e.g. Oxford Ashmolean MSS 47, B.L.Eger.MSS 2725, B.L.Add.MSS 28640, B.L.Lansd.MSS 973, 81-7, etc., etc. *DNB* XX, 1073 charts his dismissal.

20. Balfour, *Annals* II, 70; Wedgwood, 'Anglo-Scottish Relations', 44.

21. Carr, *Flags of the World*, 34.

22. *Reg.PCSc.* VII, 398 and 715.

23. *Acts Sc.Parl.* IV, 373-4.

24. *Reg.PCSc.* VII, 347: April 9th, 1607.

25. *Ibid.*, 304: 22 January 1607.

26. *Ibid.*, VIII, 8.

27. *HMC.Salis.MSS* XX, 35.

28. See e.g. the Scots Acts against export of raw materials, 1608-10: *Reg.PCSc.* VIII, 58 *et passim*.

29. Lythe, 'Union of Crowns', 226; *Larkin & Hughes*, 261; *Cal.S.P.(Dom) 1604-10* Sign Manual Vol. I, No. 50.

30. Keith, *Commercial Relations*, 17-18; *Reg.PCSc.* XI, 202 and XII, 107.

31. *Keith*, 37.

32. Watts & Watts, *From Border to Middle Shire*, 156. See also Williams, 'Northern Borderlands', 10-11.

33. Tanner, *Constitutional Documents*, 43-5.

34. *Acts, Sc.Parl.* IV, 470.

35. Williams, 'Northern Borderlands', 11-15.

36. *Calderwood*, 589-99; *Acts of Kirk*, 1046-63; Row, *History*, 248-60; Melville, *Diary*, 754-61; Scot, *Apologeticall Narratioun*, 201-7.

37. Our main — presbyterian — sources emphasise the English insistence 'that there was no substantial difference in Religion betwixt the two Realmes, but only in things indifferent concerning Government and Ceremonies': Calderwood, 589 and Row, 248. Calderwood however also makes clear 'his Majesty's will, that England should stand as he found it, and Scotland as he left it'.

38. Row, 245; Calderwood, 584.

39. Falkland, May 1609; Stirling, August 1609. The May meeting broke up in dispute over whether the proceedings should be oral or written. The bishops' delegation simply failed to turn up in August, having 'gained this muche, that no opposition wes maid againes thame at the Parliament': Melville, 780. See also Row, 260ff; *Acts of Kirk*: 1069-78; Scot, 211-15; Calderwood, 606-12.

40. Scot, 215-17; Calderwood, 612; Donaldson, *Scotland*, 206.

41. Melville, 787-92; Calderwood, 619; *Acts of Kirk*, 1078-82; Scot, 218-21.

42. Row, 276; Scot, 221; Calderwood, 621; Donaldson, 205-6. For the nomination of specified ministers, see *Acts of Kirk*, 1083; for the assembly itself, see esp. Wadsworth, 'The General Assembly of 1610'.

43. Donaldson, 206; Calderwood, 644.

44. Donaldson, 206-8. See also Matthieson, *Politics and Religion*, 313.

45. *Cal.S.P.(Ven) 1607-10*, 172-3, 187-8.

46. *Ibid.*, 390.

47. *HMC.Salis.MSS* XIX, 275.

48. *Ibid.*, 441.

49. *Ibid.*, 355.

50. *Ibid.*, 363.

51. Montagu, *Bacon* V, 83-105.

52. *Ibid.*, 84. See also Levack, 'Union of English and Scots Law', 97.

53. Montagu, *Bacon* V, 85.

54. Wormuth, *Royal Prerogative*.

55. Craig, *Ius Feudale*, ix.

56. S.P.14/27/1.

57. See above, Chapter 3, note 24. Craig clearly updated his works regularly. *De Unione*, written in 1604-5, thus contains later references to speeches in 1607 by Fuller, Piggott and Robinson: *Ibid.*, 329, 351, 356, 415.

58. N.L.S.Adv.MSS 33.1.1. Vol. II, fol. 38.

59. E.g. B.L.Sloane MSS 1786, fols. 100-4.

60. Levack, *Civil Lawyers*, 139 and 'Union of English and Scots Laws', 103-5. I am grateful to Dr Levack for our conversation and correspondence on this and other aspects of union.

61. E.g. Craig, *Right of Succession*, 431.

62. Craig, *De Unione*, 304-28.

63. See in particular McKechnie's comments in *Sources and Literature of Scots Law*, 34.

64. *HMC.Salis.MSS* XIX, 275.

65. *Ibid.*, 441 (for the demand) and 452-3 (for the arrangements).

66. Ferguson, *Scotland's Relations with England*, 104n: *Reg.PCSc.* VIII, 557-8. The difference between English and Scots nomenclature drew a typical barbed comment from Mackie, *History of Scotland*, 192n: 'The English know that the Scots are Calvinists and sometimes assume that they cannot spell their own names'.

67. *HMC.Salis.MSS* XIX, 293: 23 October 1607.

68. *Ibid.*, 297.

69. *Cal.S.P.(Dom) 1604-10*, 377 (Docquet, 29 October 1607). For the actual grant, see S.P.38/8/Oct 29 (Docquet Book).

70. Howell, *State Trials* II, Col. 608.

71. Jones, *Politics and Bench*, 49.

72. *HMC.Salis.MSS* XX, 191.

73. Wilson, *History of GB*, 41.

74. *Howell*, Col. 657.

75. Maidment, *Abbotsford Miscellany*, 219. See also S.P.14/32/40 fol. 64.

76. *Cal.S.P.(Dom)*, *1604-10*, 452.

77. *Maidment*, 219.

78. Pollard, *STC*, No. 7540.

79. *Cal.S.P.(Ven) 1607-10*, 137.

80. S.P.14/38/17.

81. *Reg.PCSc.* VIII, 557.

82. Levack, 'Union of English and Scots Law', 111.

83. *HMC.Downshire MSS*, II, 86.

84. *Ibid.*, 240.

85. *Cal.S.P.(Ven) 1607-10*, 450-1. For similar bills by Poole in 1607 and 1614, see *CJ* I, 328 and 493-4.

86. *Howell*, Cols. 608-58.

87. S.P.14/32/40.

88. S.P.14/34/10.

89. *Howell*, Col. 584.

90. This is clearest in Foster's speech: 'Law is *lex coronae, lex terrae*, not *lex regis*. There is ligeance of the subiect to ye k: to the kingdome and to ye lawes.' S.P.14/34/10 fol. 13r.

91. *Ibid.*, fol. 12v.

92. See B.L.Lansd.MSS 486, fols. 139-40.

93. Howell, Col. 579.

94. *Ibid.*, 580.

95. Cap.de Exceptionibus lib.5 fol. 47 and lib.4 fol. 297.

96. Howell, 606.

97. *Ibid.*, 587.

98. Spedding, *Bacon* III, 317.

99. Cf. Cowell, *Interpreter*, 'Alien': 'A man born out of the land, so it be within the limits of the King's obedience, beyond the sease, or of English parents, out of the King's obedience . . . is no alien'.

100. S.P.14/34/10 fol. 24.

101. *Ibid.*, fol. 26v.

102. Knafla, *Law and Politics*, 67. Knafla has also identified the sources used by Ellesmere in compiling his speech. These include the speeches of James opening the 1604 and 1606-7 sessions, the tracts of Doddridge and Savile, and Lincoln's Inn Maynard MSS 83:3 & 8.

103. Howell, 662.

104. Austin, *Allegiance Not Impeached*. Austin attempted by subtle distinctions to assert allegiance to the body politic, and justify resistance to Charles I.

105. Knafla, *Law and Politics*, 75.

106. Wheeler, 'Calvin's Case', 590ff.

107. Axton, *Two Bodies*, 21-2, 75, 131-47.

108. S.P.14/34/10 fol. 21r.

109. S.P.14/32/40 fol. 70v.

110. B.L.Sloane MSS 2716, fols. 11-12.

111. Wheeler, 'Calvin's Case', 595.

8
Conclusion

'When was their contract better driven by fate
   or celebrated with more truth of State?
The world the temple was, ye priest ye King,
   ye sponsored payre two Realmes, ye stay ye Ring.'[1]

1. Fallacies

I have concentrated on the political development of the union project.
Inevitably, this has involved excursions into aspects of religious, legal and
commercial history, as well as the history of constitutional thought, but these
have only been made where necessary to explain the political progress of the
union. My conclusions are therefore correspondingly political.

Most accounts of the union rely on a set of fallacies and misguided assumptions. This is as true of the century after 1608 as of the five preceding years. The
commonest fallacy about 1603-8 is to belittle the importance of the union
project, considering it insignificant or irrelevant to the 'real' political issues of
the period.[2] Equally, historians of the 1707 union and of Anglo-Scots relations
in the seventeenth century have frequently been misled into considering union
as inevitable, the culmination of a gradual growing together that started before
1603 and continued independently of political initiatives by James or other
rulers.[3]

Both these fallacies are implicitly Anglocentric. They assume that 'union'
meant the assimilation of Scotland into England, that this was Britain's natural
destiny, that the union of the crowns was somehow a part of this set course, and
that attempts to 'force its pace' by specific programmes were unnecessary and
counter-productive.

In examining both assumptions, let us start with the blanket dismissal of the
Jacobean project. This relies on certain beliefs about the motivations of James in
launching the union, and generally about the royal character. The project is
explained as a personal foible — not merely a pet policy, but a foolish and ill-
considered toy. The responsibility for this lies partly with Bruce[4] and James's
biographer, Willson. Willson presents the king as a political and personal
lightweight: vain, pompous, extravagant, cowardly, homosexual, concerned
more with pleasure than the detailed work necessary to run a troubled kingdom;
a good but pedantic brain overwhelmed by good fortune, egotistical theories of
divine right, and his own dreams of universal peace and brotherhood; ruled by
favourites and factions, distrusting and hectoring the loyal parliamentary
'opposition'.[5] Taught from infancy to consider union as part of his own personal
destiny, James 'was a man vouchsafed a glimpse of the awesome potential which

lay in the title "king of Great Britain", its owner mighty in stature among the rulers of Europe and God's chosen instrument for healing the breach between Catholic and Protestant'.[6] The Bellarmine campaign, the assertion of Britain's status as leading Protestant power while simultaneously seeking peace with Spain combines with the union project as a single obsession, obscuring the realities of domestic and foreign policy.

Upon this basis have been built sub-themes about the Jacobean project. One is its lack of support at any level of English society.[7] Willson doubts even Bacon's support. Cecil acted cautiously, from duty; most others saw no point in union, some covertly opposing it. Opinion on Scotland is divided. Some English historians see a parallel, citing Craig as the only 'unionist' Scot. Others, believing that union favoured Scotland, see Scots pressure behind its progress. Other themes emphasised are the excessive haste with which James promoted the question, and the absolute nature of the union advanced. Even Ferguson talks of an immediate and perfect union without proper time for discussion. A variation favoured by Wormuth invokes Jacobean theories of divine right.[8] James is held to have believed that, because all authority devolved from the monarchy, his accession automatically brought unity to the kingdoms. Parliaments were summoned merely to ratify union. This rapid unification programme was coupled with tactless importation of Scots favourites into English offices — if not of government or Council, at least of Household and Bedchamber.[9] Scots dominated James's court and favour, to the chagrin of the English.

These 'facts' are then used to justify parliamentary resistance. Since union served only to boost the grandeur of a vain king, and to gratify the Scots, English M.P.s were entirely reasonable in opposition. Trade, naturalisation etc. are all seen as being to the advantage of Scotland.

This picture of the project appears in the work of many 'whig' historians, and can be linked to their theories about the nature of parliament and its relations with the king. These trace the growth of parliamentary authority, and of the Commons within parliament, from revival under the Reformation crisis of Henry VIII through contentious sessions under Elizabeth (whose personality held off very real Puritan opposition in the Commons) to outright confrontation under the early Stuarts.[10] The growth of the Lower House, and of an 'opposition' or 'Country Party' within it counterbalancing the 'Court Party' of office-holders and courtiers, becomes a backdrop for the whig thesis on the origins of the English Civil War. During 1604-10, parliament is seen in an intermediate stage of development. Many features characterising the great Caroline parliaments may already be seen: the formalisation of procedure into three readings; the proliferation of committees, including the revolutionary Committee of the Whole House, circumventing the authority of 'royalist' Speakers; the use of the subsidy weapon to exact concessions; the alliance between gentry and common lawyers; the appeal to history to justify policy and extend parliamentary privilege. Royal management was hampered by the absence of Salisbury and almost all the Privy Councillors, in the Lords —

explaining the use of intermediaries like Thomas Wilson and Cecil's emphasis on conferences of the two Houses. This indirect control was made more difficult by the king: with no knowledge and much mistrust of English parliaments, James interrupted Salisbury's discreet daily manoeuvres with ill-considered and frequently ill-tempered speeches, full of peremptory command and divine-right abstractions uncongenial to an English mixed-monarchy tradition. Opposition was increasingly orchestrated by a cohesive group of leaders. Their programme was 'progressive', concerned with 'responsible government' (defined by Dodd as royal administration with a representative body and through ministers having the confidence of that body), parliamentary privilege, a Protestant if not Puritan religious settlement, and reform of grievances. The last — confirming the opposition as bearers of the nation's political conscience — are emphasised, at the expense of other issues such as supply or union.[11] Purveyancing, monopolies, wardships, impositions and the Great Contract are seen as the abiding issues of debate, carrying the greatest constitutional significance. Union was important only as the first occasion on which a major Stuart proposal openly backed by the king met defeat in and by the English House of Commons.

This has been a brief canter through familiar fields. Seen from a different angle, the landscape changes. Not every detail or feature is altered, but the new perspective is sufficient for the picture to carry an entirely different message. James above all gains from re-appraisal. Re-examination of the 'wisest fool in Christendom' has occupied several historians lately, scholars belatedly becoming aware of his considerable achievements in Scotland. Scots historians have always portrayed James as a much more competent and ruthless figure.[12] Aylmer poses the question: 'The basic problem with James VI and I is how far appearances deceive. Is it really the case that he was one of the most effective monarchs ever to rule over Scotland, and that, if not a disaster (that remained for his son) he was a failure as king of England?'[13]

2. The King's Project: A New Perspective

'James's actions and intentions have perhaps been more seriously misunderstood and misrepresented by historians in respect of this issue [i.e. the Union] than any other.'[14]

England and Scotland before 1560 were two of the most hostile nations in Christendom. Centuries of warfare and prejudice had isolated them from each other. Scotland's natural ally was France — natural, because both faced English aggression.[15] England claimed material, moral, spiritual, judicial and feudal superiority over Scotland — the last being a formal assertion of suzerainty, resisted steadfastly by successive Scots kings, rebutted by generations of her scholars.

How much had really changed by 1603? Changes should not be underestimated. Donaldson has shown that in certain areas like language and culture, Scotland had absorbed much that was English.[16] Unprecedented peace reigned between them — broken, however, by Border raiding and English-backed intervention in the 1580s. The two nations were united in adherence to protestantism. However much the two church settlements differed in detail, their Calvinist theology was united. There were some commercial links between the countries — though less than those connecting either to leading Continental nations.

Despite this, an enormous residue of misunderstanding and ill-will persisted. English claims to suzerainty were frequently re-stated, albeit in histories, plays and royal genealogies rather than diplomatic papers.[17] Scots like Craig continued resolute denials up to and beyond 1603.[18] It is not only significant that Shakespeare greeted the union with a play on Scotland — but equally notable that the tragedy was *Macbeth*, full of barbarous treachery and super-stition, and of English suzerainty over Scotland. As Thornborough showed, union had not removed the traditional opposition of the two nations in children's games. Differences between the two nations materially remained immense, as did the Englishman's assumption of general superiority.

The dangers posed by residual hostility after 1603 were compounded by a second factor — the existence of Scotland as a sovereign, nominally independent nation. The operative word is 'nominally'. At first, there was pride that a Scot should reign in England; yet there was equal worry, even humiliation, over the effects of James's accession.[19] Scotland would henceforth be deprived of its sovereign; the source of government and policy would be in distant London, only its executive arm remaining in Edinburgh. It is true that James surrounded himself partly with Scots counsellors and courtiers — but these were a new breed of 'native sons', Anglo-Scots with lands, titles and personal interests in the south. Russell's fears of Scotland becoming 'ane pendicle' of England could be echoed even by so ardent a unionist as Craig:

> No prince born in Scotland will ever rule that country after His Majesty's son. Our kings will be Englishmen, born and living in England, favouring Englishmen as their courtiers . . . London will be the seat of the Court and the capital of the whole island. Thence for the most part will the laws that govern us proceed, and to London we must look for directions.[20]

The prospects of a satisfied Scotland after the union of the crowns were therefore seen as poor by many contemporaries, on both sides of the Border. This dissatisfaction must pose a danger to the continuance of the union. Scotland might become generally alienated from England and Anglo-Scots government — a real possibility, given the feeling between the two peoples. With the differences between the needs, positions and interests of England and Scotland, points of conflict must inevitably arise. Alienation might produce an adverse Scots reaction, that her interests were being overlooked, and render that reaction more extreme. Possibilities for variance were considerable. At the least, the two nations might adopt different policies at variance with each other. This could produce a confrontation. Any attempt from London to break a stalemate might be interpreted in Edinburgh as another example of *reductio ad provinciam*.

Thornborough's warnings were precise: 'If union in name, bring also in deed, a composition and faithfull conjunction *bona fide*, it will doubtless by Gods goodnesse, last ever: but otherwise I feare (which God forbid) may againe rent in sunder, and make the new breach worse than the former'.[21]

The union of the crowns was thus seen to hold in itself the seeds of its own destruction: a great advancement for the Stuarts, but a great danger to their secure hold over either kingdom.

This was why James launched the union project — not vanity. The only real evidence for vanity lies in James's use of mythology. James encouraged the apocalyptic visions of men like Gordon and Galloway, and emphasised in his own speeches the direct and personal relationship between himself, divine providence and the union.[22] To assume from this that he was spellbound by a vision of 'Britannia Rediviva' is naive. No Tudor or Stuart monarch lacked a theatrical role full of Arthurian, Biblical and Classical significance. James drew eclectically from many sources to establish his roles, with a sophistication equal to Elizabeth's courtier/scholars. Yet he refused offers of 'Empire', and made no commitment to the apocalyptic mission of Gordon. Theatre was one thing: politics, quite another.

This commitment to security as the purpose of union has many implications. There is much confusion among historians about the nature of the project. Houston speaks of James's plans for the 1606-7 session as a union of law, religion and parliaments — none of which were on the agenda for discussion. A distinction must be made between James's immediate and long-term aims. Trevor-Roper and Levack alike emphasise ecclesiastical and legal union as abiding parts of the overall scheme, with parliamentary union being abandoned in 1604. Masson however believed that it was James's original intention to leave the two nations 'their separate apparatus of legislation and administration, their separate parliaments, Privy Councils and law courts'.[23] Even within the area of law, there is confusion. Did James intend a union of the whole law, as Craig and Saltern clearly favoured, its outstanding 'public' and 'fundamental' heights, as Bacon advised, or only such hostile laws as might maintain the marks of division? Levack believes the second, but James's words to the 1604 session point to the third.[24] Was this union to be by compromise on either side, or the assimilation of Scots to English law? Again, Levack's emphasis on the first is supported — and denied — by James's words. Similar questions arise on ecclesiastical union: was it to be doctrinal only, to involve the anglicisation of Scots discipline and *ecclesia*, or the subjection of both churches to a single primate? Did the appointment of five Anglo-Scots to the English Privy Council presage conciliar union?

The words and actions of the king can be used to support any of these interpretations. James was flexible, and pragmatic. The purpose of the union was to strengthen his dynastic hold over the two kingdoms. This entailed the establishment of mechanisms by which their conflicting interests could be reconciled, and the elimination of popular hostility and sense of distinctiveness — union in hearts and minds, supported by conformity in behaviour and customs. In all areas, James wanted ultimately the closest possible fusion. The more similar the kingdoms, the more conjoined by economic, political and spiritual bonds, the stronger the realm and the less the likelihood of friction. But since the aim was to eliminate friction, progress had to be gradual, each advance taking place by consent and understanding of both nations. Forced unity would be counter-productive. Unionist writers emphasised the superiority of love to fear in the creation of unity. To promote this coming together of hearts and minds, James encouraged unionist mythology, and united the outward marks or symbols of government — name, flag, seals, coinage, weights and measures etc. The Borders were pacified and re-named as part of the same fraternisation programme. Intermarriage between the nations was encouraged, and a mixture established in the court, Household and Council. This mixture was necessary for substantive as well as symbolic reasons. It was a gesture of goodwill and equality towards distant Scotland, and an insurance that, in times of conflict, there would be a point of reconciliation under the king's control.

To describe James as having any single 'plan' for union, and being forced to 'abandon' parts of it at an early stage, is to over-simplify. James was determined to seize every opportunity for unification that arose. If this meant promoting union in particular legal customs in 1604 but in 'fundamental laws' in 1607-8, or shelving parliamentary union until willing consent had been established, so be it.

This emphasis on hearts and minds, on consent and understanding as essential concomitants of union has two major implications. The first we have already stated: that James advanced his scheme cautiously, with leaden foot. Despite occasional references to the union being already settled or inherent in his accession, there is no evidence to support Wormuth's thesis. James did not consider that his accession automatically united the institutions and systems of his two countries, needing only parliamentary ratification. Nor did he press for immediate, rapid advances to union, in any parliamentary session. This connects with the second major implication: that James desired to create 'union' with the maximum possible use of either parliament. As the highest representatives of the people, the parliaments were uniquely placed to emphasise the joyful reconciliation of the two countries.[25] Thus James submitted to parliaments in both kingdoms proposals he could carry through by executive action — the change in style and removal of commercial customs being examples.

3. King and Parliament

Hitherto, we have examined mainly the aims of the union project. It is here that the most important errors of historical interpretation have been committed. The chronological account is generally more accurate, as is the central conclusion —

that the project was a failure, defeated primarily in and by the English House of Commons.

One could argue that James's plans were notably successful, outside parliament. Besides union in outward marks of government and pacification of the Borders, James was able to secure permanent naturalisation of the *Post-Nati*, abolition of hostile laws, the establishment of common law judicial arrangements in the 'Middle Shires', and several years of free trade between the nations. The last was ended only by the deepening financial crisis of the crown. Finally, James's campaign in Scotland to establish bishops and reduce the power of the General Assembly was eventually successful. Nevertheless, the union was clearly abortive, in two ways. The wider, long-term unions in law and government which James had considered essential for the elimination of friction and diversity proved unobtainable. More importantly, the project failed to inspire the hearts and minds of his peoples with any sense of unity. The years of union were marked by increasing acrimony, national self-consciousness and prejudice — indications of genuine failure, given the project's aim of reconciliation. James's progressive retreat from union after 1607 was perhaps hastened by an awareness of this paradox.

But it is in parliament that defeat seems undeniable. The whig thesis of an increasing parliamentary resistance to the Stuarts based on an aggressive Lower House has been challenged recently by many historians.[26] The attack has come from many different directions. The effectiveness of opposition has been denied. The supply weapon was dulled by the unwillingness of the Commons to wield it, and by the comparative insignificance of parliamentary revenue. The crown had little incentive to abolish or reform lucrative grievances such as monopolies, patents and wardships, unless offered a composition — which the House would not grant. Nor did parliament's place as a legislature give its debates particular importance. Stuart monarchs believed that there were already too many statutes, with few new public acts required. Proclamations, prohibitions, permissions etc. created an effective 'administrative law', bypassing not only parliament but also common law courts. Parliament did less public business and met less frequently, while the activity of Privy Council, signet office and Great Seal increased correspondingly. The steps taken by the Commons to regularise procedures, expand privileges, elaborate its committee system and 'seize the initiative' only hastened the day when its increasing inconvenience, irrelevance and opposition to the crown led it, like representative assemblies throughout Christendom, into oblivion.

Russell questions the nature of opposition in the Lower House. Opposition is considered rare, Commons cooperating with Lords and Parliament with Court on most items of the legislative programme. 'Disagreement between King and Parliament [was] regarded by all those concerned . . . as a failure . . . a cause of shame and disgrace'. 'The purpose of a successful parliament was not to engage in constitutional conflict, but to do business.'[27] There was no recognised or organised opposition 'party'. Resistance on particular issues was *ad hoc*, by varying, ill-defined groups of men under different spokesmen, reacting to events happening elsewhere. The 'party' had no particular programme save opposition to crown proposals. Aspiring politicians saw parliament not as a career, but as a stepping-stone to favour. People wanting something done would seek to influence the king or a court patron, not work through the Commons. Opposition in the House reflected divisions of opinion within powerful court factions. To speak of a permanent, aggressive opposition intent on constitutional and political changes within Stuart government is therefore seen as simplistic. Many M.P.s were, after all, office-holders in their local shires or towns. They were tied to 'Court' and 'Country' alike, and had a vested interest in the elimination of friction.

Where does the union fit into this controversy? Initially, it provides some conformation of the whig interpretation. The project *was* the first occasion when a proposal openly and vigorously supported by a Stuart king met defeat in and by the Lower House. It *did* produce strident, argued opposition by a coherent group of M.P.s, fighting what Notestein has called 'a rearguard action' by 'a policy of delay and objections'.[28] Many specific factors stressed by the whigs are confirmed. The shortage of Councillors, the absence of Cecil, the use of committees (and particularly the Committee of the Whole House) were all tactically important in the defeat. The use of conferences *is* as notable as Willson and Notestein suggest. James's management of the Commons *was* unsuccessful — although qualification is necessary here. James has been condemned by the whigs for hectoring, pedantic and self-important speeches. In fact, his speeches on the union were made in reaction to extreme provocation, and compare favourably in tone with those of his predecessor. They also provided detailed and moderate justifications of the project, cogently answering many objections advanced to individual proposals. He was generally much more 'constitutional' in his treatment of parliament than Elizabeth.[29] His main fault, correctly identified by Willson, was his undoubted unwillingness to become involved in detail, and his frequent absences at Royston. But the scant attention paid by the Commons to his words says rather more about the House itself than about James.

On detailed inspection, the union shows rather less support for the whig thesis. Despite Notestein,[30] there is no evidence of prior consultation by leaders of the resistance. The extent to which the resistance group can be called a *party* of 'opposition' is doubtful. Even Willson calls its operations 'unpremeditated and individual', without 'the organised leadership of political chiefs'.[31] Resistance came from a range of individuals, differing greatly in their method of opposition. It is only necessary to mention the names of Fuller and Yelverton on one hand, and Sandys on the other, to see this. Attempts to create an opposition party in 1604-7 from those opposing union have revealed some incongruous names — minor court officials, members of provincial Councils like Owen and Crofts, people with prominent local positions dependent on good working relations with the crown. These are precisely those persons you would expect to support James, and who do so on other issues. Attempts to define a single opposition 'policy' on union are similarly doomed. The same speakers who vehemently opposed the change in style in 1604 because it might lead to a union of laws as stoutly pressed three years later for the 'perfect union'. The 'opposition' was just that: it *reacted* against the royal proposals, using many, often contradictory, objections as seemed tactically most suitable.[32]

Having decided the whig picture of a coordinated opposition is inadequate, what are we left with? One could substitute Russellian faction as the motive force behind resistance. Throughout the project there are rumours of support for the Lower House from peers and courtiers. Ambassadors speak of collusion, and the anger of James with nobles who defied the official line. Holles sees the division between the Houses as illusory, the Lords using the Commons as a screen for their own opposition.[33] But it is difficult to identify which 'faction' at court is spearheading the resistance. Some have considered Cecil privily opposed to the union, yet manuscript records show him working painstakingly in support, both personally and through dependants in the Commons. His willingness to make concessions is matched by his anger when the Lower House persists in 'unreasonable' resistance. Ellesmere, another possibility (given his later clashes with Scots at court) was similarly active in support, both in parliament and Chancery.[34] The most likely name would be Northampton. He too was prominent in opposition to the Scots at court, after 1610, and generally recognised as Cecil's main rival. A few fragments of evidence point his way: James's letter of condemnation, the ambiguous references in the Paper Booke, and the appeal from the disfavoured Yelverton are the principal examples. In his speeches on union, however, Northampton is notably fulsome.[35] This may suggest covert resistance; it does not really support the Russellian thesis of open faction at court spreading into the halls of Westminster.

Union was, *sui generis*, attracting a much wider resistance throughout the political nation than other issues. The conventional picture of a project launched by James and supported by none is a gross exaggeration. The tracts demonstrate considerable support for union, in both nations. Nevertheless, James clearly failed to convince sufficient people in England or Scotland of the necessity for the union, despite a massive campaign of explanation and propaganda. His strong, persuasive message simply did not get across. In 1606-7, even loyal servants of the crown are found supporting limitations on naturalisation, and the 'perfect union'. This was why union was defeated. It was not through 'Court vs Country', or even faction, but a general revolt on a specific issue. Union cannot therefore be taken as indicative of normal relations between king and parliament. This cuts both ways. By demolishing the thesis of an organised opposition party, it denies the whig interpretation. On the other hand, it simultaneously demonstrates that, on a political or constitutional issue of particular importance, normal political guidelines ceased to apply. King and Parliament, Lords and Commons might cooperate happily on normal issues, if faction did not intervene; but a 'whiggish' reaction *was* possible — given the right issue.

M

4. Forces Working for and against the Union Project

Section three has examined *how* the union was defeated, in the English Commons. This section explains *why*, briefly summarising the factors working for and (predominantly) against acceptance of union, in either country.

Forces for union are notable mainly by their absence. There was some appreciation in England, and more in Scotland, of the need for unity in affections. Many writers spoke of the instability of the existing settlement, and of the dangers of future conflicts of interest between the nations. Without the growth of sympathy and identity between English and Scots, Hayward said, all other changes would be worthless. Alongside this realisation was the potentiality for union: the existing 'unions' or similarities in language, geography, behaviour and religion. Trevor-Roper and Tyacke amongst others have confirmed the implications of the tracts regarding the assumptions of an identity in doctrine.[36] This was a powerful incentive to union — as serious doctrinal differences would have constituted an absolute disincentive. This religious unity made possible a second line of propaganda — arguing not only union's necessity, but its place within the universal scheme of God. As Williamson has demonstrated, the absence of a separate, apocalyptic, missionary dogma in Scotland strongly impelled many there to acceptance of 'Britain', with its revolutionary and messianic overtones.[37] In England, too, the British vision had great success, notwithstanding the rival tradition of an English Elect Nation. This success reflected official encouragement by James. The king's personal involvement in the project may be counted as the most important factor working for its success — not merely for its own sake, but its effects on royal servants and those seeking favour. The greatest weakness of the union was correspondingly its failure to gain any other coherent interest group. Individuals might be inspired by its political logic or spiritual possibilities, but no major group in either kingdom declared itself clearly in favour of the programme. The few groups attracted were generally minorities — civil lawyers in England, Episcopalians in Scotland. Even in the 'Middle Shires', where arguments about security might be expected to carry most weight, there was ambivalence towards the idea of union, and the pacification measures proposed in its name.

Against this weak range of factors can be serried four major countervailing forces: prejudice, nationhood, self-interest and conservatism. These themes have recurred so regularly as to need only brief re-statement here. There can be no doubt about the importance of the residual animosity and prejudice between the peoples. It is one factor on which every historian since Bruce is agreed.[38] At each point of tension during the project, hostilities were resumed. The two nations reacted to the Gunpowder Plot — a 'British' crisis — by separate, even antagonistic expressions of anger and loyalty. At all times. Englishmen would make derogatory remarks about Scotland, to which Scots would over-react. James's attempts to establish a necessary mixture of the nations at court provoked innumerable squabbles.

A closely allied theme was nationhood. Each nation was established in a separate identity, defined in part by historical opposition to the other. The two kingdoms also had different, indeed contradictory, ideas about their correct relationship. Most Englishmen clearly wanted either no union, or one (such as the 'perfect union') confirming English superiority. That 'superiority' was expressed differently; some saw it in material terms, others as a moral or spiritual affair. Lawyers and scholars were likely to invoke the panoply of suzerainty. Whichever justification was used, Scotland as resolutely rejected such claims. The only union acceptable to her was one that was demonstrably equal. This impasse endangered the entire project. Fears of inequality recur continually in Scots tracts, and even in letters to the king.[39] The absence of the court in London, the danger to Scots religion, laws, privileges, rights and dignities were all raised.[40] The English chronicler Arthur Wilson said it all:

> There is an inequality in the Fortunes of the two Nations; and by this Commixture, there may ensue advantage to them, and Losse to us.

> The Scots would not lessen, nor in the least derogate from the dignity of their long continued Monarchy, and the English thought they had no reason to come to them to derogate from themselves.[41]

The third major factor against the union was self-interest. This was apparent in the arguments over naturalisation and trade. Naturalisation involved offices, and the careers of aspiring English courtiers and politicians: hence the restrictions proposed in the Commons during March-April 1607. Bickering against Scots at court continued throughout the ensuing decade.[42] Commerce drew enormous protestation from English M.P.s and merchants, prophesying ruin. In practice there was no flood of Scots into high offices in England, while free trade threatened the underdeveloped Scots mercantile marine more than the English. Wedgwood, Lythe and Riley alike dismiss the arguments used as based upon prejudice and false premises. It is obvious that perceptions of self-interest were distorted by dislike and fear of the Scots.

The fourth factor was a deep conservatism, going beyond merely rational caution. It comprised a particular set of beliefs, about the law and constitution. English beliefs about the superiority, immemoriality and quasi-immutability of common law, and about the intimate relationship between law and the health of the body politic, were widespread enough to create an ambivalent attitude towards union.[43] The prospect of uniting English law with Scots appalled many; but such a union was seen as the only way to ensure the success of 'Great Britain', the only safeguard against Scots exploitation of naturalisation. The two alternatives were therefore again to have no union, or to have one involving submission of Scots law to English — the 'perfect union'. This was confirmed by arguments from the 'historical philosophy of union' — a conservative dogma that in effect if not intent matched the revolutionary, Providential Philosophy of James. Scotland could see law and national institutions in a more utilitarian manner, as Williamson has pointed out; but her concern for equality and sovereignty created an intransigence just as implacable as English legalism, which saw in the alteration of a name the dissolution of the entire common-wealth.[44]

The operation of these factors in England is patent; but one must not forget the Scots dimension simply for lack of documentary evidence. The Scots political nation *did* obey James faithfully on the union. The Council and parliament *were* normally as docile as the king had claimed.[45] No bill put before them for union went unpassed. However, the influence of Scotland on political developments was considerable. Too much has been made by Levack and others of the savings in the Scots Act of Commission. These merely parroted royal policy decided in April 1604. More significant is the lobbying of the king by Mar to produce that policy in the first place. The concern of the Scots Council with equality and sovereignty is everywhere evident — in the controversy over the flags, in their commendation of Craig, in their outrage at English Piggotry in 1607. Ferguson's talk of the Scots parliament 'smuggling' a condition into their 1607 act making it conditional on English parliamentary ratification is nonsense. The condition reflected the Act's inclusion of free trade and naturalisation — an inclusion effected to assert Scots loyalty against the 'unnatural' resistance of the English Commons. In general, the prior meetings of the English parliaments removed the onus for opposition from Scotland; but resistance there was, and one whose effect on royal policy and the stance of the English Commons was occasionally crucial.

5. Aftermath

I have examined the political development of the Union project, isolating the main factors working for and against its success. Strictly speaking, the history of Anglo-Scots Union after James is irrelevant. Nevertheless, something may be said, to show how the principal themes of this conclusion fit into the overall picture of union.

At the beginning of this conclusion, I dismissed the thesis of inevitable growth towards union. This is a thesis which has inevitably come under attack, notably from Ferguson, who considers each union project to be 'a phenomenon dominated by its own immediate and usually far from simple circumstances'.[46] This is true; but such atomisation should not obscure the very real continuity between these projects. This continuity is partly direct. Papers, tracts, methods of approach and blocks of argument from the Jacobean project recur during other attempts. More importantly, the projects illustrate the same factors as James's programme.

This is best demonstrated by the first revival of unionism in the seventeenth century: the dialogue between Englishmen and Scots in the '30s and '40s. The history of the Scottish revolution after 1637 and its close connections with the outbreak of the English Civil War have been clarified by much useful modern work.[47] One prominent theme is the effect of English domination on the Scots during the National Covenant. Riley emphasises the instability of the settlement left behind by the failure of the Jacobean Union.[48] It was an Anglocentric union, in which the centre of power was London; yet Scotland remained a separate, sovereign nation, with its own institutions and methods of determining policy. This not only made possible the *national* revolution of 1637 — it also made it more likely. Stevenson has shown how absentee rule, effective loss of nationhood and the continuation of prejudice led to Scottish alienation from the seat of government.[49] This alienation increased under Charles, for two allied reasons. One was the anglicisation of the Court. Charles had little sympathy for or experience of Scotland; his advisers were English, his religion and court culture likewise. As Craig had predicted, the 'British' court of James I did not survive his death. The second, compelling reason for alienation was the attempted Anglicanisation of the Kirk. Many Scots thought this part of a stealthy programme of incorporation into England. Trevor-Roper accepts the existence of such a programme, under James and Charles alike.[50] James, however, prudently abandoned ecclesiastical Anglicanisation in 1621. The decision to allow Laud a free rein in Scotland offended more than the men of property threatened by Acts of Revocation, or the Presbyterian clergy. It also offended the ecclesiastical independence of Scotland. The Kirk became the rallying point of Scottish nationhood, rather than the fanatical *organiser* of resistance postulated by Trevor-Roper.[51] 'Constitutional and other secular grievances contributed powerfully to the revolt.'[52]

The Scottish revolution confirmed the instability of the Union of the Crowns and the wisdom of James's project. Perhaps the most interesting feature of the Covenanters over the ensuing years was their awareness of the situation. This was forced on them by the situation itself. Since the origin of the dispute lay in the Anglocentric nature of the settlement, they were compelled to consider changing the ground rules of union. This was never truer than in the early years of the Civil War. Scotland might in theory have its own independent treaty with Charles, defending her Kirk and privileges; but Royalist victory in England would in short time negate any separate, Scottish arrangement. The Solemn League and Covenant both rejected this realisation, and renewed the pressure for alterations in the union.

What were these 'alterations'? The options were many. Scots might reject the union entirely, or accept incorporate union on the best terms possible — or strive for links between the countries giving Scotland the national voice at the centre of power she so badly needed. The last meant an equal, federal union, necessary as a tactical move coordinating resistance to Charles, and as a long-term constitutional arrangement guaranteeing Scots interests. Scots sought permanent links between the two Parliaments — either by 'Conservators', as in the 1641 peace treaty and the Solemn League and Covenant, or by a formal Committee of Both Kindoms.[53] Matters of mutual interest would be discussed, including foreign policy and the making of war and peace. Naturalisation would be confirmed, free trade established.[54] Privy Councils and Households would contain natives of either kingdom. These demands persisted during the 1640s, in negotiations with the English Parliament and the King (for example the

Propositions of Newcastle and the Engagement). Stevenson's thesis of a genuine, prolonged attempt to convince England of the need for federal ties is unassailable. His de-emphasis of the importance or (to England) revolutionary nature of the commitment to Presybterianism in the Covenant should, however, be deplored. Trevor-Roper is perhaps wrong in believing that England could never have become Presbyterian, but there is no doubting that, by 1643, Scots resistance had taken on a particular apocalyptic vision and reforming zeal. This later drastically split Scotland, and fuelled existing English prejudices against alliance.

The breakdown of the alliance between the English and Scots showed the fragility of the links set up after the personal Union of the Crowns. Yet it was that personal Union which created the Engagement, the second Civil War, and eventually the Cromwellian conquest of Scotland. Unable to live together or apart, the two nations were like unruly horses fighting in the shafts.

The 'Covenanter' period of union illustrates very clearly the insecurity and alienation brought on by the Union of the Crowns, and the solution preferred by Scotland. The Cromwellian Union, examined painstakingly by Dow,[55] was by contrast an English settlement reflecting English 'solutions'. At one time, the possibilities of using the Historical Philosophy of Union were considered, with Scotland being treated as a conquered province or a consolidated fief.[56] This was rejected in favour of a 'consensual' union, with ratifying assemblies in Scotland and a deputation of Scots to London. In practice, the unification and settlement that resulted were Anglocentric. Resistance to union was submerged by force, Scotland receiving a Cromwellian army and heavy taxes to pay for the same. The union was incorporative, Scotland sending a few M.P.s, mainly Englishmen and tame native officials, to Parliament at Westminster.[57] As Ferguson has said, 'The ultimate aim . . . was one unified nation, an enlarged England'.[58]

Cromwell sought to build up a party of 'godly men', from the 'middling sort', bound to neither of the presbyterian factions. This was combined with attempts to set the middling and lesser sort free from excessive aristocratic power, by the abolition of hereditary jurisdictions. Attempts to replace Scots with English law failed, while the judicial system established was *ad hoc*, not geared to long-term unification.[59] The failure of this policy reflected the absence of any anti-aristocratic, anti-clerical party or educated gentry in Scotland. Broghill's attempt after 1655 to enlist moderate Resolutioners similarly failed — not so much because of their fanatical zeal, as Trevor-Roper asserts, but the unwillingness of Scots to accept the dictates of an occupying power. Not even free trade and common citizenship compensated for loss of sovereignty or equality. Most Scots agreed with Robert Blair that 'As for the embodying of Scotland with England, it will be as when the poor bird is embodied into the hawk that hath eaten it up'.[60] The retreat from the Anglocentric, incorporating union at the Restoration was in many ways a watershed. Henceforth, no legal or religious union would be possible, not merely because these were hallmarks of pride and national identity, especially in Scotland, but also because English and Scots systems increasingly diverged. The Scots adherence to presbyterianism and the codification of Scots law by Stair are relevant here. The return to two 'independent', contiguous sovereignties under one monarch — one country being much weaker than the other and distant from the centre of power — inevitably created further insecurity. The first trouble was commercial. The English mercantile economy boomed, the Scots lapsed. English Navigation Acts treated Scots as foreigners, yet Scotland was involved in wars with her best trading partners, to foster English commercial aspirations. The consequence was a renewed union project, beginning first as commercial negotiations and ending in a full-blown Commission for parliamentary and political union.[61] It is worth noting that 'the proposals submitted for discussion at that time were modelled point by point on the modified recommendations of King James in 1604', using papers from the Jacobean project to support national positions.[62] The same issues of sovereignty and equality arose, Englishmen pointing to their 'suzerainty', Scots denying same and demanding at least the retention of fundamental laws.[63] Scots opinion was against union, with reminders of the Cromwellian 'Union'; and the project eventually foundered on a remarkable demand by the Scots, as an equal nation, for equal representation with England in the proposed British Parliament!

We are getting so far now from the Jacobean union that individual analysis of projects becomes meaningless. Nevertheless, the remaining union projects (1689, 1702-3 and 1704-7) display many familiar themes. They arose not from a withering away of differences, but from moments of high tension when the Union of the Crowns threatened finally to break down into international confrontation. They were launched by monarchs conscious of the situation's inherent instability,[64] and reflected the different commercial, diplomatic, religious and political interests of the two countries. Scotland strove for an equal union, often stressing federal solutions against the Anglocentric and incorporative plans sent up from London. An incorporative settlement was eventually achieved only by the exclusion of religion and law. It was a settlement that did little to bring about the union in identity for which James had striven. Scotland was not fully subordinated to 'Britain' until after 1745; even thereafter, residual nationalist feelings remained, waiting to surface in more propitious times.

In 1603, a close and truly national union had seemed possible, despite all the hostility and prejudice, to submerge the identity of the two kingdoms in one, at least as far as Wales had done with England, Brittany with France, and Aragon with Castile. Prejudice, conservatism, and the rival demands for superiority and equality defeated the Jacobean project, and with it the best opportunity for secure union in Britain. The same factors operated throughout the seventeenth century, wherever the patent insecurity of the 1603 settlement impelled a move towards union. Eventually conceived almost by accident in the political manoeuvrings of 1702-7, the new child of Britain remained a weakling and, in some ways, a Siamese twin.

NOTES

1. Oxford Ashmolean MSS 47, fol. 45: 'Epitaph on the Union'.
2. See e.g. Gardiner's dismissal of the union in a few pages: *History* I, 170ff. and 330ff. The effect on lesser works is pronounced: Houston, *James I* gives twenty times the space to the Goodwin-Fortescue Case as to the union in 1604, not even mentioning the Commission or the change in the style!
3. Even Nobbs has fallen into this trap! 'In the course of the seventeenth century, Scotland developed politically and economically to such an extent that by 1700 a union with England closer than the union of the two crowns became possible and, at least to some minds, a necessity' — *England and Scotland*, xi.
4. See Bruce, *Report on the Union*, I, 31ff.
5. Willson's general verdict is tempered by occasional appreciation of the king's wider abilities: see *James VI and I*, 166-8, 186.
6. Willson, 'James and Anglo-Scottish Unity', 43; Riley, *Union of England and Scotland*, 4.
7. Gardiner, *History*, I, 332.
8. Wormuth, *Royal Prerogative*, 52.
9. Willson, 'James and Anglo-Scottish Unity', 47 and 53 is the clearest summary of these pervading themes.
10. For the period before 1603, see Neale, *Elizabethan Commons* and *Parliaments of Elizabeth*. Gardiner, Notestein, Willson, Mitchell and Rabb continue the whig interpretation into the early Stuart period.
11. Several writers note with a dismissive air the lack of any royal programme save for union and supply, Willson, *Privy Councillors*, 24 and Russell, *1621-9*, 46 being examples.
12. See e.g. Donaldson, *Scotland*, 214-15; Mackie, *History of Scotland*, 179-82; Masson, in *Reg.PCSc.*VII, xxvii. See also Lythe, *Economy of Scotland*, 250.
13. Review of Smith, *James VI and I*, in *S.H.R.* LIII (1974), 228.
14. Munden, 'Growth of Mutual Distrust', 62.
15. This is how Scotland is portrayed in Shakespeare: an ally of France (*Henry V*), a refuge of rebels and ex-kings (*I and II Henry IV*, *III Henry VI*). Particularly explicit is *Henry V*, Act I, Sc.ii, lines 166-73.
16. Donaldson, 'Foundations of Anglo-Scottish Unity'.
17. B.L.King's MSS 396 fol. 28v is a particularly magnificent and explicit genealogical expression of suzerainty.
18. Craig, *De Hominio* and *Right of Succession* (e.g. 350).
19. At James's departure, there was 'such a mourning and lamentation of all sorts, as cannot be well expressed. For albeit they joyed not a little at first to hear of that accession of honour to their King, yet considering they should be deprived of his presence, and have no more a resident among them, they were grieved out of all measure'. *Spottiswoode*, 476.
20. Craig, *De Unione*, 440-1.
21. Thornborough, *Discourse*, 218.
22. See e.g. his 'corner-stone' speech: Spedding, *Bacon* III, 68-9.
23. *Reg.PCSc.* VII, xxix. Trevor-Roper believes that James originally wanted parliamentary union, but dropped this in 1604 after experiencing the English parliament: 'Union of Britain', 451.
24. Levack, 'Union of English and Scots Law', 97-102.
25. Russell, *1621-9*, 54 for the central publicising function of parliament; Munden, 'Growth of Mutual Distrust', 63 for its application to 1604.
26. Russell, *1621-9*, 'Parliamentary History in Perspective', 'Parliament and the King's Finances' (in *Origins of ECW*; Hinton, 'Decline of Parliamentary Government'; Myers, 'Parliaments of Europe', etc.
27. Russell, *1621-9*, 5 and 35.

28. Notestein, *Winning of the Initiative*, 167.

29. Wormuth, *Royal Prerogative*, 93 agrees: 'He never did undertake any action for which there was not fairly good legal warrant; he was certainly a more moderate and "constitutional" monarch than Henry VII, Henry VIII or Elizabeth . . . a reexamination of the reign of James would disclose far less apprehension on the part of subjects, far less jealousy of the Crown, than the Whigs have taught us to believe'.

30. Notestein, *House of Commons*, 504.

31. Willson, 'Earl of Salisbury', 283; *Bowyer*, xx.

32. Munden, 63-4; Rabb, 'Sir Edwin Sandys', 649.

33. *Cal.S.P.(Ven) 1603-7*, 151, 494; *De la Boderie* II, 89-90, 136; B.L.Add.MSS 30641, fol. 98v; HMC.Portland MSS I, 12-13.

34. Knafla argues that Ellesmere supported Union 'to strengthen the regional character of the kingdom': *Law and Politics*, 87.

35. See: B.L.Harl.MSS 1314, 146-7; B.L.Cott.MSS Tit.CVI fols. 178, 186, 415-26 and 429-34.

36. Trevor-Roper, 'Union of Britain', 448; Tyacke's remarks are in Russell, *Origins of ECW*, 120-1.

37. Williamson, *Scottish National Consciousness*, 31, 95-6 etc.

38. E.g. Munden, 63-4: 'The specific objections employed by these opponents were not, on the whole, objections to the name as much as to the whole idea of a Union. What is more, they were permeated by fear, hatred and a national pride that verged on racial intolerance'.

39. See e.g. the Scots Council's insistence on 'a trew and friendlie Unioun, not a conquered and slavishe province to be governed by a Viceroy or Deputye': Wedgwood, 'Anglo-Scottish Relations', 34. Also relevant: Gordon, *Ενωτικον*, 40; Craig, *De Unione*, 271, etc., etc.

40. Riley perceptively calls these 'the visible signs of their independence': *Union of England and Scotland*, 4.

41. Wilson, *History of GB*, 35, 41.

42. Willson, *Privy Councillors*, 154n; Wedgwood, 'Anglo-Scottish Relations'.

43. For these beliefs, see Pocock, *Ancient Constitution*; Gough, *Fundamental Law*, esp. 56; Judson, *Crisis of Constitution*, esp. 44, 47.

44. Williamson, *Scottish National Consciousness*, 139.

45. *Reg.PCSc.* VII, xxvi.

46. Ferguson, *Scotland's Relations with England*, 142.

47. See esp: Stevenson, *1637-44* and *1644-51*; Trevor-Roper, 'Union of Britain' and 'Scotland and the Puritan Revolution'; Cowan, 'Covenanters'; Ferguson, *Scotland's Relations with England*.

48. Riley, *Union of England and Scotland*, 4-5: 'In 1603 there was created a system of three kingdoms — England, Ireland and Scotland — within which the political forces were finely balanced. For such a structure to function effectively there had to exist one dominant power, either through the Crown's imposing its will on all kingdoms alike or through the primacy of a particular kingdom'.

49. Stevenson, *1637-44*, 313-14 and 319-24. Stevenson's use of reference theory is particularly apt.

50. Trevor-Roper, 'Union of Britain', 451-4; Wedgwood, 32; Stevenson, *1637-44*, 313; Smout, *Scottish People*, 66.

51. Trevor-Roper, Ibid., 446 and 'Scotland and the Puritan Revolution', 78-130 *passim*. As Russell has said in *Origins of ECW*, 12-13: 'Many of the Scottish nobility who allied with Puritan ministers were not really Puritans at all. For them, there was an issue of Scottish dignity and independence: a protest against reduction to the status of a neglected frontier province'.

52. Stevenson, 'Trevor-Roper and the Scottish Revolution', 35. Trevor-Roper's Anglocentric analysis of the Kirk during this period is rightly considered simplistic.

53. Notestein, 'Committee of Both Kingdoms'.

54. Stevenson, *1637-44*, 221 and *1644-51*, 218-23.

55. Dow, *Cromwellian Union*. See also Firth, *Scotland and the Protectorate* and *Scotland and the Commonwealth* and *Last Years of the Protectorate*, Terry, *Cromwellian Union*.

56. Note the collection of papers on suzerainty drawn up by Bulstrode Whitelocke: B.L.Harl.MSS 1300.

57. Firth, *Last Years of Protectorate*, II, 85. Pinckney, 'Scottish Representation in 1656', 95, emphasises however that 'by 1656 nearly half the members could be said to have represented true Scottish interests'.

58. Ferguson, *Scotland's Relations with England*, 138.

59. Levack, 'Union of English and Scots Law', 112.

60. Firth, *Scotland and Commonwealth*, xxv.

61. Hughes, 'Negotiations for a Commercial Union'; Terry, *Cromwellian Union*.

62. Levack, 113.

63. See esp: Terry, *Cromwellian Union*; Ferguson, 'Imperial Crown'; N.L.S.Adv.MSS 31.7.7 (Mackenzie's 'Discourse Concerning the Three Unions betwixt England and Scotland'); Prynne, *The History of King John etc.* (London, 1670); B.L.Add.MSS 32094, fols. 246-58 (answering Prynne's allegations of suzerainty). Omond, *Scottish Union Question* remains the best (almost the only) general account of the 1667-70 union project.

64. Riley, *Union of England and Scotland*, 3: 'The most powerful incentives to the union of England and Scotland had always been political: security and ease of government, considerations present throughout the whole catalogue of union projects. Any ruler who thought he was strong enough tried to impose unity on the island. Such designs had their origin in the need for military security . . . and invariably the policy was foisted on the nation from the top'. See also Ferguson, *Scotland's Relations with England*, 197.

Bibliography

This Bibliography contains a comprehensive list of the manuscript and printed sources used in my research. It does not include materials that have been consulted, but which have not been directly used in writing this book.

The list of materials used is divided into the following sections:
- A: Manuscript Sources,
- B: Primary Printed Sources.
- C: Secondary Printed Sources.
- D: Unpublished Dissertations.

Section B includes contemporary manuscript sources subsequently published in a printed work: e.g. Sir Thomas Craig's 'De Unione Regnorum Britanniae Tractatus' (written 1605-7, first published 1909).

Section C includes both books and articles.

Section A is listed numerically, by manuscript collection. The other sections are listed alphabetically, by author or occasionally by title (in anonymous works or official collections such as *Acts of the Parliaments of Scotland*).

SECTION A. MANUSCRIPT SOURCES

Numbers appearing in the main reference after colons refer to the identifications given in the appropriate catalogue. Thus 'B.L.Add.MSS 4161:2' = the second item listed in B.L.Add.MSS catalogue for volume 4161.

Conventional abbreviations used in the chapter notes are identified after the Collection, in inverted commas.

PUBLIC RECORD OFFICE

State Papers (Domestic) = 'S.P.'

14/6/42.
14/7/29, 38, 39, 40, 41, 48, 49, 52, 57, 58, 59, 60, 61, 62, 63, 64, 65, 66, 67, 68, 69, 70, 72, 73, 74, 75, 76, 77, 78, 79, 80, 80b, 81, 85.
14/8/2, 3, 4, 5, 6, 9, 10, 37, 38, 61, 63, 82, 93, 100, 101, 102.
14/9/35, 36, 37, 37.1, 42, 82.
14/10/12, 15, 16, 17, 18, 19, 21, 22, 39, 40, 41, 55, 56, 82, 83.
14/17/98, 99.
14/19/1.
14/21/15, 16, 21.
14/22/3.
14/23/60, 61, 62.
14/24/2, 3, 4, 5, 6, 7, 8, 9, 10, 11, 12, 13, 16, 20, 23.
14/26/50, 53, 54, 55, 64, 65, 66, 68, 69, 70, 72, 73, 74, 75, 76, 77, 78, 79, 80, 81, 85, 86, 87, 88, 92.
14/27/1, 2, 9, 14, 30, 42, 43, 44, 45, 53, 54, 60, 61, 62.

14/28/51.
14/32/40.
14/34/10.
14/38/17.
14/51/3.
14/57/100, 104.
14/216/18, 37, 39. (Gunpowder Plot Book).

BRITISH LIBRARY

Additional MSS = 'B.L.Add.MSS'.

3479.
4149: 14, 15.
4160: 122, 123, 126, 130.
4161: 2.
4164: 49.
4173: 3.
4176: 6, 8, 9, 10, 11, 12, 13, 14.
6128.
6178 pps 561, 763.
8981.
12497 fos 153-60.
14289.
17747.
23132 fol. 100.
26635.
29975 fol. 12.
30639.
30640.
30641.
30666: 1, 3, 6.
32094, fos 246-58.
35864.
38139, fos 24-102.
38170.
41613, fos 37-47, 119v-30, 149-51.

Egerton MSS = 'B.L.Eger.MSS'.

2877, fol. 170v.

King's MSS = 'B.L.King's MSS'.

124.
396.

Harleian MSS = 'B.L.Harl.MSS'.

158, fos 165-6.
292: 48, 50, 54, 55, 56, 57, 58, 59, 60, 61, 62, 63, 64.

383.
532: 7.
1130: 3.
1300: 1, 2, 3, 5, 6, 7, 9, 10, 13, 35, 36, 37, 38.
1305: 1, 2.
1314: 1, 2, 3, 4, 5, 6, 7.
1583: 40, 41.
1607, fos 17-18.
1875: 58.
3787: 26, 28.
6797: 2, 3, 10.
6798: 2, 3, 4, 5, 6.
6806: 209, 210.
6842: 1, 2, 3, 52.
6846: 56.
6850: 8 (fos 35-64).
7189: 1.

Stowe MSS = 'B.L.Stowe MSS'.

132, fos 55-6, 141-2, 183-8.
158, fos 34-9.
180: 7.

Hargrave MSS = 'B.L.Hargrave MSS'.

17: 4.

Lansdowne MSS = 'B.L.Lansd.MSS'.

216: 4 (fol. 65v).
245.
486: 1, 6, 7, 8, 9, 10, 11, 12, 13, 14, 15, 17, 18, 19, 20, 21.
512: 13, 14, 18, 20, 21.
513: 2, 3.

Cottonian MSS = 'B.L.Cott.MSS'.

Julius ('Jul.') F. VI.: 39, 62.
Titus ('Tit.') C. VI.: 13, 14.
Titus ('Tit.') F. IV.: 6, 7, 8, 9, 10, 12.
Faustina ('Faust.') C. II.: 25.

(See also MSS indexed under 'Scotland: Supremacy of England over'.)

Royal MSS = 'B.L.Royal MSS'.

12A.LIII.
17A.LVI, fos 1-103.
17B.VI.
18A.XIV.
18A.LI.
18A.LXXVI.

Sloane MSS = 'B.L.Sloane MSS'.

78, fos 109-15.
2716, fos 1-38.
3479, fos 59-67.
3521.

BODLEIAN LIBRARY, OXFORD

Miscellaneous MSS = 'Bod.Misc.MSS'.

3499: 7e.

Willis MSS = 'Bod.Willis MSS'.

16352: 13.

Rawlinson MSS = 'Bod.Rawl.MSS'.

A.123.
C.206.
D.918.

LINCOLN'S INN LIBRARY, LONDON

Maynard MSS = 'Lincoln's Inn Maynard MSS'.

83: 1, 2, 3, 4, 5, 6, 7, 8, 9, 10, 11, 12, 13.

CAMBRIDGE COLLEGE LIBRARIES

Caius College = 'Cam.Caius College MSS'.

73/40 No. XVII.
291/274 No. XV, pps 407-10.

Trinity College = 'Cam. Trinity College MSS'.

R5.15.

EDINBURGH UNIVERSITY LIBRARY

Laing MSS = 'E.U.L.Laing MSS'.

III.249.

NATIONAL LIBRARY OF SCOTLAND

Advocates' MSS = 'N.L.S.Adv.MSS'.

31.7.7.
31.12.19, pps 135-44.
33.1.1, Vol I: 16, 18, 19, 20, 21.
Vol II: 10, 15, 30.
34.2.2.
81.1.4, pps 78-80.

Other MSS = 'N.L.S.MSS'.

2092, fol. 3.
2517, fos 67-8.
3648, fos 4-8.
7036, fos 11-14.

SCOTTISH RECORD OFFICE

Gifts & Deposits = 'S.R.O.MSS.GD'.

45/1/8.
124/10/83.
124/15/25.
156/6/3.

SECTION B: PRIMARY PRINTED SOURCES

Later reproductions or editions of works by known authors are listed under the name of the original author. Reproductions of anonymous works, and collections of material (Acts, ballads etc.) are listed under the name of the editor or collator, or the title of the volume.

A listing marked with an asterisk indicates that the work was not originally printed.

The short titles in inverted commas after each listing are those used in notes, for reference.

*Acts of the Privy Council of England, 1601-1604. London, 1907. 'Acts, PCE'.
*Acts of the Parliament of Scotland, 1124-1707, ed. T. Thomson and C. Innes. 12 vols. Edinburgh, 1814-75. 'Acts Sc.Parl.'
*Acts and Proceedings of the General Assemblies of the Kirk of Scotland, ed. T. Thomson.

Bannatyne Club. 3 vols. Edinburgh, 1845. 'Acts of the Kirk'.

Albericus Gentilis, *Regales Disputationes Tres*. London, 1605. 'Albericus Gentilis'.

Austin, R., *Allegiance Not Impeached*. London, 1644. 'Austin, Allegiance'.

Ayscu, E., *A Historie Contayning the Warres, Treaties, Marriages and other occurrents betweene England and Scotland*. London, 1607. 'Ayscu, Historie'.

*Bacon, Sir F., *Henry VII*, ed. Rev. J. Lumby. 2nd edn. Cambridge, 1892. 'Bacon, Henry VII'.

*Bacon, Sir F., *Letters and Life of Lord Bacon, Vol. III*, ed. J. Spedding. London, 1868. 'Spedding, Bacon III'.

*Bacon, Sir F., *Works, Vol. V*, ed. B. Montagu. London, 1826. 'Montagu, Bacon V'.

*Balfour, Sir J., *Balfour's Annals of Scotland, Vol. II*. London, 1825. 'Balfour, Annals II'.

*Bowyer, R., *The Parliamentary Diary of Robert Bowyer*, ed. D. H. Willson. Minneapolis, 1931. 'Bowyer'.

'Bristol, Jo.' See Thornborough, J.

*Brown, P. H., ed., *Early Travellers in Scotland*. Edinburgh, 1891. 'Brown, Early Travellers'.

*Brown, P. H., ed., *Scotland before 1700 from Contemporary Documents*. Edinburgh, 1893. 'Brown, Scotland before 1700'.

*Brown, T., ed., *Miscellania Aulica*. London, 1702. 'Brown, Misc.Aul.'

Buchanan, G., *De Jure Regni apud Scotos*. Edinburgh, 1579. 'Buchanan, De Jure Regni'.

*Calderwood, D., *The True History of the Church of Scotland*. Edinburgh, 1678: reprinted Menston, 1971. 'Calderwood'.

Calendar of State Papers (Domestic), Vol. VIII, 1603-1610. London, 1857. 'Cal.S.P. (Dom)'.

Calendar of State Papers (Venetian), 1603-1607 and *1607-1610*. 2 vols. London, 1900. 'Cal.S.P.(Ven)'.

*Chambers, R., *Domestic Annals of Scotland, Vol. I*. Edinburgh, 1858. 'Chambers, Annals I'.

*Cobbett, W., *The Parliamentary History of England, Vol. I*. London, 1806. 'Cobbett, Parl.Hist.I'.

*Collier, J. P., *The Egerton Papers*. London, 1840. 'Collier, Egerton'.

Commons, Journal of the House of, Vol. I. London. 'CJ I'.

Cornwallis, Sir W., *The Miraculous and Happie Union of England and Scotland*. Edinburgh and London, 1604. 'Cornwallis, Miraculous and Happie Union'.

Cowell, J., *Institutiones*. London, 1605. 'Cowell, Institutiones'.

Cowell, J., *The Interpreter*. London, 1607. 'Cowell, Interpreter'.

*Craig, Sir T., *De Unione Regnorum Britanniae Tractatus*, ed. and trans. C. S. Terry. Scottish History Society. Edinburgh, 1909. 'Craig, De Unione'.

*Craig, Sir T., *Ius Feudale*, ed. and trans. J. A. Clyde. 2 vols. Edinburgh, 1934. 'Craig, Ius Feudale'.

*Craig, Sir T., *Right of Succession to the Kingdom of England*. Edinburgh, 1703. 'Craig, Right of Succession'.

*Craig, Sir T., *Scotland's Sovereignty Asserted*, ed. G. Ridpath. Edinburgh, 1695. 'Craig, de Hominio'.

*De la Boderie, *Les Ambassades de M.de la Boderie, 1606-1611*. Paris, 1750. 'De la Boderie'.

*Firth, C. H., ed., *Scotland and the Commonwealth*. Scottish History Society. Edinburgh, 1895. 'Firth, Scotland & Commonwealth'.

*Firth, C. H., ed., *Scotland and the Protectorate*. Scottish History Society. Edinburgh, 1899. 'Firth, Scotland & Protectorate'.

*Forbes, J., *Certaine Records Touching the Estate of the Kirk in the Years 1605 and 1606*. Wodrow Society. Edinburgh, 1846. 'Forbes, Certaine Records'.

Forset, E., *A Comparative Discourse of Bodies Natural and Politique*. London, 1606. 'Forset, Comparative Discourse'.

Gordon, J., Ενωτικοη, *or, A Sermon of the Union of Great Brittaine*. London, 1604. 'Gordon, *Ενωτικοη*'.

Gordon, J., *The Union of Great Brittaine, or, England and Scotland's Happinesse in being reduced to unitie of Religion*. London, 1604. 'Gordon, Union of Great Brittaine'.

Harington, Sir J., *Tract on the Succession to the Crown*. London, 1602: reprinted Roxburghe Club, Edinburgh, 1880. 'Harington, Succession'.

Hayward, Sir J., *An Answer to the First Part of a Certain Conference*. London, 1603. 'Hayward, Answer to Parsons'.

Hayward, Sir J., *A Treatise of Union of the Two Realmes of England and Scotland*. London, 1604. 'Hayward, Treatise of Union'.

*H.M.C. Buccleuch MSS, Vol. III. London, 1926. 'HMC. Bucc.III'.

*H.M.C. Cowper MSS, Vol. I. London, 1888. 'HMC. Cowper I'.

*H.M.C. Downshire MSS, Vol. II. London, 1936. 'HMC. Downshire II'.

*H.M.C. Montague of Beaulieu. London, 1900. 'HMC. Montague'.

*H.M.C. Salisbury MSS, Vols. XV-XX. London, 1930-68. 'HMC. Salis.XV' etc.

*Holinshed, R., *Chronicles of England, Scotland and Ireland*, ed. H. Ellis. 6 vols. London, 1807-8. 'Holinshed, Chronicles'.

*Howell, T. B., *State Trials, Vol. II*. London, 1809. 'Howell, State Trials II'.

Hume, D., *De Unione Insulae Britanniae, tractatus primus*. 1605. 'Hume, Tractatus Primus'.

*James VI and I, King, *The Political Works of James I*, ed. C. H. McIlwain. Cambridge, Mass., 1918. 'James I, Works'.

*Laing, D., ed., *Original Letters relating to the Ecclesiastical Affairs of Scotland*. Bannatyne Club. 2 vols. Edinburgh, 1851. 'Laing, Ecclesiastical Letters'.

*Larkin, J. F., and Hughes, P. L., ed., *Stuart Royal Proclamations, Vol. I*. Oxford, 1973. 'Larkin & Hughes'.

Lords, Journal of the House of, Vol. II. London. 'LJ II'.

*Maidment, E., *State Papers and Miscellaneous Correspondence of the Earl of Montrose*. Abbotsford Club. 2 vols. Edinburgh, 1837. 'Maidment, Melrose Papers'.

*Maidment, J., ed., *Abbotsford Miscellany*. Abbotsford Club. Edinburgh, 1837. 'Maidment, Abbotsford Miscellany'.

*Maidment, J., ed., *Letters and State Papers during the Reign of King James VI*. Abbotsford Club. Edinburgh, 1838. 'Maidment, Letters and State Papers'.

*Major, J., *History of Greater Britain*, ed. and trans. A. Constable. Scottish History Society. Edinburgh, 1892. 'Major, History'.

*Marston, J., Jonson, B., and Chapman, G., *Eastward Hoe*, ed. J. M. Harris. New Haven, 1926. 'Marston, Eastward Hoe'.

*Melville, J., *Autobiography and Diary*. Wodrow Society. Edinburgh, 1842. 'Melville, Diary'.

Monipennie, J., *Certeine Matters Concerning the Realme of Scotland*. London, 1603. 'Monipennie, Certeine Matters'.

*Murray, J. A. H., ed., *The Complaynt of Scotlande*. Early English Text Society. London, 1872. 'Murray, Complaynt of Scotlande'.

*Nichols, J., *The Progresses . . . of James I*. London, 1828. 'Nichols, Progresses'.

Nicolson, W., *Leges Marchiarum*. London, 1705. 'Nicolson, Leges March.'

Nicolson, W., *Scottish Historical Library*. London, 1702. 'Nicolson, Sc.Hist.Lib.'

Osborne, F., *Historical Memoires on the Raigne . . . of James I*. London, 1658. 'Osborne, Historical Memoires'.

*Palgrave, Sir F., ed., *Documents and Records of Scotland*. London, 1837. 'Palgrave, Documents and Records'.

Parsons, R. (alias Doleman), *A Conference touching Succession to the Crowne*. Antwerp, 1594. 'Parsons, Conference'.

Pont, R., *De Unione Britanniae Dialogus*. Edinburgh, 1604. 'Pont, Dialogue'.

*Pollard, A. F., ed., *Tudor Tracts, 1532-1588*. London, 1903. 'Pollard, Tudor Tracts'.

Rapta Tatio: The Mirrour of his Maiesties present Gouernment, tending to the Union of his whole Iland of Brittaine. London, 1604. 'Rapta Tatio'.

Register of the Privy Council of Scotland, Vols. VI-VIII, ed. D. Masson. Edinburgh/London, 1884. 'Reg.PCSc. VI' etc.

*Row, J., *History of the Kirk of Scotland*. Wodrow Society. Edinburgh, 1842. 'Row, History'.

Sanderson, W., *A Compleat History of the Lives and Reigns of Mary Queen of Scots and . . . James VI*. London, 1656. 'Sanderson, Compleat History'.

*Scot, W., *An Apologeticall Narratioun of the State and Government of the Kirk of Scotland since the Reformation*. Wodrow Society. Edinburgh, 1846. 'Scot, Apologeticall Narratioun'.

Saltern, G., *Of the Antient Lawes of Great Britaine*. London, 1605. 'Saltern, Antient Lawes'.

*Scott, Sir W., *Somers Tracts, Vol. II*. London, 1809. 'Somers Tracts II'.

*Scott, Sir W., ed., *Bannatyne Miscellany*, Vol. I. Edinburgh, 1827. 'Scott, Bannatyne Miscellany'.

*Shakespeare, W., *Collected Works*. London, 1966. References by plays.

Skene, Sir J., ed., *Regiam Maiestaem and the Auld Lawes*. Edinburgh, 1609, 'Skene, Regiam Maiestatem'.

Skene, Sir J., *De Verborum Significatione*. Edinburgh, 1597. 'Skene, De Verb.Sign.'

Solemn League and Covenant for Reformation, and Defence of Religion, The Honour and the Happinesse of the King, and the Peace and Safety of the three Kingdoms of England, Scotland and Ireland. Edinburgh and London, 1643. 'Solemn League and Covenant'.

Speed, J., *The Theatre of the Empire of Great Britaine*. London, 1611. 'Speed, Empire of Gt Britaine'.

*Spottiswoode, J., *The History of the Church of Scotland*. Edinburgh, 1655, reproduced Menston, 1972. 'Spottiswoode'.

*Tanner, J. R., *Constitutional Documents of the Reign of James I, 1603-1625*. Cambridge, 1961. 'Tanner, Documents'.

*Terry, C. S., ed., *The Cromwellian Union: Papers concerning Negotiations between England and Scotland, 1651-1652*. Scottish History Society. Edinburgh, 1902. 'Terry, Crom. Union'.

Thornborough, J., *A Discourse plainly proving the evident Utility and urgent Necessity of the desired happy Union of England and Scotland*. London, 1604. 'Thornborough, Discourse'.

Thornborough, J., *Joyful and Blessed Reuniting the two mighty and famous kingdoms of England and Scotland*. London, 1605. 'Thornborough, Joyful and Blessed Reuniting'.

Weldon, Sir A., *Letter out of Scotland*. Printed as *A Perfect Description of the People and Country of Scotland*, by J. Howel. London, 1659. 'Weldon, Letter from Scotland'.

Willett, A., *Ecclesia Triumphans*. Cambridge, 1603. 'Willett, Ecclesia'.

Wilson, A., *History of Great Britain, etc.* London, 1653. 'Wilson, History of GB.'

Wilson, T., *The State of England*. London, 1600; reprinted in Camden Miscellany Vol. XVI, 1936. 'Wilson, State of England'.

*Winwood, Sir R., *Memorials of Affairs of State*. 3 vols. London, 1725. 'Winwood, Memorials'.

SECTION C: SECONDARY PRINTED SOURCES

The section includes books, articles and pieces contained in collections and festschrifts. Short
titles as Section B.

Allen, J. W., *A History of Political Thought in the Sixteenth Century*. London, 1928. 'Allen, Political Thought'.

Ashton, R., *The City and the Court, 1603-1643*. Cambridge, 1979. 'Ashton, City and Court'.

Ashton, R., *The English Civil War. Conservatism and Revolution, 1603-1649*. London, 1978.

Axton, M., *The Queen's Two Bodies*. London, 1977. 'Axton, Two Bodies'.

Benjamin, E. B., 'Sir John Hayward and Tacitus', *R.E.S.* New Series VIII (1957), 275-6. 'Benjamin, Sir John Hayward'.

Bindoff, S. T. *et al*, eds., *Elizabethan Government and Society (Essays presented to J. E. Neale)*. London, 1961. 'Bindoff, Eliz.Govt.'

Bindoff, S. T., 'The Stuarts and their Style, *E.H.R.* LX (1945), 192-216. 'Bindoff, Stuart Style'.

Birch, T., *The Court and Times of James I*. London, 1848. 'Birch, James I'.

Bradshaw, B., *The Irish Constitutional Revolution of the Sixteenth Century*. Cambridge, 1979. 'Bradshaw, Irish Constit.Revolution'.

Braudel, F., *The Mediterranean and the Mediterranean World in the Age of Philip II*, trans. S. Reynolds. 2 vols. London, 1972-3. 'Braudel, Mediterranean World'.

Brown, P. H., *George Buchanan*. Edinburgh, 1890. 'Brown, Buchanan'.

Brown, P. H., ed., The Union of 1707. Glasgow, 1907. 'Brown, Union of 1707'.

Bruce, J., *Report on the Union with Scotland*. 2 vols. London, 1799. 'Bruce, Report on the Union'.

Bush, M. L., *The Government Policy of Protector Somerset*. London, 1975. 'Bush, Protector Somerset'.

Campbell, L. B., 'The Use of Historical Patterns in the Reign of Elizabeth', *H.L.Q.* I (1938), 135-67. 'Campbell, Hist.Patterns'.

Carr, H. G., *Flags of the World*. London, 1953. 'Carr, Flags'.

Cochran-Patrick, R. W., *Records of the Coinage of Scotland from the earliest period to the Union*. 2 vols. Edinburgh, 1876. 'Cochran-Patrick, Coinage of Scotland'.

Cooper, J. P., 'Differences between English and Continental Governments in the Early Seventeenth Century', in J. S. Bromley and E. H. Kossmann, eds., *Britain and the Netherlands*. London, 1959. 'Cooper, English and Continental Governments'.

Cooper, Lord T. M., *The Dark Age of Scottish Legal History*. Glasgow, 1952. 'Cooper, Dark Age'.

Cowan, I. B., 'The Covenanters: A Review Article', *S.H.R.* XLVII (1968), 35-52. 'Cowan, Covenanters'.

Daiches, D., *Scotland and the Union*. Edinburgh, 1977. 'Daiches, Union'.

Dicey, A. V., and Rait, R. S., *Thoughts on the Scottish Union*. London, 1920. 'Dicey & Rait, Thoughts'.

Dictionary of National Biography. 'DNB'.

Dodd, A. H., *The Growth of Responsible Government*. London, 1956. 'Dodd, Responsible Government'.

Donaldson, G., *Scotland: James V — James VII* (Edinburgh History of Scotland, Vol. III). Edinburgh, 1965. 'Donaldson, Scotland'.

Douglas, D. C., *English Scholars, 1660-1730*. London, 1939. 'Douglas, Scholars'.

Dow, F. D., *Cromwellian Scotland, 1651-1660*. Edinburgh, 1979. 'Dow, Crom.Sc.'

Dowling, M., 'Sir John Hayward's troubles over his "Life of Henry IV"', *The Library* XI (1930-1), 212-25. 'Dowling, Hayward's Troubles'.

Eaves, R. G., *Henry VIII's Scottish Diplomacy, 1513-1524*. New York, 1971. 'Eaves, 1513-24'.

Enright, M. J., 'King James and his Island — an archaic kingship belief?', *S.H.R.* LV (1975), 29-40. 'Enright, James and his Island'.

Ferguson, A. B., 'John Twyne: A Tudor Humanist', *J.B.S.* IX (1969), 24-44. 'Ferguson, John Twyne'.

Ferguson, W., 'Imperial Crowns: a neglected facet of the background to the Treaty of Union of 1707', *S.H.R.* LIII (1974), 22-44. 'Ferguson, Imperial Crowns'.

Ferguson, W., *Scotland's Relations with England to 1707*. Edinburgh, 1977. 'Ferguson, Scotland's Relations'.

Firth, C. H., 'Ballads illustrating the relations of England and Scotland during the seventeenth century', *S.H.R.* VI (1908-9), 114-28. 'Firth, Ballads'.

Fussner, F. S., *The Historical Revolution in English History Writing and Thought, 1580-1640*. London, 1962. 'Fussner, Historical Revolution'.

Gardiner, S. R., *A History of England from the Accession of James I to the Outbreak of Civil War, 1603-1642*. 10 vols. London, 1883-4. 'Gardiner, History of England'.

Goldberg, S. L., 'Sir John Hayward, "Politic" Historian', *R.E.S.* New Series VI (1955), 233-44. 'Goldberg, Sir John Hayward'.

Gough, J. W., *Fundamental Law in English History*. Oxford, 1955. 'Gough, Fundamental Law'.

Grant, I. F., *Social and Economic Development of Scotland before 1603*. Edinburgh, 1930. 'Grant, Scotland before 1603'.

Haller, W., *Foxe's Book of Martyrs and the Elect Nation. London, 1963*. 'Haller, Elect Nation'.

Hannay, R. K. *The College of Justice*. Edinburgh, 1933. 'Hannay, College of Justice'.

Hannay, R. K., 'General Council and Convention of Estates', *S.H.R.* XX (1922), 263-84. 'Hannay, Council and Convention'.

Hannay, R. K., 'Officers of Scottish Parliaments', *Juridical Review* XLIV (1932), 125-38. 'Hannay, Officers of Parliament'.

Hannay, R. K., 'On "Parliament" and "General Council"', *S.H.R.* XVIII (1921), 157-70. 'Hannay, Parliament and Council'.

Harrison, G. B., *A Jacobean Journal*. London, 1941. 'Harrison, Journal'.

Hay, D., 'The Term "Great Britain" in the Middle Ages', *P.S.A.S.* LXXXIX (1956), 55-67. 'Hay, GB'.

Hinton, R. W. K., 'The decline of parliamentary government under Elizabeth and the Early Stuarts', *C.H.J.* XIII (1957), 116-30. 'Hinton, Decline of parliamentary government'.

Houston, S. J., *James I*. London, 1973. 'Houston, James I'.

Hughes, E., 'Negotiations for a Commercial Union between England and Scotland in 1668', *S.H.R.* XXIV (1926), 30-47. 'Hughes, Negotiations for a Commercial Union'.

Hurstfield, C. J., 'The Revival of Feudalism in Early Tudor England', *History* XXXVII (1952), 131-45. 'Hurstfield, Feudalism'.

Ives, E. W., ed., *The English Revolution*. London, 1968. 'Ives, English Revolution'.

Jones, W. J., *Politics and the Bench*. London, 1971. 'Jones, Politics and Bench'.

Judson, M. A., *The Crisis of the Constitution*. New Brunswick (N.J.), 1949. 'Judson, Crisis of Constitution'.

Kantorowicz, E., *The King's Two Bodies. A Study in Medieval Political Theology*. Princeton, 1957. 'Kantorowicz, The King's Two Bodies'.

Keith, T., *Commercial Relations of England and Scotland, 1603-1670*. Cambridge, 1910. 'Keith, Commercial Relations'.

Kendrick, Sir T., *British Antiquity*. London, 1950. 'Kendrick, British Antiquity'.

Kenyon, J. P., *The Stuart Constitution: Documents and Commentary*. Cambridge, 1966. 'Kenyon, Stuart Constitution'.

Kenyon, J. P., *The Stuarts*. London, 1958. 'Kenyon, the Stuarts'.

Knafla, L. A., *Law and Politics in Jacobean England*. Cambridge, 1977. 'Knafla, Law and Politics'.

Koebner, R., 'The Imperial Crown of this Realm: Henry VIII, Constantine the Great and Polydore Vergil', *B.I.H.R.* XXVI (1953), 29-53. 'Koebner, Imperial Crown'.

Lamont, W., *Godly Rule*. London, 1969. 'Lamont, Godly Rule'.

Lee, M., 'James VI's Government of Scotland after 1603', *S.H.R.* LV (1975), 41-53.

'Lee, Government of Scotland'.

Levack, B. D., *Civil Lawyers in England, 1603-1641*. Oxford, 1973. 'Levack, Civil Lawyers'.

Levack, B. D., 'The Proposed Union of English Law and Scots Law in the Seventeenth Century', *Juridical Review* 1975, 97-115. 'Levack, Union of Laws'.

Levy, F. J., *Tudor Historical Thought*. San Marino (Cal.), 1967. 'Levy, Historical Thought'.

Loades, D. M., *Politics and the Nation, 1450-1660*. London, 1974. 'Loades, Politics & Nation'.

Lythe, S. G. E., *The Economy of Scotland in its European Setting, 1550-1625*. Edinburgh, 1960. 'Lythe, Economy of Scotland'.

Lythe, S. G. E., 'The Union of the Crowns in 1603 and the Debate on Economic Integration', *S.J.P.E.* V (1958), 219-28. 'Lythe, Union of Crowns'.

Lythe, S. G. E., and Devine, B., 'The Economy of Scotland under James I', *S.H.R.* L (1971), 91-106. 'Lythe & Devine, Economy under James I'.

MacGregor, Rev. M. B., *Sources and Literature of Scottish Church History*. Glasgow, 1934. 'MacGregor, Scottish Church'.

Mackie, J. D., *The Earlier Tudors*. Oxford, 1966. 'Mackie, Earlier Tudors'.

Mackie, J. D., 'Henry VIII and Scotland', *T.R.H.S.* 1947, 93-114. 'Mackie, Henry VIII and Scotland'.

Mackie, J. D., *A History of Scotland*. Harmondsworth, 1964. 'Mackie, History of Scotland'.

Maitland, F. W., 'The Crown as Corporation', in *Selected Essays*, ed. H. D. Hazeltine. Cambridge, 1936, 104-27. 'Maitland, Crown as Corporation'.

Manning, B., *The English People and the English Revolution*. London, 1978. 'Manning, English Revolution'.

Mathieson, W. L., *Politics and Religion in Scotland, 1550-1695*. Glasgow, 1902. 'Mathieson, Politics and Religion'.

McKisack, M., *Medieval History in the Tudor Age*. Oxford, 1971. 'McKisack, Medieval History'.

Merriman, M. H., 'The Assured Scots: Scottish Collaborators with England during the Rough Wooing', *S.H.R.* XLVII (1968), 10-34. 'Merriman, Assured Scots'.

Mitchell, W. M., *The Rise of the Revolutionary Party in the English House of Commons*. New York, 1957. 'Mitchell, House of Commons'.

Munden, R. C., 'James I and the "Growth of Mutual Distrust": King, Commons and Reform, 1603-1604', in K. Sharpe, ed., *Faction and Parliament*, 43-73. Oxford, 1978. 'Munden, "Growth of Mutual Distrust"'.

Myers, J. L., 'The Parliaments of Europe and the Age of the Estates', *History* LX (1975), 11-27. 'Myers, Parliaments of Europe'.

Neale, J. E., *The Elizabethan House of Commons*. London, 1949. 'Neale, Elizabethan Commons'.

Neale, J. E., *Elizabeth I and Her Parliaments*. 2 vols. London, 1953. 'Neale, Parliaments of Elizabeth'.

Nobbs, D., *England and Scotland, 1560-1707*. London, 1952. 'Nobbs, England and Scotland'.

Notestein, W., 'The Establishment of the Committee of Both Kingdoms', *A.H.R.* XVII (1912), 477-96. 'Notestein, CBK'.

Notestein, W., *The House of Commons, 1604-1610*. New Haven, 1971. 'Notestein, House of Commons'.

Notestein, W., *The Winning of the Initiative by the House of Commons* (Raleigh Lecture on History, 1924). 'Notestein, Winning of the Initiative'.

Ogg, D., *Selden's 'Ad Fletam Dissertatio'*. Cambridge, 1925. 'Ogg, Selden'.

Omond, G. W. T., *The Early History of the Scottish Union Question*. Edinburgh, 1897. 'Omond, Scottish Union Question'.

Pinckney, P. J., 'The Scottish Representation in the Cromwellian Parliament of 1656', *S.H.R.* XLVI (1967), 95-114. 'Pinckney, Scottish Representation in 1656'.

Pocock, J. G. A., *The Ancient Constitution and the Feudal Law*. Cambridge, 1957. 'Pocock, Ancient Constitution'.

Pollard, A. W. *et al*, *A Short-Title Catalogue of English Books, 1475-1640*. London, 1926. 'Pollard, STC'.

Rabb, T. K., 'Free Trade and the Gentry in the Parliament of 1604', *P & P* 40 (1968), 165-73. 'Rabb, Free Trade in 1604'.

Rabb, T. K., 'Sir Edwin Sandys and the Parliament of 1604', *A.H.R.* LXIX (1964), 646-70. 'Rabb, Sir Edwin Sandys'.

Rae, T. I., *The Administration of the Scottish Frontier, 1513-1603*. Edinburgh, 1966. 'Rae, Scottish Frontier'.

Rait, R. S., *The Parliaments of Scotland*. Glasgow, 1924. 'Rait, Parliaments of Scotland'.

Reinmuth, H. S., ed., *Early Stuart Studies* (Essays in Honour of D. H. Willson). Minneapolis, 1970. 'Reinmuth, Stuart Studies'.

Ridpath, C., *The Border History of England and Scotland*, revised by P. Ridpath. Berwick, 1848. 'Ridpath, Border History'.

Riley, P. W. J., *The Union of England and Scotland*. Manchester, 1978. 'Riley, Union of England and Scotland'.

Robertson, J., *A Handbook to the Coinage of Scotland*. London, 1878. 'Robertson, Coinage of Scotland'.

Rowse, A. L., *The England of Elizabeth*. London, 1950. 'Rowse, Elizabeth'.

Russell, C., *The Crisis of Parliaments: English History, 1509-1660*. Oxford, 1971. 'Russell, Crisis of Parliaments'.

Russell, C., ed., *The Origins of the English Civil War*. London, 1973. 'Russell, Origins of ECW'.

Russell, C., 'Parliamentary History in Perspective', *History* LXI, (1976), 1-28. 'Russell, PHIP'.

Russell, C., *Parliaments and English Politics, 1621-1629*. Oxford, 1979. 'Russell, 1621-9'.

Scottish Legal History, An Introduction to. Stair Society. Edinburgh, 1958. 'Scottish Legal History'.

Sharpe, K., *Sir Robert Cotton, 1586-1631*. Oxford, 1979. 'Sharpe, Cotton'.

Skeel, C. A. J., 'The Influence of the Writings of Sir John Fortescue', *T.R.H.S.* 3rd Series X (1916), 77-114. 'Skeel, Fortescue'.

Skinner, Q., 'History and Ideology in the English Revolution', *H.J.* VIII (1965), 151-78. 'Skinner, History and Ideology'.

Slavin, A. J., *Politics and Profit: A Study of Sir Ralph Sadler, 1507-1547*. Cambridge, 1966. 'Slavin, Sir Ralph Sadler'.

Smith, A. G. R., ed., *The Reign of James VI and I*. London, 1972. 'Smith, James VI'.

Smout, T. C., *A History of the Scottish People, 1560-1830*. London, 1969. 'Smout, Scottish People'.

Sources and Literature of Scots Law, An Introduction to the. Stair Society. Edinburgh, 1936. 'Sources & Literature of Scots Law'.

Stafford, H. G., *James VI of Scotland and the Throne of England*. New York, 1940. 'Stafford, James and the Throne of England'.

Stevenson, D., 'Professor Trevor-Roper and the Scottish Revolution', *History Today*, February 1980, 34-40. 'Stevenson, Trevor-Roper and the Scottish Revolution'.

Stevenson, D., *Revolution and Counter-Revolution in Scotland, 1644-1651*. London, 1975. 'Stevenson, 1644-51'.

Stevenson, D., *The Scottish Revolution, 1637-44*. Newton Abbott, 1973. 'Stevenson, 1637-44'.

Stone, L., *The Causes of the English Revolution, 1529-1642*. London, 1972. 'Stone,

1529-1642'.

Stone, L., *Crisis of the Aristocracy, 1558-1641*. Oxford, 1965. 'Stone, Crisis of the Aristocracy'.

Stone, L., 'The Fruits of Office: The Case of Robert Cecil, First Earl of Salisbury, 1596-1612', in F. J. Fisher, ed., *Essays in the Economic and Social History of Tudor and Stuart England*. Cambridge, 1961, 89-116. 'Stone, Fruits of Office'.

Styles, P., 'Politics and Historical Research in the Early Seventeenth Century', in L. Fox, ed., *English Historical Scholarship in the Sixteenth and Seventeenth Centuries*. London, 1956. 'Styles, Politics and Historical Research'.

Terry, C. S., *The Scottish Parliament, Its Constitution and Procedure, 1603-1707*. Glasgow, 1905. 'Terry, Scottish Parliament'.

Tough, D. L. W., *The Last Years of a Frontier*. Oxford, 1928. 'Tough, Last Years of Frontier'.

Trevor-Roper, H. R., *Buchanan and the Ancient Scottish Constitution. S.H.R.* Supplement, 1966. 'Trevor-Roper, Buchanan'.

Trevor-Roper, H. R., 'Scotland and the Puritan Revolution', in H. E. Bell and R. L. Ollard, eds., *Historical Essays, 1600-1750*, 78-130. 'Trevor-Roper, Scotland & Puritan Revolution'.

Trevor-Roper, H. R., 'The Union of Britain in the Seventeenth Century', in *Religion, the Reformation and Social Change*, 445-67. London, 1967. 'Trevor-Roper, The Union of Britain'.

Tyacke, N. R. N., 'Wroth, Cecil and the Parliamentary Session of 1604', *B.I.H.R.* 50 (1977), 120-5. 'Tyacke, Session of 1604'.

Tytler, P. F., *Life of Sir Thomas Craig*. Edinburgh, 1823. 'Tytler, Life of Craig'.

Usher, R. G., 'Nicholas Fuller: A Forgotten Exponent of English Liberty', *A.H.R.* XII (1907), 743-60. 'Usher, Nicholas Fuller'.

Wallace, W. M., *Sir Edwin Sandys and the Parliament of 1604*. Philadelphia, 1940. 'Wallace, Sir Edwin Sandys'.

Walton, F. P., 'The Relationship of the Law of France to the Law of Scotland', *Juridical Review* XIV (1902), 17-34. 'Walton, Law of France and Scotland'.

Watts, S. J., and Watts, S. J., *From Border to Middle Shire: Northumberland, 1586-1625*. Leicester, 1975. 'Watts & Watts, From Border to Middle Shire'.

Wedgwood, C. V., 'Anglo-Scottish Relations, 1603-1640', *T.R.H.S.* 4th Series XXXII (1950), 31-48. 'Wedgwood, Anglo-Scottish Relations'.

Wheeler, H., 'Calvin's Case and the McIlwain-Schuyler Debate', *A.H.R.* LXI (1956), 587-97. 'Wheeler, Calvin's Case'.

Williams, P., 'The Northern Borderland under the Early Stuarts', in H. E. Bell and R. L. Ollard, eds., *Historical Essays, 1600-1750*, 1-17. London, 1963. 'Williams, Northern Borderland'.

Williamson, A., *Scottish National Consciousness in the Age of James VI*. Edinburgh, 1979. 'Williamson, Scottish National Consciousness'.

Williamson, H., *The Gunpowder Plot*. London, 1951. 'Williamson, Gunpowder Plot'.

Willson, D. H., 'The Earl of Salisbury and the "Court" Party in Parliament, 1604-1610', *A.H.R.* XXXVI, 274-94. 'Willson, Earl of Salisbury'.

Willson, D. H., 'King James VI and Anglo-Scottish Unity', in W. A. Aiken and B. D. Henning, eds., *Conflict in Stuart England*. London, 1960. 'Willson, James and Anglo-Scottish Unity'.

Willson, D. H., *King James VI and I*. London, 1956. 'Willson, James VI'.

Willson, D. H., *The Privy Councillors in the House of Commons, 1604-1629*. Minneapolis, 1940. 'Willson, Privy Councillors'.

Wormuth, F. D., *The Royal Prerogative, 1603-1649*. Ithaca, New York, 1939. 'Wormuth, Royal Prerogative'.

Yates, F. A., *The Occult Philosophy in the Elizabethan Age*. London, 1979. 'Yates, Elizabethan Occult Philosophy'.

Zagorin, P., *The Court and the Country: the beginning of the English Revolution*. London, 1969. 'Zagorin, Court and Country'.

Zupko, R. E., 'The Weights and Measures of Scotland Before the Union', *S.H.R.* LVI (1977), 119-45. 'Zupko, Weights & Measures'.

SECTION D: UNPUBLISHED DISSERTATIONS

Munden, R. C., The Politics of Accession — James I and the Parliament of 1604, East Anglia (1976).

Roberts, P., The "Acts of Union" and the Tudor Settlement of Wales, Cambridge (1966).

Seddon, P. R., Patronage and Officers in the Reign of James I, Manchester (1967).

Wadsworth, G. C., The General Assembly of 1610, Edinburgh (1930).

Index

Albericus Gentilis 30, 31, 40
Alford, —, English MP 95, 118
Altham, —, judge 149
Anglo-Scots Union Commission (1604) 58
    achievements 63, 74; composition 62-3; delay of debate on Instrument 79-81; hostile and Border laws 65-8; James's attitude to 75-6; naturalisation 71-3; preparations for 59-62; trade and customs 68-71; working of 64-5
Apology of the House of Commons 19, 24
Argyll, earl of 59

Bachler, John 139
Bacon, Sir Francis 22, 31, 94, 95, 116, 118
    and Anglo-Scots Union Commission 62, 63, 64, 67; and Calvin's Case 149, 151, 152, 157; and debate on change of royal style 20, 21; and escuage 97; on hostile and Border laws 99, 121, 122, 123, 125, 126; and legal union 41, 146; on naturalisation 71, 99, 105-8 *passim*, 112, 115; on parliamentary union 42, 43; tracts and treatises 32, 41, 42, 43, 48, 61, 68, 71; on trade 68, 99
Balmerino, James Elphinstone, 1st lord 17, 24, 61, 62, 63, 70
Bancroft, Richard, archbishop of Canterbury 74, 86, 88
Barkley, Sir Maurice 20, 115
Barrington, Sir Francis 117
Barrow, Lord of 122
Bennett, Sir John 67, 108, 109, 113
Berwick, Lord of 61
Billingley, —, member Anglo-Scots Commission 70
Bingley, —, defendant, Calvin's Case 148
Black Acts (1584) 6
Blantyre, Walter Stewart, Lord 70
Bond, —, English MP 95
Border Commission 85, 86
Border Laws 65-6, 95, 96-8, 120-7

Borders
    abolition of March laws 16; escuage 97-8; justice in 66-8, 84-6, 142-3; role in James's campaign for recognition as heir to English throne 10
Bowyer, Sir William 142
Britain
    historic use of name 35; *see also* Great Britain
Brock, —, English MP 121
Brooke, —, English MP 95, 118, 125
Buchanan, George 3

Calderwood, David 144
Calvin's Case 148-57
Carew, —, English MP 107, 109
Carleton, Dudley 61, 72, 115, 118
Carlisle, Treaty of (1597) 10
Carnegie, —, member Anglo-Scots Commission 70
Carr, Sir Robert 139
Cecil, Robert, earl of Salisbury 17, 24, 94, 114, 115, 169
    and Anglo-Scots Union Commission 60-4 *passim*, 67, 68, 70, 73, 75; and conference on trade and hostile laws 99, 103; and Gunpowder Plot 79; on hostile and Border laws 97, 125; and legal union 146; on naturalisation 109, 113; and prorogation of Parliament (1605) 79
Chamberlain, Sir Robert 139, 150
Chapman, George 80
Charles I, union under 173-4
Charles II, union under 174-5
Charlton, Edward 142
Charteris, Robert 85
Chirnside, Patrick 85
Churches
    England, at March 1603 5; Scotland, at March 1603 5-6; union 43
Coinage 82, 141
    proclamation of 59-60; *see also* Currency
Coke, Sir Edward 110
    and Calvin's Case 149, 154, 155, 156-7

Colville, Robert 148
    see also Calvin's Case
Commerce *see* Trade
Commission, Act of
    English 22; Scots 24-5
Constitution
    England, at March 1603 2;
    Scotland, at March 1603 3
Convention of Royal Burghs 4
Cope, Sir Anthony 113
Cornwallis, Sir William 31
    tracts and treatises 31, 33, 42, 48
Cotton, —, English MP 97, 99, 108
Councils
    English
        admission of Scots 17, 18; at
        March 1603 2-3
    Scottish
        at March 3-4, 1603 2; division
        into Edinburgh and London
        groups 17; letter to James,
        March 3 1607 119; letter to
        James Aug 1607 129-30
    union of 41
Court
    mixture of English and Scots at 17,
    18; under Charles II 173
Covenanters 173-4
Craig, Sir Thomas 31, 147
    Anglo-Scots Union Commission 67;
    and ecclesiastical union 43; fears for
    Scotland 164; and legal union 40,
    146-7; tracts and treatises 30, 32-7
    passim, 40, 42, 43, 52, 53
Cranston, Sir William 85
Crofts, —, English MP 115, 117, 139,
    168
Cromwell, union under 174
Crooke, —, and Calvin's Case 149, 154
Cumberland, earl of 142-3
Currency 16, 59-60
Customs duties 69-71, 84

Daniel, —, judge 149, 154
Dannett, —, English MP 95
De Beaumont, —, French ambassador
    58
Delaval, Sir Robert 85
Discourse of Naturalisation 59, 62, 69-72
    passim
Doddridge, Sir John 31, 118
    tracts and treatises 37, 39, 41-4
    passim, 48, 50; and trade 99
Douglas, Thomas, execution of 79

Dunbar, George Home, earl of *see*
    Home, George
Duncombe, —, English MP 115
Dunfermline, Alexander Seton, 1st earl
    see Fyvie
Dunne, —, English lawyer 67

Economy
    English, at March 1603 7; Scottish,
    at March 1603 6
Ellesmere, Sir Thomas Egerton, lord 94
    95, 169
    and Calvin's Case 149, 155, 156; and
    hostile and Border laws 126; and
    naturalisation 109, 113; and trade
    70, 99, 100, 103
Elphinstone, Sir James *see* Balmerino
Erskine, John, earl of Mar 17, 23, 24, 63
Erskine, Sir Thomas 17, 62
Escuage 97-8
Extradition 122-3, 142-3

Fenner, —, judge 149
Fenwick, Sir William 142
Fischer, —, Scots merchant 98, 103
Flags, union of 82-4
Fleming, —, chief justice 110, 149, 154
Forbes, —, minister of the Kirk 87
Foster, —, judge 149
France
    alliance with Scotland, English mis-
    trust of 70; fears of disadvantage
    from union 58-9; mercantile sub-
    commission to 84, 98, 101; Scots
    trade with 70, 98, 101-2, 142
Fuller, —, English MP 63, 94, 95, 111,
    112
    and change of style 20; downfall
    138; and escuage 97; and hostile and
    Border laws 120-1, 124, 126; and
    naturalisation 105, 117, 118
Fyvie, Alexander Seton, lord 61-4
    passim, 72
    and legal union 145

General Assemblies
    Aberdeen (1605), prorogation of 87;
    Glasgow (1610) 144; James's inter-
    ference with 86; Linlithgow (1606)
    89, 143; Perth (1618) 145; St.
    Andrews (1617) 145
Gordon, John 30, 31
    tracts and treatises 31, 33, 34, 43,
    48, 51, 52, 60

Governments
  English
    appointment of Scots to 17, 42;
    at March 1603 2
  Scots
    at March 1603 3-4; March
    1603-July 1604 17
  union of 41-2
Gray, Sir Ralph 142
Great Britain, adoption of name 20-2
  Bacon's collation of objections to
  28-9; effect on international re-
  lations 37; effect on law 36; historic
  precedents 35; proclamation of 59,
  60-1, 67; tracts and treatises on 35-8
Great Seal, changes in 16
Greenwich, Treaty of (1543) 9
Grey, Edward 85
Griffin, Richard 148
Gunpowder Plot 79-80

Hamilton, Sir Thomas 61, 62, 63, 67,
  141
Hastings, —, English MP 22
Hay, Alexander 63
Hayward, John 31
  tracts and treatises 30, 35, 36, 37,
  40, 42, 48
Hedley, —, English MP 107, 112
Henry VIII and Scotland 8-9
Herbert, —, English lawyer 67
Herne, —, judge 154
Hesketh, —, English lawyer 67
Hitcham, —, English MP 124
Hobart, Sir Henry 118
  and Calvin's Case 149, 152, 153-4;
  and hostile and Border laws 67, 99,
  103, 124, 126; and legal union 124,
  146
Hoby, —, English MP 62, 63, 95, 111,
  126
Holles, Sir John 23
Holt, —, English MP 107, 118
Home, George, earl of Dunbar 17, 18, 62
  and Kirk 88, 89; and legal union
  145; and Borders justice 85, 86,
  142-3
Home, Sir William 85
Hubbard, —, English lawyer 67
Hume, D. 31
  tracts and treatises 39, 41, 42, 52
Huntly, George Gordon, 6th earl 59, 62
Hutton, Serjeant 145, 152
Hyde, —, English MP 94, 99, 111, 115

Hyde, Laurence 149

James, Frances 112
James IV, marriage to Margaret Tudor 8
James VI
  aims for the union 165-6; alleged
  rush to achieve union 15, 17;
  attitude to Anglo-Scots Union
  Commission 75-6; desire to reconcile the two peoples 15-16, 20, 166;
  divine mission 33-4, 48, 61; eagerness to leave Scotland 15; encomia
  30; historians' views of 161-3;
  personal servants 18; preferment of
  Scots 17, 73; reasons for promoting
  union 165; relationship with English
  Parliament 19-23, 116-17, 119-23,
  162, 167-9; speeches to English
  Parliament 20, 93, 116-17, 118-19;
  suppression of opposition to union
  138-40; vainglory 15, 165
Johnson, —, English MP 95
Jones, —, English MP 124
Jonson, Ben 80
Judicial systems
  Border shires 66; English, at March
  1603 5; Scots at March 1603 5
Justices of the Peace, introduction into
  Scotland 145, 150

Kinloss, Edward Bruce, lord 17, 148
Kirk
  Charles I policy towards 173; con-
  ference on future (1606) 88; James
  VI policy towards 24-5, 86-9, 143-5,
  173; and union 24-5, 43; *see also*
  General Assemblies

Language, extension of English into
  Scotland 7-8
Law
  conference on reconciliation (1607)
  145-7; effects of change in royal
  style on 36; English 2; Scots 5, 24-5;
  union of 38-41
Laws
  Border 65-6, 95, 96-8, 120-7; hostile
  65-6, 95, 96-8, 120-7
Lawson, Sir Wilfrid 85
Leigh, Sir Henry 85
Lennox, Louis (Ludovick), 2nd duke 17,
  59, 63

Leveson, Sir Richard 22
Linlithgow, Alexander Livingstone, 1st
    earl 70

Mar, John Erskine, earl of 17, 23, 24, 63
March Treasons 66
Margaret Tudor (daughter of Henry
    VII), marriage to James IV 8
Marischal, George Keith, 5th earl 59
Marston, John 80
Marten, —, English MP 118
Martin, —, English MP 94, 95, 98-9
Maxwell, J. 31
    tracts and treatises 48, 51, 52
Melville, —, member Anglo-Scots Com-
    mission 70
Melville, Andrew 6, 88
Melville, James 24, 88
'Middle Shires' *see* Borders
Monarchy
    status at March 1603 2-4; 'Two-
    Body' theory 106-7, 156
Montague, —, English MP, 99, 103,
    111, 118, 124
Moore, Francis 113
Moore, George 95, 126
Moore, Sir George 113
Moray, James Stewart, 3rd earl 59
Morrice, Sir William 21, 81, 94, 150
Murray, Sir David 61
Murray, Gideon 85
Murray, John 63

Naturalisation 71-3, 95
    after 1608 149-50; Calvin's Case
    148-57; great conference 108-10;
    legal position 106-10; parliamentary
    session 1607 103-19
Nevill, —, English MP 113
Neville, —, member Anglo-Scots Com-
    mission 70
Northampton, Henry Howard, earl of
    18, 45, 171
    Anglo-Scots Union Commission 70;
    and hostile and Border laws 125;
    and naturalisation 109, 113
Northumberland, Henry Percy, 9th earl
    80, 85, 86

Owen, —, English MP 118, 168
    fall from favour 139; and hostile and
    Border laws 123, 126; and natural-
    isation 106, 108, 112, 115

Parliaments
    Act of Commission 24-5
    English
        at March 1603 2; in 1604
        18-23; 1606-7 session 93-128;
        Act of Commission 22; Apology
        of 19, 24; debates on change of
        royal style 20-2; nature of 19,
        167-9; prorogation (1605) 79;
        relationship with James VI
        19-23, 116-17, 119-23, 162,
        167-9
    Scots
        at March 1603 3; 1606-7
        session 128-30; opposition to
        union 23-5, 172
    union of 41
Pennington, Joseph 85
Percival, —, English MP, 63
Percy, Thomas 80
Phellips, Sir Edward 114, 117, 120, 122,
    123, 126
Piggott, Sir Christopher 104, 105
Pont, Robert 31
    tracts and treatises 33, 40, 43, 48,
    52, 53
Poole, —, English MP 95, 111, 121
Popham, —, judge 110
Post between Edinburgh and London 17
Precedency, English claims to 11, 20, 37,
    38, 50
Prejudices
    Anglo-Scottish, effect on union 11,
    170; suppression of 140
Prerogative, royal 146
Pro Unione 34, 35, 36, 42, 43

Ramsay, —, gentleman of bedchamber
    104
Rapta Tatio 34, 40, 42, 48
Recusants, campaign against 80
Reformation
    effect on Anglo-Scottish relations 8,
    10; in England 6; in Scotland 5-6
Religion
    England, at March 6, 1603 5;
    Scotland, at March 1603 5-6; union
    in 43
Remand 122-3, 142-3
Ridgeway, —, member Anglo-Scots
    Commission 70
Robinson, Rev. Edward 139
Ross, Thomas 140
Rough Wooing 9

Russell, John 31
    tracts and treatises 30-4 *passim*, 36,
    39, 43, 48, 51-3 *passim*

Salisbury, earl of *see* Cecil, Robert
Saltern, George 31
    tracts and treatises 40
Sandys, Sir Edwin 20, 21, 63, 94, 95
    and hostile and Border laws 123,
    124; and naturalisation debate 108,
    110, 112, 114, 117
Sanquhar, Lord 140
Savile, Sir Henry 31, 46, 71
    tracts and treatises 38, 39, 43-6
    passim, 48, 50
Scone, David Murray, lord 61
Scots language, anglicisation of 7-8
Seals, changes in 16, 82
Seaton, Sir William, 85, 122
Selby, Sir William 85, 86, 122, 123, 142
Sharpe, —, Scots lawyer 67
Skene, —, Scots lawyer 67
Snigg, —, judge 149
Somerset, Edward Seymour, duke of 9,
    53
Speir, —, Scots merchant 98, 103
Spelman, Sir Henry 31, 106
    tracts and treatises 34, 38, 39, 42,
    43, 50, 71
Stafford, —, member Anglo-Scots Com-
    mission 70
Strode, —, English MP 107
Stroud, —, English MP 95
Suffolk, Thomas Howard, 1st earl 18
Suzerainty, English claim to 9, 11, 20,
    37, 38, 51, 106, 115, 164, 171

Talbot, —, member of Commission on
    Border Justice 142
Tanfield, —, judge 67, 149, 154
Thornborough, John 31
    tracts and treatises 23, 30, 33, 35-7
    passim, 42, 43, 48
Tracts and treatises
    on adoption of Great Britain in royal
    style 35-8; English 50-1; on further
    union 38-46; on government and
    offices 41-2; influence of 46-7; on

legal union 38-41; on opposition to
    union based on historical precedent
    44-6; on principle of unity 32-4; on
    religion 43; royal 48-50; Scots 51-3;
    on trade 43-4; variety of 30-2, 46
Trade
    1607 onwards 141-2; Anglo-Scots
    Union Commission 68-71; Franco-
    Scottish 70, 98, 101-2, 142; parlia-
    mentary session 1606-7 98-103;
    relaxation of restrictions 16;
    Scottish, at March 1603 6; union in
    43-4
Twysden, —, English MP 107

Union
    factors for and against 170-2; Scots
    and English attitudes to 11-12
Union Flag 82-4
Unity, principle of, tracts and treatises
    32-4

Walmsley, Sir Thomas 149
Warburton, Sir Peter 149
Warden Courts 66-7
Wars, Anglo-Scottish
    medieval 8; 16th century 8-9
Weights and measures 141
Weldon, Sir Anthony 140
Wentworth, —, English MP 107, 117,
    118
Widdrington, Sir Henry 85, 122
    fall from favour 139
Wilbraham, —, 145, 148
Williams, —, judge 149
Wingfield, —, English MP 107, 111,
    115, 118, 120
Worcester, Edward Somerset, 4th earl 18

Yelverton, Sir Henry
    and Calvin's Case 149, 154, 157;
    downfall 138; and hostile and
    Border laws 120, 121, 123, 125; and
    naturalisation 117, 118

Zouch, —, member Anglo-Scots Com-
    mission 62, 64